The Muslim Brotherho[
Contemporary Egypt

The Muslim Brotherhood is one of the oldest and most influential Islamist move-ments. As the party ascends to power in Egypt, it is poised to adopt a new system of governance and state–society relations, the effects of which are likely to extend well beyond Egypt's national borders. This book examines the Brother-hood's visions and practices, from its inception in 1928, up to its response to the 2011 uprising, as it moves to redefine democracy along Islamic lines. The book analyses the Muslim Brotherhood's position on key issues such as gender, reli-gious minorities and political plurality, and critically analyses whether claims that the Brotherhood has abandoned extremism and should be engaged with as a moderate political force can be substantiated. It also considers the wider political context of the region, and assesses the extent to which the Brotherhood has the potential to transform politics in the Middle East.

Mariz Tadros is a Research Fellow at the Institute of Development Studies at the University of Sussex. She spent three years as an Assistant Professor at the American University of Cairo, has worked as a consultant for both local and international NGOs, and was a journalist for *Al-Ahram Weekly* newspaper for almost ten years, covering human rights, women's rights, civil society organisa tions and activism, poverty and a plethora of development-related topics.

Durham modern Middle East and Islamic world series
Series Editor: Anoushiravan Ehteshami
University of Durham

The Muslim Brotherhood in Contemporary Egypt

Democracy redefined or confined?

Mariz Tadros

Routledge
Taylor & Francis Group

LONDON AND NEW YORK

First published 2012
by Routledge
2 Park Square, Milton Park, Abingdon, Oxfordshire OX14 4RN

Simultaneously published in the USA and Canada
by Routledge
711 Third Avenue, New York, NY 10017

First issued in paperback 2014

Routledge is an imprint of the Taylor and Francis Group, an informa business

British Library Cataloguing in Publication Data
A catalogue record for this book is available from the British Library

Library of Congress Cataloging in Publication Data
A catalog record for this book has been requested

ISBN 978-0-415-46596-0 (hbk)
ISBN 978-1-138-81580-3 (pbk)
ISBN 978-0-203-11570-1 (ebk)

Typeset in Times New Roman
by Wearset Ltd, Boldon, Tyne and Wear

To my daughters Mariam and Merit, may they come to live in an Egypt where there is freedom, dignity and justice *for all*.
To my dear husband Akram and my parents for their enduring dedication and love.

Contents

Preface

Well before the Muslim Brotherhood won a majority in Egypt's first post-Mubarak parliament, the writing on the wall was unmistakable: their ascension to power was imminent. The youth revolutionaries who had instigated the uprisings, in collaboration with coalitions, groups and various movements, had failed to translate their popular legitimacy into a political constituency. Concurrently, many observers noted that there was a clear pact between the Islamists and the Supreme Council for Armed Forces, whereby in return for the Islamists regulating/controlling the streets, the latter would create an enabling environment for them to thrive socially and politically. Weeks after the ousting of Mubarak in February 2011, the stage was set for a struggle between the legitimacy of Tahrir Square, represented in the revolutionary forces who believed that the revolution had been hijacked, and the legitimacy of formal politics which became represented in the parliament where the Islamists had a clear majority. While the battle for legitimacy was ongoing, and the dust had yet to settle, it was clear that at no other time since the movement's conception in 1928 had the Brotherhood enjoyed so much political power. Their rise to power was, on the whole, favourably looked upon. Western delegations flocked to Egypt in the summer and autumn of 2011 to build bridges with the Brothers, the media was not altogether unsympathetic and public opinion, in particular overseas, tended to empathise with the new developments on several accounts. First, the argument was that if this was the choice of the people, then how could anyone object? Second, the Muslim Brotherhood will, by virtue of their political engagement, adapt to their surroundings and contextual dynamics. Third, why should we not assume that the Muslim Brotherhood will move in the direction of the APK in Turkey and become another Islamist force championing democracy and reform? Fourth, is it not time for organic, authentic movements to have an opportunity to rule? This book seeks to address these questions by exposing some of the nuances in political thought and practice. By February 2012, there were clear indicators that the Brothers' policies had served to undermine social cohesion, deepen gender inequalities and significantly narrow the normative parameters through which contentious issues can be discussed. This book seeks to contribute to the understanding of why this happened.

Acknowledgements

This book has been six years in the making, a task begun against the backdrop of the Muslim Brotherhood's rise to formal political power in the parliamentary elections of 2005, when they won eighty-eight seats in parliament, roughly 20 per cent of all seats. It was completed in September 2011, a couple of months before the parliamentary elections that secured them a majority in the country's first post-Mubarak People's Assembly. Well before they took their seats in parliament, less than a month after the revolution that ousted Mubarak, it became clear that the path to their ascension to power had already been laid. It is in this context that the urgency to finally complete the manuscript consumed me, and I am deeply indebted to my husband, my family, my friends and my colleagues for encouraging and pushing me to complete it. I am especially indebted to Akram Habib, my husband, for his unwavering support in data collection and helping me sharpen the analysis, in acting as a sounding board for emerging ideas, and in meticulously reviewing many chapters of this book. It is no exaggeration to say that, without his support, it would have been impossible to complete this work.

I am very grateful to my parents, Fikry and Mary, who afforded me many opportunities to pursue my research and supported me in many ways. I am grateful for all the members of the Muslim Brotherhood who gave their time, formally through interviews or informally through highly instructive conversations and reflections.

I am indebted to the many friends in Egypt and elsewhere, who are too many to name here. However, I would like to single out Professor Deniz Kandiyoti, whose mentorship I am unworthy of, and my colleagues John Gaventa, Andrea Cornwall and Rosalind Eyben for their constant encouragement and support.

Finally, I would like to thank the team at Routledge for preparing the manuscript for publication, in particular Gail Welsh for her tireless and meticulous copy-editing work.

All disclaimers apply.

A note on transliteration

In this text, Arabic words have not been fully transliterated. An apostrophe (')
has been used to render the letter 'hamza' and a reverse apostrophe (') has been
used to render the letter ' 'ayn'. Macrons have not been used, nor have dots been
put under consonants unique to Arabic.

Introduction

The 25 January 2011 uprisings in Egypt that led to the ousting of Hosni Mubarak opened the floodgates for civil and political activism. The political landscape in post-Mubarak Egypt comprised more than fifty new political parties and youth-based coalitions. The Muslim Brotherhood's political power reached a great height in the six months after the demise of Mubarak's regime. Throughout the Arab world, as the uprisings were ignited from one country to the next, all eyes were focused on the Muslim Brotherhood, be they in Egypt, Yemen or elsewhere. Questions were asked: are they edging closer to the revival of the Islamic Caliphate? Will the establishment of an Islamic state, be it called a civil state with an Islamic reference (marja'iyya) or an Islamic democracy, bring them one step closer to the unification of the Islamic Ummah across borders and territories?

Concurrently, in the immediate aftermath of the eruption of the revolution, another set of counter questions were being deliberated: are we in fact entering a post-Islamic phase? In view of the fact that the uprisings had strong civil – not Islamic – overtones, does this not indicate that this is an era of the demise of Islamist identity politics (Louer 2011; Zeghal 2011; Bayat 2011)? This book argues that a more nuanced understanding of the dynamics of Islamist agency during and after the ouster of Mubarak is needed. The youth who led the protests on 25 January 2011 were adamant on making their call for public action a civil one. However, when the Muslim Brotherhood joined in full force on 28 January, the political forces agreed that all messages, slogans and other idioms would be Egyptian in character and absent of any Islamist overtones. This was symbolised in that no flag would be raised except the black, red and white Egyptian one. However, this was not a reflection of the demise of Islamist identity politics but a strategic deployment of the appropriate framing by the Muslim Brotherhood and the Islamists seen to be most conducive to the positive representation of their struggle against Mubarak's regime (see Chapter 2).

The significance of the youth having laid conditions on the Brotherhood to make the uprisings of a civil character and their resistance to the Islamisation of the revolution in that it challenged the previous political analyses suggesting that the Brotherhood is the greatest and the only force capable of mobilising the masses and having a populist base. It showed that they were not the only ones who can make 'claims' to the street. Rather than indicating a mani-festation of the fading of identity politics, it suggests a political struggle over Egypt's future. The battle over who can claim the Egyptian street as theirs is being contested and it is no longer assumed that the Brothers are the only ones who have a constituency. On the other hand, the fact that the Brothers and the Islamists were able to mobilise the majority in the March constitutional refer-endum and in the one-million-plus protest calling for the implementation of the Shar'ia on 29 July 2011 suggests that we are far from being in a post-Islamist era (see Chapter 2).

The Muslim Brotherhood continues to represent the strongest contender for leading on the fulfillment of the vision of the establishment of an Islamic state. The new political spaces that have opened up following the demise of Mubarak have created an enabling environment for their full flourishing – and a test to their ability to engage politically. This book seeks to examine the political thought of the Muslim Brotherhood, against the backdrop of their activism since their inception in 1928 and up to six months after the uprisings (July 2011). The questions guiding the research are: how far have the new freedoms following the demise of Mubarak changed the Brotherhood's positions on the kind of state they aspire to establish? How have the Brotherhood engaged with fiqh (jurispru-dence) in developing their own political thought on matters such as the relation-ship between the ruler and the citizenry, and within society? How do we acquire a better understanding of the expression of political agency of the rank and file who account for its constituency and grassroots base, in particular since the exposure to the Muslim Brotherhood is often limited to the views and statements of a few members of the political office at the top of the hierarchy?

These questions are approached by examining the interface between the Brotherhood's Islamic political thought, historical experience and contemporary political agency. It is argued here that the question of how the Brotherhood relate to Al-Siyassa al Shari'yya is fundamental to understanding of their vision of positive change, and how they wish to pursue it. In Islamic jurisprudence Al-Siyassa al Shar'iyya (legitimacy politics) differs from general politics in that the former is based not on human normative frameworks that are subject to change, but is based on the decrees and ordinances of God. Unlike politics which con-cerns itself strictly with matters of this world, Al-Siyassa al Shar'iyya concerns itself with the bridge between the worldly and the other-worldly (El Masry 2006).

While Al-Siyassa al Shar'iyya covers a wide array of areas, among the most important identified are:

1   the Shari'a and its laws;
2   the shura;
3   ijma' and ijtehad;
4   the Caliphate;
5   jihad;
6   the opposition;

7   the People of Dhimma and non-Muslims;
8   *Dar al Harb* and Dar al Islam;
9   the *hisba* (the equivalent of the General Prosecution);
10   finances and *Kharaj*;
11   the police; and
12   the judiciary.

These core central issues broached by Islamic legitimacy politics (or Al-Siyassa al Shar'iyya) have received varying degrees of attention by Muslim Brotherhood jurists and political thinkers.

This book does not seek to tackle all twelve areas, but focuses specifically on four areas fundamental to the question of freedoms and liberties. The first of these elements is the application of the Shari'a and Shura as instituted through the concept of a civil state with an Islamic reference. The second is the question of the positioning and role of the opposition and the political minorities whose views deviate from the majority (in other words the question of the terms of political pluralism in an Islamic state). The third dimension of legitimacy politics addressed here in this book is that of the People of Dhimma and the non-Muslims specifically in Dar el Islam (i.e. non-Muslims in a Dar el Islam context such as Egypt, not those in Europe or the United States). Finally, although the question of gender relations has hardly featured as an area of its own until more recently, it often appeared as a cross-cutting issue broached in all of the twelve areas (i.e. women in jihad, women in the judiciary, relations with women of the People of Dhimma or non-Muslims, etc.) and will be tackled here as a social category of analysis on its own.

This is not to suggest that the other areas of Al-Siyassa al Shar'iyya are of any less importance, only that these areas have been especially prominent in the debates on the Islamic state in Egypt because of their particular contextual relevance.

Why the Muslim Brotherhood?

There has been a proliferation of literature on the Muslim Brotherhood in both Arabic and English, which reflects the increasing awareness of the growing importance of the movement not only for its implications on the Egyptian context, but for the wider ripple effect it has on other Arab contexts and beyond. This explosion of scholarship on the Brotherhood has been particularly notable since 2005, when the Muslim Brotherhood won eighty-eight seats or 20 per cent of the seats in the Egyptian parliament, generating intense debate over whether they were edging closer to political power. The 25 January uprisings of 2011 that led to the demise of the Mubarak government brought the Brotherhood closer to the centres of political power,[1] making the understanding of their vision of governance more pressing than ever before.

Imam Hassan El Banna, the founder of the Muslim Brotherhood offered one of the most insightful, comprehensive definitions of what the movement is. He said that the Muslim Brotherhood is:

1   A Salafi call (da'wa): because they call for returning Islam to its purist meaning from God's Book and the Sunnah of his Prophet

2   A Sunni way (tariqa[2]): because they take it upon themselves to work according to the pure Sunna in all things especially in beliefs, *'badat*, whenever they find a way for that

3   A Sufi truth: because they know the essence of goodness is purity of soul and purity of heart and persistence in work [...]

4   A political entity: because they call for the reform of internal government, and the revision of the Islamic Ummah's relations with other nations [...]

5   A sports group: because they care about their bodies and believe that a strong believer is better than a weak one [...]

6   A scientific, cultural solidarity: because Islam makes the quest for knowledge a *fareeda* (ordinance from God) for every Muslim man and woman and because the Muslim Brotherhood clubs are in reality schools for education and enculturation and institutes for pedagogy for the body, mind and spirit.

7   A commercial company [...]

8   A social idea: because they are concerned with the ills of Islamic society and they try to reach ways of remedying and healing the Ummah from them.

(Amin 2006)

This representation of the Muslim Brotherhood made in 1939 is as relevant today as it was then. The contemporary Muslim Brotherhood is also a political party, a network of charity-providing organisations and an international solidarity of like-minded organisations. Yet the movement continues to be characterised by the same eclecticism and heterogeneity in its pursuit of its aim, unifying and reforming the Muslim Ummah.[3] A number of important caveats are worthy of mention here.

The first is the notion that they are a political 'entity'. Any attempt to separate the political from the apolitical is anathema to the ethos of the Brotherhood. While initially the Muslim Brotherhood was established as a civic association prohibiting political engagement (see Chapter 3), this discourse quickly changed to one of recognising no separation of religion and state. Hence, the Muslim Brotherhood has historically sought to gain political legitimacy without reducing their agency to a political party. By the same token, it is unlikely that the Muslim Brotherhood will ever separate its political essence from its da'wa role, as some authors have recommended it does (see Conclusion).

The second important inference from Hassan El Banna's definition is that of the Muslim Brotherhood as an all-encompassing movement that can accommodate different schools of jurist thought/orientations/ways – even those that are in enmity or opposition to each other such as the Salafis in relation to the Sufis by focusing on agreeing on the fundamentals that unite, not on the secondary matters that divide. The Salafis are a movement comprised of many different groups who believe in the return to *al Salaf al Saleh*, which refers to the righteous past, as lived by the Companions of the Prophet in the first three centuries of Islamic society.[4] One of the distinctive markers of the Salafis is their extreme condemnation of other Islamist groups and movements whom they would argue have deviated from the path of Al Salaf al Saleh and are not considered as being true Muslims (Shallatah 2011: 35). The Brotherhood's ability to incorporate all under one umbrella is one of the distinctive features of the movement which has continued to characterise the movement to this day, to varying degrees. The significance of this all-embracing nature of the movement, as we will see below, is that it makes the movement's heterogeneity and internal political fluidity more difficult to capture but, simultaneously, enables it to be pragmatic in dealing with the volatility of changing political power configurations. Further, it also enables the movement to assume coalitional work with other Islamist forces.

The third key characteristic of Hassan El Banna's definition above is that it is neither a social movement that acts solely to contest the hegemonic powers of the state, nor is its politics reduced to that of a political party aspiring for power, nor is it a religious movement strictly concerned with the spiritual rejuvenation of Muslims. The Islamisation of society and politics are two sides of the same coin. They rest on the fundamental idea of the consciencisation of the people in an all-pervasive manner as absolutely integral for creating the enabling environment for acquiescence to the implementation of the Shari'a. Hassan El Banna exercised power at the invisible level by diffusing the values of a normative framework in which all aspects of life are mediated by Islam. Such a strategy of power is far more influential than an approach focused exclusively on acquiring formal power in key political posts. El Banna's use of the mosque as a powerhouse for education, awareness raising and social activities, continues to be key to the process of the Islamisation of society. Such a process of Islamisation of society from below has also been pursued through a variety of other key strategic entry points including the university campus, the professional syndicates and unions, the media, and the extension of charity and development work (Ibrahim 1988; Pieretti 2008; Ismail 2001; Wickham 2002). The Islamisation of society was an end in itself, but also served as a precursor for laying the foundation for the establishment of an Islamic state.

Reversed realities? The rise of the Brotherhood and the demise of the Mubaraks

It is rather ironic that Gamal Mubarak and his entourage were incarcerated in the prison cells that were normally 'reserved' for the Muslim Brothers, who frequently received sentences that required long sojourns in the infamous Torah prison. This is a far cry from the political standing of the Brotherhood up to January 2011 when they were subjected to one of the most systematic and ruthless repression campaigns. The historical account of the Muslim Brotherhood's relationship with the Egyptian regime is marked by periods of extreme antagonism and high levels of amicability.

Despite the fact that the Muslim Brotherhood was established as a civic association (non-governmental organisation) in 1928–1929 by Hassan El Banna, it quickly developed from engaging as a religious organization proselytizing adherence to true religious values to becoming a highly influential actor in the social and political life of the nation. Rashwan (2006) identifies the time since the inception of the Brotherhood up to the late 1940s as a time of building the foundation of the movement and expanding its outreach. The dissolution of the movement in 1949 was never technically overridden but, practically, their political legitimacy was subject to the nature of the relationship with prospective governments.

There was a honeymoon period between 1951 and 1954 in the wake of the new revolutionary government that was very sympathetic to the Brotherhood. This ended with the great confrontation between the Muslim Brotherhood and Nasser and signalled the beginning of the systematic repression of members of the movement. Under the new leadership of President Sadat, the movement entered a second phase as it witnessed the release of imprisoned members of the Muslim Brotherhood as part of a strategy of strengthening the Islamist movement in Egypt in order to contain the perceived 'communist threat' emanating from groups that were sympathetic to Nasser's socialist beliefs such as communist and Marxist leaning groups. It is in this political context, as well as an economic one, in which Sadat adopted an open market policy, characterised by the state's retreat from free welfare provision, that the Muslim Brotherhood movement was revived. During this historical period, they successfully reached out to the middle class that formed its new rank and file (after the previous membership had all but dissolved under the Nasserite government) and that were to occupy key policy- and decision-making positions in the government and civil society organisations (Rashwan 2006: 41).

The assassination of President Sadat in 1981 at the hands of a member of the more radical and militant Islamist group, Jihad, brought President Mubarak to power in the same year. Rashwan characterises the Muslim Brotherhood's relationship with the government under the Mubarak regime as undergoing three stages. The first is from 1981 to 1988 in which the government treated the movement with clemency and tolerance, and which enabled the Brotherhood to build a populist base, especially through its much needed social services and benefits that were extended to a population that did not share in the wealth accumulated by a small class of entrepreneurs under the open market economy. From 1988 to 1992, the Brotherhood's relationship with the government began to sour as the latter's suspicions and fears were heightened when faced with the scale of Brotherhood activity and membership and in the light of the movement's lack of condemnation of the militant Islamist terrorist attacks on tourists and government figures (Rashwan 2006: 42).

It is possible, however, to speak of the relationship between the Brotherhood and the Mubarak government as having gone through a series of ebbs and flows between 1993 and 2011. Although officially outlawed, the movement was active on the political, social and economic landscape to various degrees throughout.

The Brotherhood arrived at an entente with the government between 2005 and 2007, which coincided with the period of a more relaxed policy on the part of Mubarak towards political liberalisation mainly in response to President Bush's democratisation push. It is one in which a *safka* (deal) was made between the government and the Brotherhood allowing the latter more political representation in parliament than they ever had before.

From 2007 up to 2011, the Mubarak government returned to its policy of systematic repression of the Muslim Brotherhood. From 2007 onwards we also saw President George Bush retreat from his policy of promoting democratisation in the Middle East and the increased tightening of political space in Egypt and other Arab countries. The second half of the 2000s also witnessed the increased visibility of Gamal Mubarak and more aggressive leadership coinciding with the steady retreat of his father. Widespread repression and corruption culminated in the Brotherhood's official withdrawal from the 2010 elections in reaction to the flagrant violations of basic electoral laws and practices.

Finally, the demise of the Mubarak regime marked a new dawn for the Brotherhood, marked by the sealing of a pact with the armed forces and the forging of joint work with the well-supported Salafi movement. The Brotherhood established the Freedom and Justice Party and Muslim Brotherhood members formed four other additional parties while the Brotherhood as a movement was allowed to function freely (see Chapters 2 and 3). While the Brotherhood did not instigate the uprisings of 25 January 2011 (see Chapter 2), nonetheless, questions of ownership of the revolution and who represents the will of the Egyptian people will ultimately affect the power struggle with other political forces for a long time to come.

Mapping the movement

The internal organisation of the Muslim Brotherhood has not changed radically since its establishment by Hassan El Banna. Mitchell provides an authoritative account of the internal governance structure and organisational hierarchy (Mitchell 1969), although Khalil El Anani's recent study (El Anani 2007) argues that following their success in the parliamentary elections of 2005, the Brotherhood sought to activate and streamline some policies to enhance the internal functioning of the movement.

Organisationally, at the top of the power hierarchy stands the Supreme Guide. Since the assassination of Hassan El Banna in 1949, the Muslim Brotherhood has had seven leaders serving as Supreme Guides (Hassan el Hodeiby, Omar el Telmesany, Hamed Abou el Nassr, Mustapha Mashour, Ma'moun el Hodeiby, Mahdi Akef and the current Muhammad, Bad'ie). None have been so influential in the direction of the Muslim Brotherhood as the founder. The Supreme Guide presides over the Guidance Bureau comprised of thirteen members who retain significant decision-making power on an ideological and organisational level. The Shura Council comprised of ninety members elects the members of the Guidance Bureau. The technical operation unit supports the decision-making apparatus (the Guidance Bureau) with information and background, be it religious, political, legal or otherwise. An elaborate field apparatus structure exists on the ground: at the top lies the administrative office (usually existing at a governorate level), followed by the district level, then branch, then family. The family, or cell as it is known, is comprised of between seven and ten persons and meets for about two hours on a weekly basis to study the prescribed curriculum (El Anani 2007: 96). The family is the building block of the movement and the institution for 'membership organization and indoctrination' (Mitchell 1969: 205). Each five or six families comprise a branch (around thirty members), and each district comprises about three or four branches which then feed into the administrative office which is answerable to the Guidance Bureau. The districts elect the members of the administrative office (El Anani 2007).

Like other political movements, the Muslim Brotherhood is a site for power struggles between different factions. Some Egyptian political and social analysts and scholars such as Shobky, Rashwan, El Anani and Ali have argued that the power struggle at the leadership level lies between the old guard representing the conservative elements and the reformists who tend to be of the 1970s generation. This is based roughly on the notion that the older generation tend to represent the old guard within the Brotherhood, such as the late Mustapha Mashour and the late Ma'moun el Hodeiby, while the younger generation, represented by Essam el Erian and Abdel Moneim Aboul Fotouh, tend to represent the reformist trends in the movement (Abd el Rehim Ali 2005).

The personal trajectories of the old guard who spent many years in prison during the Nasserite era, and became disconnected from what was happening in the outside world and the internal developments within the Brotherhood, may partly account for the generational gap with the reformers. They tend to be therefore more faithful to the teachings of El Banna whom they knew personally. Ali contrasts them with the reformers of the 1970s generation who became politically active at the time of the revival of the Brotherhood in the same decade and who were keen on integrating the movement fully into the political life of the nation.

Abou el Ela Mady, one of the founders of the El Wasat Party provides a slightly more complex analysis of group differentiation. He suggests that the first group comprises the special or secret squad (al Tanzim el Sirry) and the 'group 65', those who were imprisoned and tried at the time of Sayed Qutb's assassination (both of which condoned the use of violence to elicit change). The second group comprises those who were leaders in *al nizam al 'am* (the general organisational structure) of the Brotherhood at the time of Hassan El Banna and were involved in the early formation years such as Omar el Telmesany and were later joined by the 1970s generation such as Essam el Erian, Ibrahim el Zafarany, Saeed Mahmoud Eissa, Salah 'Abd el Sattar and Anour Shehata. Such a group classification is corroborated by times in the movement's history during which the simple 'old guard, new reformers' dichotomy was challenged. For example, when Omar el Telmesany was Supreme Guide he established a strong relationship with the youth in the movement and the configuration of the 'camps' was not strictly generational.

Concepts such as old guard vs. reformers are analytically useful because they do, to a certain extent, correspond to generational gaps between the founders and the generations that followed, but they do not represent the full political spectrum within the Brotherhood, nor do they explain single-handedly the nature of power dynamics. The challenge of understanding the power map in the Muslim Brotherhood lies in the obvious gap between the political image mediated – and who conveys it – and the internal relations with the movement. For example, at the tip of the pyramid – not of power but of political visibility – are the members of the political office of the Guidance Bureau and prominent MPs of the Muslim Brotherhood. Both groups combined give the movement its political face vis-à-vis the outside world, whether in Egypt or internationally. They are numerically few and highly visible in the press and in scholarship about the Muslim Brotherhood. Throughout the 1990s and 2000s the most popular faces from among this group were Essam el Erian, Abdel Moneim Aboul Fotouh and Mohammed Habib (until he was voted out from the Guidance Bureau). Once in political office, some became less connected with members from the other layers in the pyramid by virtue of their engagement with an outside audience. The political office has spearheaded the reformed discourse of the Brotherhood on democracy, pluralism and human rights, yet it is this very discourse that has led to some of the members' alienation from the rank and file at the two other tiers of the pyramid.

The second tier in the pyramid comprises the movers and shakers who have substantial ideological and organisational powers within the movement. They include some of the less conspicuous members of the Guidance Bureau, thinkers whose works bear an influence on the political strategies and positions of the Guidance Bureau more generally. A significant number of those who are the movers and shakers are not known to the wider public and academia. This is partly because some are fully immersed in da'wa and are not concerned with the political dimensions of the Brotherhood's work and partly because it allows them to work behind the scenes without hassles.

The second tier also includes the political activists who have gone up the ladder from being rank and file to being leaders, strategising, organising, mobilising the members. It also includes the da'eya as well as those who have excelled in the fundamentals of Islam and jurisprudence, including the Mufti of the Ikhwan, who is the authoritative source of issuing religious opinions (fatwas) for members of the movement. The list also includes those who do not have an organisational position in the Muslim Brotherhood but whose influence over the Brotherhood is definitive – such as the renowned Youssef El Qaradawy who was once a member of the Brothers and was at one time nominated to serve as Supreme Guide and who is an authoritative source on jurisprudence matters for the movement (he currently serves as head of the international union of Muslim scholars). Mohammed 'Emara, renowned Islamist scholar, and Fahmy Howeidy a prominent Islamist writer, both of whom were repreatedly cited by the Brothers as important references.

Finally, the last tier in the pyramid, that of the rank and file, constitutes the overwhelming bulk of the members of the Brotherhood. While some have political ambitions and are therefore keen to follow the movement's news, a significant proportion see themselves as primarily engaged in da'wa. While most of the 'movers and shakers' are highly influential organisationally within the overall movement, it does not follow that the rank and file are completely in tune with their political thought because their exposure to it in their curriculum is very limited. On the other hand, they are very much exposed to preachers such as Sheikh Youssef El Qaradawy and their own Mufti.

The Brothers at the tip of the pyramid are much more accessible to researchers and the media, yet what will be argued here is that they may not necessarily represent the movement in all its diversity and fluidity. There is a great disconnect between what is conveyed outwardly, and how matters are perceived inwardly. What is proposed here is that to understand the dynamics of power in the Brotherhood, we need to turn the pyramid upside down – and look at rank and file and movers and shakers, rather than exclusively at those in political office.

On an ideological level, it would be inaccurate to draw clear demarcations between one ideological camp and another within the Brotherhood, because there is much fluidity and overlap. However, it is possible to talk of particular ideological orientations assuming hegemonic entrenchment within the Brotherhood and, as a consequence, the marginalisation of other ideological strands. This has been the case with the triumph of the Salafi movement within the Brotherhood, or what has been called the Salafisation of the Brotherhood (Tammam 2010).

From its very foundational stage, the Muslim Brotherhood had organisational links with the Saudi movement that propagated Wahabi-Salafi ideology,[5] and was heavily influenced by the Salafi political thought prevalent in Egypt at the time. Hassan El Banna was very close to the famous preacher Rashid Reda who championed Salafi-Wahabi ideology.[6] El Banna's own autobiography (*The Da'wa and the Preacher*) talks of spending many hours with Sheikh Reda. The association was so close that some considered the Muslim Brothers an offshoot of Reda's da'wa and its magazine, *Al Manar*, and that Reda was the connecting link between the Saudi monarchy and El Banna. From El Banna's own autobiography, it is clear he had links with the Saudi monarchy. Moreover, it is believed that that he was a regular recipient[7] of Saudi funding for his organisation (El Nimnim[8] 2011: 115; El Es'ad 1996: 99–100). Moreover, Sheikh Moheb el Din el Khatib, the founder of the Salafi publishing house in Egypt was also a close friend of Hassan El Banna and was appointed as the managing editor of *Al Ikhwan al muslimeen*, the Muslim Brotherhood's regular weekly publication and its mouthpiece at the time (El Shobashy 2000: 32).

At the time of the establishment of the Brothers, El Banna was open to both Salafi thought and that of the *Hassafiyya*, one of the Sufi ways which had shaped his own approach to spirituality.[9] Some argue that as his association with Wahabi-Salafi Islam became stronger, he became more dismissive of the Sufi ways, to the point that his second deputy and member of the Guidance Bureau, Mustapha el Teir, exited the organisation in objection.[10] Moreover, there is much overlap between the curriculum taught by the Muslim Brotherhood to its members and the curricula taught among many Salafi groups (see Chapter 2).

It was, however, in the 1950s that the Saudi Wahabi strain of Salafi ideology became increasingly influential in the Brotherhood's political thought. The escape from Nasser's persecution led many of the key Muslim Brotherhood leaders to flee to Saudi Arabia where they and their families became exposed to Wahabi ideology over a sustained period. Many were key figures in crafting the political and fiqh thought of the Brotherhood and, in effect, what happened was the Salafisation of the old guard, whether they be the Qutbists or their offshoots the Sororyeen or those from the original core group of the movement. Whether they remained in exile (such as Mohammed Qutb, the brother of Sayed Qutb and one of the Sororyeen, and Sallah El Sawi whose intellectual contribution to the Muslim Brotherhood's political thought cannot be underestimated) or whether they returned to Egypt later (Gom'a Amin, Mahdi Akef), their diffusion of Salafi ideology into the Brotherhood was thorough and insidious.

The 1970s saw the diffusion of the Wahabi-Salafi ideology among the rank and file by the older generations within the Brotherhood but also directly from other sources. It is in this period that due to its notable enrichment with petrodollars, the Saudi government took a more proactive approach in injecting large funds into exporting Wahabi ideology, which supported a large sympathetic constituency in Egypt. Moreover, many of the Brothers who were released from prison during this period went to Saudi Arabia in search of employment in large numbers, again enlarging the group within the Brotherhood that had pro-Wahabi sympathies.

Back on Egyptian university campuses, where the political battle between the leftist and Nasserite leaning students and the Islamists was being fought out, the Brothers sought to win the Gama'at to their ranks. Given that the Gama'at thought that the Brothers were too lax in their commitment to Islam and its observance, compromises had to be made in order to win them over by adopting a more orthodox approach.

In the 1990s and 2000s, the increasing popularity of religious satellite television shows among the Egyptian public came to be one of the most strategic entry points to spreading the Wahabi-Salafi ideology. There was a great public demand for it, and the more religiously conservative, the greater its appeal. It is in this period that independent Muslim Brotherhood preachers came to be television stars, and many of them, such as Safwat Hegazy who presented on the *Al Nas* television programme, had lived many years in Saudi Arabia and had close ties with the Salafis. Many of these Salafi-oriented Muslim Brotherhood preachers not only built a strong constituency among the rank and file through their television-broadcast da'wa but also among the Egyptian public as a whole. It is also notable that pro-Salafi sheikhs were assuming key leadership positions in the tamkeen section of the Brotherhood (those responsible for organising the rank and file), resulting in considerable influence over the curriculum taught (see Chapter 2).

One of the rank and file's triumphs in influencing the power configurations within the Brotherhood has been to expel some of the eminent politically visible reformists such as Mohammed Habib and Abdel Moneim Aboul Fotouh in the elections of the members of the Guidance Bureau and replace them with those more aligned with their Wahabi-Salafi thinking, such as the Qutbists (further outcomes on the politics and organisational engagement of the Brotherhood are drawn in Chapter 2).

Whose Brotherhood? Whose political thought?

At the commencement of this research, the author sought direction from the former Supreme Guide Muhammad Mahdi Akef, as well as other members of the Guidance Bureau, as to the appropriate methodological approaches to pursue in understanding the agency of the Muslim Brotherhood. Given the complexity and diversity within the movement, it was important to know which sources would be considered representative, credible and legitimate. A virtually unanimous opinion expressed by members of the Brotherhood was that any official endorsement by the Supreme Guide should be taken as the authoritative, undisputed source of reference on the Muslim Brotherhood's viewpoint, i.e. the writings that have 'resala min al ikhwan' (message from the Brothers) inscribed on them or books that have the signature of the Supreme Guide and the Brothers' stamp (emblem of two swords with 'prepare' inscribed below). Official documents such as the 1994 political platform, the 2005 initiative on the principles of reform in Egypt and the 2007 draft party platform were all considered as authoritative sources representative of the Brothers' position. Akef argued that all other sources are representative of the views of the individual author, and do not necessarily represent the views of the Muslim Brotherhood as a whole. This presented a real dilemma for this research, for to have to rely strictly on these sources is very limiting, since these documents present very minimal detail and have very little explanatory power as to what informs stances, political agendas and choices, to say nothing of their agency within the Brotherhood.

The methodology adopted here for understanding the political thought of the Brothers and its relationship to policy and practice relied on a combination of sources. It combined historical accounts (written by the Brothers as well as analysts), critical theoretical texts considered to be 'key references' on these subjects, the writings of Imam Hassan El Banna[11] and former Supreme Guides of the Brothers, interviews with some members of the Guidance Bureau, analysis of fatwas (El Banna 1986: 62–63) issued by the Brotherhood's Mufti, parliamentary stances adopted by Muslim Brotherhood MPs as well as vignettes from case studies collated through participant observation.

Moreover, there is a wealth of material on the Muslim Brotherhood in English and in particular in Arabic which this study draws on. While much of the material overlaps, it is possible to categorise the literature according to disciplinary approaches (history, politics, sociology).

The historical accounts of the Brotherhood are many, although most end around 2008. In addition to Mitchell's account of the Muslim Brothers (1969), other key accounts include: Abd el Azim Ramadan's *The Muslim Brotherhood and the Secret Apparatus* (1982), Mohsen Mohammed's *Who Killed Hassan el Banna?* (1987) and Abd el Rehim Ali's series on the Brotherhood comprising four books on the internal reform process (2004), the fatwas on Copts, democracy, women and art (2005), 'pre-Fall' scenarios, from El Banna to Mahdi Akef (2007), and readings of secret classified files (2011).

The Muslim Brotherhood's own historical accounts are of central importance at the forefront of which is Gom'a Amin's series titled 'Papers from the History of the Muslim Brotherhood'. Abbas el Sissy, also a renowned Muslim Brotherhood historian, provides a historical account of the Brotherhood as he experienced and witnessed it in seven books. Also significant is Youssef El Qaradawy's own historical account of the movement (1999).

Sociological accounts including those that engage with the movement through a social movement theory lens include those of Khalil El Anani, Carrie Wickham and Ziad Munson (2001).

There is a wealth of literature examining the political performance and role of the Brotherhood including the works of Brown and Hamzawy (2010), Abd el Moneim Said (2008), El Dellal (2007), El Shobky (2009), Haqqani and Fradkin (2008) and Langohr (2001).

Exclusive reliance on only one source tends to present a highly distorted representation of the Brothers. For example, as mentioned earlier, reliance on interviews with a select number of members from the political office of the Muslim Brotherhood tends to convey the progressive, liberal image of the movement, without revealing much about the internal contestations on these issues. Reliance exclusively on parliamentary performance does not tell us much about how the rank and file perceived matters. Similarly, a reliance on the rank and file exclusively through sociological approaches does not reveal the developments in the political and fiqh thoughts of those who influence the overall directions of the movement.

Understanding the position of the Muslim Brotherhood requires examining the reasoning behind positions adopted, and where relevant the theoretical premises upon which they are grounded. This is not to reduce the agency of Muslim Brotherhood actors to a blind adoption or enactment of fiqh, but that only by examining a constellation of factors: context, interests, relationships and political thought, is it possible to arrive at a more nuanced understanding. For example, examining political stances and discourses without examining El Qaradawy's postulation of different fiqhs severely undermines our ability to understand what informs particular readings of fiqh, and the political stances informed by them. The concept of *fiqh al mouwazanat* for example weighs al masalih (interests or benefits) with al mafasid (harms or ills) and if the interests advanced are more than the ills, then there is flexibility in the way an Islamic principle or decree is applied. For example, *fiqh al mouwazanat* has been applied by key Muslim Brotherhood thinkers to arrive at a stance that while non-Islamic political parties are anathema to the principle of unity in Islamic governance, nonetheless, it is possible to cooperate and create coalitions with them in a phase in which the Islamists are in a position of weakness and not of power (see Chapter 4). Similarly it is possible to understand one key Muslim Brother's position on the permissibility of a woman being head of state, if it is understood within the context in which he was using it, i.e. comparing Noha el Zeiny with Ahmed Ezz by looking at fiqh al masaleh (see Chapter 8).

In addition to the political thought of the Supreme Guides, that of key political thinkers was analysed. After Hassan El Banna, Abd el Kader Ouda is
believed to be one of the founding fathers responsible for theorising the details
of political governance (Khallaf Allah 1987: 51–59). Sayed Qutb is the third
leading figure to have immensely influenced the political thought of the movement and his works continue to feature on the Brotherhood's curriculum for the
rank and file. Other political thinkers who are critical for influencing the interpretation of fiqh and the operationalisation of ideas into policies include Tawfik
el Shawi, Gom'a Amin, El Wa'i, Mohammed Qutb, Ahmed El Sawi, Mohammed el Bahi and El-Bahnasawy. The third source is the political thinkers and
leaders who are not organisationally part of the Brotherhood but whose influence
on their political thought is beyond measure, such as the late Sheikh Mohammed
el Ghazali and Sheikh Youssef El Qaradawy. The selection of the political thinkers to be studied was arrived at through interviews with the Brothers about who
is considered as influential, from what is being taught in the curriculum to the
rank and file, and through informants and historical accounts.

Positionality

The author is aware that being a liberal Egyptian non-Muslim researching the
Muslim Brotherhood makes her suspect among some Islamists and sympathisers
of having a hidden agenda of undermining the movement and Islam itself. Certainly, the Brotherhood have been subject to the most voracious smearing campaign in the pro-government press and to the most ruthless and brutal systematic
state-sponsored repression at the time of Mubarak. The author has purposely
sought to avoid press sources from Mubarak's era, in view of their inherent
biases towards the Brotherhood and their consistent reference to the movement
as el mahzoura (the forbidden). However, it is also unacceptable to self-censor
oneself to present a positivist portrayal of the movement in order to avoid being
called an Islamophobe/Ikhwanphobe. Moreover, the implicit interchangeable use
of the terms Islamophobia and Ikhwanophobia means that critical perspectives
of Islamist movements are immediately tagged as assaults on Islam. For
example, a recent article in *Ikhwanweb* criticised the Quillam Foundation, a
think tank in London, for its negative reaction to the visit made by a delegation
from the British Foreign Office to the Muslim Brotherhood's administrative
office in Alexandria. The author of the article comments that the Quillam's accusation of the Muslim Brotherhood masterminding the engagement (with the
British delegation) to further its own anti-Western agenda and to sideline liberal
Muslim voices, and its claim that these were aimed to whitewash its own extrem-
ist beliefs, was a case 'demonstrating a model example of both Islamophobia
and Ikhwanophobia' (Mazin 2011). While it is understandable (though not
necessarily justifiable) that attacks on the Brotherhood should be seen as a form
of Ikhwanophobia, to also describe an attack on the Brothers as an attack on
Islam is highly disconcerting, as it indicates the intention of giving the Ikhwan
the sacrosanct veneer of religion.

The issues and the debates

This book will seek to critically engage with three contestations relating to the Brotherhood's vision of rights and freedoms in an Islamic state. The first contention stems from the prediction made prior to January 2011 and during the transition phase that once the authoritarian shackles of the Mubarak regime are removed, the Muslim Brotherhood will become increasingly democratised, both internally as an organisation, and externally, vis-à-vis its positions and practices. The second contention, very much associated with the first, is that the Brotherhood represents a moderate Islamist political force with a reformist agenda and their political inclusion is the key to building Arab democracies. The third contention is that the democracy credentials of the Muslim Brotherhood would be greatly enhanced if they clarified their position on certain grey areas around which there is much ambiguity. Each of these will be briefly flagged here and revisited in the upcoming chapters.

The first contention flagged here is that the Brotherhood will undergo positive change once they are no longer burdened by having to freeze internal reform and prioritise cohesion. It has been argued that the internal process of reform has been stalled because the leaders of the movement have focused their attention and efforts on shielding themselves against the assaults of an authoritarian state. Consequently, analysts proposed that this will change once the political environment changes. This earlier contention (El Hamzawy 2005; El Shobky 2006; Hamzawy and Brown 2008; Diaa Rashwan 2008) that in a politically free setting, the progressive and reformist elements within the movement will become stronger and more influential, needs to be set against the unfolding reality in Egypt after the demise of Mubarak. Amr el Shobky, for example, had argued that if the Muslim Brotherhood are allowed to establish their own political party and be granted legitimacy as a political actor, a number of positive transformative reforms will incur, such as: that there will be a separation between the da'wa or the proselytizing and the political work (with the former pursued through the Muslim Brotherhood as an organisation, the latter through the political party); that the movement will become a democratising force in its own right in the wider political sphere and that this will lead to the emergence of an:

> 'Islamic democratic' force that believes in political pluralism, human rights, non-discrimination against citizens on the basis of religion or ethnicity and also believes in the principles of a republican system and the civility of the state, the constitution and the legal system.
>
> (2006: 31)

It is important to note however, that the above hypothesis was written by political analysts before the Egyptian uprising and therefore their perspectives may have changed substantially since then.

While this book covers the period only up to July 2011, this six-month phase is one in which the Brotherhood enjoyed a level of political freedom not seen since the 1970s. Unlike the youth coalitions, some of whose members were harassed and incarcerated by the armed forces, the Muslim Brothers were given virtually carte blanche to engage politically as they wished. While still not in power, it is nevertheless useful to examine how issues of political and religious pluralism played out in the Muslim Brotherhood's actions, how issues of internal democracy and dissent within the movement were handled and how relations between the movement and the newly established political party were mediated. The second contention is that the endorsement of democracy in the region requires that moderate Islamists be fully integrated into the political systems (Ibrahim 2006; Hamzawy 2005; Al Sayyid 2003; Brown *et al.* 2006; Asseburg 2007). Moderate Islamists, according to Hamzawy, are those that 'reject violence and endorse competition through pluralistic politics and it is they with whom the western governments now should engage' (2005: 2). They have also been labelled as part of the 'reformist' Islamist tradition. Such reformist currents are deemed as 'becoming much more sophisticated and flexible in their thinking, and that recent political success in some countries is increasing their influence within their respective organizations' (Brown *et al.* 2006: 19). Abou el Fotouh, one of the former members of the Guidance Bureau of the Muslim Brotherhood and prospective presidential candidate, commended the authors' description of the Muslim Brotherhood as reformist. Another use of the term 'moderate' is that commonly used by El Qaradawy who sees himself as heralding the jurisprudence school of Islam al wassatiyya, 'the moderates', a term that many of the politically visible members of the Muslim Brotherhood use to describe the movement.

The value of supporting 'moderate' Islamist movements such as the Brotherhood is based on the recognition of their legitimacy on the streets (a wide populist constituency), their representation of counter-force to more radical Islamist militant groups and movements (Khan 2007) and because of their

> genuine commitment to both the principles of Islam and cultural identity on the one hand, and to meeting the challenge of modern political life on the other, centrist Islamic politics are the only credible way forward for many countries in the Arab world.
>
> (El Anani 2009)

The authors presented such projections at a time when the Brotherhood was still politically contained by Mubarak's regime, and it is possible that their views have changed, given the unexpected ouster of the former president. However, there are still a number of issues that need to be flagged with respect to defining the movement as 'moderate'. Who determines the yardstick of what is 'moderate' and what is not? And what does it mean to be reformist? Reformist according to whose criteria and vision? Hassan El Banna labelled his vision for the movement as reformist with a view to reviving the Islamic Ummah. Yet his political choices may clash with what is referred to in some Western scholarship as 'reformist'.

On the level of fiqh, it is also highly problematic if one is examining the full spectrum of ideological orientations within the Brotherhood to assume that the Brotherhood has chosen to be reformist. There is no doubt that Youssef El Qaradawy is a highly influential figure within the Brotherhood, yet some of these very same supporters would also be followers of the Wahabi strain of Salafi ideology. What will be highlighted in the forthcoming chapters is that the lines are far more blurred, in political thought, affiliations and configurations, than conventionally conveyed. The third contention is around what Nathan *et al.* term 'the gray zones' or areas around which there is ambiguity within the Islamist movement. They identify the question of the implementation of the Shari'a, the question of civil and political rights, minority rights, political pluralism and the use of violence as issues the resolution of which will 'determine whether the rise of Islamic movements leads the countries of the Arab world, finally, towards democracy or, conversely to a new form of authoritarianism with Islamic character' (2006: 17). What will be suggested in this book is that some of the ambiguity and murkiness around those areas[12] can be removed if we examine the political thought of Muslim Brotherhood thinkers and triangulate those with the views among rank and file. What is proposed here is that through triangulation with the sources of influential political thought within the Brotherhood and with other sources of knowledge, it is possible to arrive at a fairly clear articulation of positions on these areas dubbed murky. What the author discovered is that despite the media's focus on the seeming polarization of viewpoints on key matters within the Brotherhood, there is often a surprising consistency within the Brotherhood's constituency and the logic that guides a 'progressive viewpoint' is often the one that guides a viewpoint that is dubbed 'reactionary/conservative'.

Outline of the book

Chapter 1 analyses some of the constellation of factors that led to Egypt reaching tipping point, or what is commonly referred to domestically as the 25 January revolution. In particular, it uncovers how the corporatist-pluralist configuration of power delicately balanced by President Mubarak was replaced with a highly repressive policy led by his son, Gamal, and his entourage of businessmen. The rupture of Mubarak's management of corporatist-pluralist arrangements and the possibility of Gamal's ascendency to the presidency led to a number of oppositional forces turning completely against the president, the most important of which was the army, which, in the end, played a central role in toppling him. The chapter also situates the waxing and waning of the relations between the Muslim Brotherhood and the Mubarak government in the light of the above and the impact of the increasing use of repression on uniting the opposition against the regime.

Against this backdrop, Chapter 2 begins with the moments before the outbreak of 25 January uprisings, analyses what the response of the political leadership of the Brotherhood meant for its own internal legitimacy vis-à-vis their youth and in relation to the wider question of who represents the Egyptian street.

This is contextualised in relationship to other political forces and actors in Egypt and how they were reacting to the unfolding events. In the second part, the chapter tracks how the Brotherhood engaged politically through the formation of new pacts (armed forces and Islamist groups) and the abandonment of the old ones (non-Islamist political forces). The millioniyya of 29 January 2011 is discussed as a vignette that was indicative of these new political configurations. The ideological and political nuances of these realignments of power are discussed in detail in Chapter 4 on the question of the relationship between an Islamist political force and non-Islamic forces at different phases and stages.

Chapter 3 begins with a discussion of the concept of a civil state with an Islamic reference, one of the most critical messages delivered by the Brothers to withstand accusations that they are demanding the establishment of a religious state. The origin and development of the concept is examined, as well as its contemporary uses and its meanings and the extent to which the application of Shari'a as envisioned by the Brotherhood will be possible without undermining the civility of the state. This is followed by a discussion of the concept of shura, which is seen by the Brothers as one of the greatest guarantors of the civility of the state. Shura is presented as the Islamic equivalent of – but not the same as – democracy. The qualifiers to this are examined at length.

Chapter 4 discusses the Brotherhood's perspective on engaging politically and discusses why the proposal of separation of politics and da'wa is anathema to the foundations of their political thought. It then discusses in detail the concept of political pluralism as theorised in Muslim Brotherhood political thought. It discusses the dilemmas that political pluralism posed for the movement itself and its members in the transition phase after Mubarak's ouster as shown in Chapter 2. Finally, the question of what will political pluralism look like if the Brothers come to power is discussed at length.

Chapter 5 uncovers the relationship between the movement and the Copts from the time of El Banna to Bad'i. Against this backdrop, the ideological and political debates around the place of non-Muslims more generally are discussed in Chapter 6 on Islamic citizenship. Chapter 7 seeks to historicise the Brothers' engagement with the question of women's agency within the Brotherhood and wider society, which again, is integral for understanding the position of the Brothers on gender matters, discussed in Chapter 8.

Finally, some of the possible scenarios under the rise or demise of the Brotherhood that can be inferred from a study of political thought and power configurations within the movement and society will be expounded in the conclusion.

1 Egypt and the Brotherhood in a pressure cooker

> Far from enhancing the governability of authoritarian regimes, the abrupt shift to repressive corporatist policies may merely provide a new recipe for revolution.
>
> (Bianchi 1989: 26)

This chapter narrates the political, social and economic crises in the months preceding the 25 January 2011 uprisings in Egypt. It argues that the disintegration of pacts, deals and coalitions of both a formal and informal nature between Mubarak and his regime on the one hand, and various political and social forces including the armed forces on the other, is critical for understanding how Egypt arrived at the tipping point. The political ascendency of Gamal Mubarak and his business group led to the breakdown of the pluralist-corporatist strategies previously pursued by President Mubarak. The exclusion of all political forces from any power-sharing arrangement in the elections of 2010 catalysed the opposition parties and the Muslim Brotherhood to coalesce into a counter-force against the status quo. Further, Gamal Mubarak's aspirations for presidency led to the rupture of one of the most important sources of Mubarak's power: the pact with the military.

The ruptures in amoebic engagements

Egypt's authoritarian regime has been characterised by its plasticity manifest in its pursuit of both pluralist and corporatist strategies of engagement with its allies and enemies (Bianchi 1989: 6). Pluralism was never allowed to thrive freely enough so as to pose a threat to the power base of the regime, while corporatism was never fully adopted as a governance mechanism such that it would obliterate all political space. In effect, strategies of engagement have sought to accommodate various interest groups through a careful balancing act combining both pluralist and corporatist elements. These interest groups have included a wide variety of economic and political actors.

It is the hybridity of the approaches (corporate-pluralist) that allows the regime room to adapt to changing political and economic circumstances. The adoption of a certain level of restrained pluralism grants the facade of a commitment to democratisation, so important for Western consumption, while also allowing the survival of weak political actors who can be manipulated and discarded by government patrons. When subject to pressure from the Bush government to democratise in 2005, Mubarak's government increased press freedom and political party activism, but regulated through the security investigations apparatus. Moreover, a certain dose of corporatism allows the government to make strategic concessions when in a politically vulnerable situation. So, for example, following the bread riots of 1977, the government backed down on removing subsidies and maintained the previous arrangements with the public. This eclectic and alterable mixture of corporatist, pluralist and hybrid strategies grants the regime flexibility and room for responding to unpredictability and, very importantly, 'corporatism supplementing pluralism increases governability, societal fragmentation and prevents the emergence of strong coalitions' (Bianchi 1989: 24, 25).

We can imagine the Egyptian regime as operating like an amoeba; it contracts and expands its space and parameters according to various internal and external pressures in a highly dynamic manner. For political and civil society, it means that the ground is constantly shifting in unpredictable ways. However, ruptures in the corporatist-pluralist policies tend to destabilise this placatory arrangement, provoke political disorder and facilitate 'the rise of a more powerful opposition demanding the transition to pluralist democracy' (Bianchi 1989: 12). For example, President Sadat's tightening of political pluralism led to the opposition turning against the regime in its later years and as was evident with Mubarak in January 2011.

Two important changes happened to alter this corporatist-pluralist political arrangement from 2009 onwards. First, Mubarak became disinterested in governing and increasingly delegated matters to his son and his entourage (the young businessmen and a corps within the security sector). Whilst the reasons for Mubarak's conspicuous retreat from politics are unknown, the timing is significant. The first step towards political disengagement manifested itself in his indefinite cancellation of a high-profile policy meeting with President Obama in the United States. This happened one week after the sudden and tragic death of his grandson in May 2009, which sources close to him say left him deeply bereft, to the point of not being able to attend the funeral. It is no coincidence that from that point onwards, President Mubarak's involvement in the day-to-day governance of the country declined, and he became increasingly disconnected from many of the important political dynamics occurring around him.

The second change destabilising the pluralist-corporatist balancing formula and which is closely related to Mubarak's retreat in May 2009 is a radical reworking of the rules of the game, leading to the exclusion of important actors and interest groups, and their increasing radicalisation. The highly elaborate corporatist arrangements handled by President Mubarak and his politically seasoned entourage, which allowed for a wide diverse set of actors and their interests to be represented was radically reconfigured with the gradual power takeover by Gamal Mubarak and his entourage.

An understanding of the breakdown of the corporatist-pluralist arrangement requires an analysis of the process, the actors and the relationships through which Gamal Mubarak came to govern. Gamal Mubarak's pathway into politics was primarily through the ruling National Democratic Party (NDP). Political writer and analyst Waheed 'Abd el Meguid argues that Gamal Mubarak's appropriation of a leadership position in the ruling NDP coincided with the disappointing results of the ruling party in the elections of 2000,[1] which they won only by a third. The party needed new blood and new leadership to revitalise it, it was argued, and hence the justification for Gamal Mubarak's entry and his new motto for the NDP, 'towards new thinking'. Within the NDP, a new layer of governance was especially carved for Gamal Mubarak to assume a leadership role, the 'High Policy Committee'. Leadership of the High Policy Committee allowed him to establish a new oligarchy from within, which came to gradually rule over the party and the country more generally ('Abd el Meguid 2011). It is too early at this stage to draw out a full mapping of Gamal's elite group responsible for the governance of the economic and political affairs of the oligarchy and the country, however, there are some key figures, known to and loathed by the Egyptian public, who merit mention here. The first is iron and steel business tycoon Ahmed Ezz who was also secretary for organisational affairs in the NDP and head of the budget committee in parliament. Second is Mahmoud Mohieddin who served as minister of investment from 2004 until his appointment as the World Bank's managing director in October 2010. The General Prosecution is examining several cases filed against Mahmoud Mohieddin accusing him of privatising Egyptian assets at below their valuation price to benefit the buyers.

The powers of Gamal Mubarak's oligarchical group of businessmen expanded and was consolidated through the appointment of Ahmed Nazif (Gamal's close ally) as prime minister in July 2004, and the appointment of Gamal Mubarak's businessmen friends to key ministerial posts: Ahmed Maghraby (minister of tourism then minister of housing), Zoheir Garana (minister of tourism), Rashid Mohammed Rashid (ministry of industry), Mansour (minister of transport) and of course Youssef Boutros Ghali whose appointment as minister of state for the economy was renewed. In effect, the appointment of Nazif's government marked the business appropriation of state resources through the same actors who happened to be the prime advocates of the scenario of the inheritance of the presidency from Mubarak the father to Mubarak the son ('Abd el Meguid 2011: 26). The impact was widespread corruption, made possible through the appropriation of state land to businessmen for luxury housing projects and large scale tourism enterprises (both bought for nominal prices from the government).

President Mubarak's own elite corps, the 'old guard', was not going to readily and easily relinquish power to Gamal and his entourage in particular since the latter's circle was small and exclusive and challenged the broader, more inclusive corporatist arrangements that were in place. As Gamal's rein on power tightened, and his group became more conspicuously involved in running the country, acts of vengeance from those who were excluded manifested themselves. Documents and other snippets of evidence were leaked to the press by the old guard in the NDP exposing the corrupt and illegal deals being made by key ministers and businessmen in Nazif's government.

However, Gamal Mubarak's oligarchic corps was able to offset the escalation of scandals into fully fledged political and economic crises through the support of the security apparatus. By the end of the 2010, the State Security Investigations Apparatus (the SSI, mabaheth amn al dawla) was playing a key role in governing the internal affairs of the country. The SSI became the primary instrument used to uncover Gamal Mubarak's enemies, negotiate with the disgruntled, and strategically engineer how to advance his agenda and interests. SSI used hard and soft power in their political manoeuvrings to advance the interests of the Mubaraks. The SSI came to control almost every aspect of Egypt's public life (excluding all that is related to the military and the ministry of defence, which were under the tutelage of the army). It mediated in worker–employer disputes; it ran 'profile checks' on candidates before they were given the go-ahead to nominate themselves whether they sought representation on a student body, workers' committee in a factory, local council or parliament. They also infiltrated almost all public action movements or political forces. It was no secret that the Muslim Brotherhood and political parties were heavily infiltrated by the SSI. Rumours among many activists in Egypt were that they had in recent times also managed to infiltrate the renowned Kefaya movement. Very few aspects (such as social networking) were out of the reach of the SSI.

Yet as Bianchi warned in the 1980s, when the corporatist-pluralist model of governance tilts towards less pluralism and more repression under the backdrop of a dire economic and political situation, the regime is bound to collapse. This is precisely what happened in the months preceding the Egyptian revolution of 25 January, very much encapsulated in the increasing repression with which voices of discontent were dealt with in the press and media and through wide-scale incarcerations, the conspicuous violation of the absolute minimal human rights in parliamentary elections of November 2010 and the emergence of powerful oppositional forces keen to wreck Gamal Mubarak's presidential aspirations. Below we will discuss the unfolding of some of these political forces as elements of the ruptures in the rules of the game.

'Let them amuse themselves' (President Mubarak remarked on the opposition's formation of a counter [informal] people parliament parallel to the NDP-led parliament in 2010). The parliamentary elections handled by Ahmed Ezz and Gamal Mubarak's core group showed a clear rupture in the earlier NDP's corporatist arrangements with political parties and forces. In the elections of 2005 (and previous elections) the ruling powers (primarily the old guard from the NDP) negotiated with the other political forces some sort of 'arrangement': the NDP would propose a number of seats with the opposition party, but they would have a say in to whom these seats would go. In return, the political parties would agree to participate in the parliamentary theatrical performance that would render an image of authenticity and credibility. In a highly revealing interview with *Al-Masry Al-Youm*, Mahdi Akef, the then Supreme Guide of the Muslim Brotherhood, formally admitted to entering a pact with the authorities prior to the elections of 2005:

This [the pact between the government and the Muslim Brotherhood] happened in 2005, when I was visited by a senior official who talked with me about the president's upcoming visit to the United States. He said he hoped that the movement [the Muslim Brotherhood] would not create a furore in light of the visit. I expressed my readiness, and the man visited me twice more. My deputies attended the meeting and we agreed on several terms. At the time, ahead of the 2005 elections, there were a number of Muslim Brotherhood members behind bars, the most famous of which was Essam el-Erian. We wanted the election results to be in our favour, so I acquiesced to their demands and we nominated 150 people, and kept our word at the meeting with the security officials. Members of the Brotherhood began holding seminars and staging protest marches, and all those in jail were released. I was also surprised to see the sweeping success of the Brotherhood in the first and second rounds of the elections. However, in the third round, someone contacted me, saying Israeli President Sharon contacted George W. Bush, who contacted President Mubarak. They told me that no one will succeed in the third round, although we expected 50 nominees to make it, especially in Mansoura and Sharqiyya, which are famous strongholds for the Brotherhood.

(*Al-Masry Al-Youm* 2009)

El Anani points to a number of indicators of a relaxed government position towards the Muslim Brotherhood prior to the elections which corroborate Akef's important statement. These include the release of hundreds of detained Muslim Brotherhood members, including leaders Essam el Erian and Mahmoud Ghozlan, prior to the elections, as well as the freedom which the movement was given to engage in electoral campaigning free of hassles and the government's overlooking of the movement's campaign election financing[2] as well as allowing it to campaign under the Muslim Brotherhood banner (Islam is the solution) (El Anani 2007: 231–239).

These kinds of corporatist pacts, such as that between the government and the Brotherhood, were missing in the parliamentary elections of 2010 which saw the abandonment of any real political bargaining with different forces (no matter how inequitable) in favour of a heavy-handed security approach. When the regime sought to excessively control the configuration of political actors and present it to the public as a fait accompli, it created the conditions that allowed for the emergence of counter-coalitions. The parliamentary elections were characterised by the use of excessive violence exercised by thugs hired by the ruling party against contenders, and against the citizenry who were suspected of voting for non-NDP candidates. Ballot box rigging and other election irregularities were also reported. Right before the second round in the elections, Mohammed Bad'i, the Supreme Guide of the Brotherhood, announced the withdrawal of the movement from the elections because of widespread fraud. This was one of the first signs that a strategy of political thuggery will have its side-effects. The withdrawal of one of the country's largest and most organised political forces was embarrassing for the government's international image – it could not tick the box of having organised a transparent and inclusive election process. Shortly after pronouncing their withdrawal, the Mufti of the Brotherhood Abd el Rahman el Bir issued his very first fatwa (El Souweify 2010) stipulating that the withdrawal of the movement is religiously sanctioned (hallal) and the rigging of the elections is religiously prohibited (haram), thus effectively crowning the movement's retreat with a religious mantra. The decision to pull out of the elections served to enhance the Brotherhood's own legitimacy; the outcome of the elections only put the parliament's own legality in question. The ruling party won more than 86 per cent of the 508 parliamentary seats, with 424 MPs in power, while the opposition won 3 per cent or sixteen seats. The liberal Wafd Party won six seats and the leftist Tagammu won five seats and the Brotherhood won zero seats,[3] down from eighty-eight seats or 20 per cent of the 2005–2010 parliament.

Independent candidates won sixty-five seats, representing 12.5 per cent of the People's Assembly but since many of these were actually NDP defectors; they were to be considered NDP aligned.[4] The MPs who won the seats were dubbed by one writer as 'the State Security Investigations Apparatus MPs' in view of the way they were handpicked by the apparatus, and in reference to the fact that no less than fifty generals had won parliamentary seats (Amin 2010). As famous media figure Amr Adeeb commented, the NDP's handling of the parliamentary elections managed to antagonise just about everybody: the Brotherhood whose animosity towards the regime intensified, the Copts who became increasingly disillusioned about the possibility for any fair representation and the international community who were shocked by the level of 'open' defiance of any pretence of abiding by the rules of electoral procedures (Zalat 2010). The Brotherhood's response to their political exclusion was far more confrontational than their stances on other government violations. Bad'i announced in a press conference that there simply is no alternative to the dissolution of the existing parliament on grounds of lack of legality and legitimacy. The Brotherhood participated in several protests and stand-ins to express their rejection of the flawed elections (Khayal 2010).

The 2010 parliament may have killed the scope for opposition within its walls, but it radically increased it from without, unifying and strengthening the opposition who overcame their ideological and political differences to express their rejection of the NDP's hegemony over the new parliament. On 11 December, days before the new MPs were to be sworn in the formal parliament, ninety MPs who had won seats in the 2005 parliament formed a parallel popular People's Assembly, led by the Democratic Front (El Guindy and Masoud 2010). When President Mubarak was asked what he thought of the parallel people's parliament, he responded: 'Let them amuse themselves' (khalihom yetsalou). The comment only served to add fuel to fire, further reinforcing the contemptuous attitude adopted by the ruling regime towards the people.

'The people have suffocated' (Al nass' itkhana'et) became a popular saying on the streets of Egypt. The old regime's motto, as Bianchi suggested, was 'live and let live'. Let the subsidies continue for the poor, while the few accumulated large bank accounts. This formula was being gradually eroded as the masses found it increasingly difficult to live: youth unemployment was having dire economic and social consequences and the manifestations of relative deprivation were becoming more difficult to ignore.

One of the fundamental elements of the new oligarchic set-up was the extent to which it was disconnected from what was happening on the streets of Egypt, despite being propped up by a large and sophisticated State Security Investigations (SSI) apparatus. The economic crises had further exacerbated the severe economic predicament, in particular in 2010–2011.

Mark Robinson and Gordon White (1998) have shown that non-democratic regimes tend to be less able to survive economic crises than democratic regimes. Economic crises undermine the ability of the ruling government to maintain contracts or pacts that involve political acquiescence in return for minimal economic concessions. Not only was Ahmed Nazif's government unable to maintain the same contract, but denied there was a crisis in the first place, emphasising Egypt's projected high economic growth rates as evidence that the economic situation was promising. The level to which it was disconnected from the acute economic crisis experienced by the majority of Egyptians is no better represented than in the statements issued at the wake of the 25 January uprising.

Perhaps one of the reasons why Ahmed Nazif's government thought it could afford to remain disconnected from the growing populist disenchantment is the belief that the security services, in particular the SSI apparatus was managing to keep the lid on the pressure cooker. The SSI apparatus had its informants in every alley, street or square across the country. Public space was entirely securitised. The paranoia, the fear and the mistrust that had gripped citizens in Egypt, Yemen and Tunisia could not be sustained from generation to generation. However, what the uprisings of 25 January showed was that the SSI was not as fully in tune with all forms of mobilisation as was believed – in particular that happening through social networking (see Chapter 2).

Citizens tried to accommodate the security services but with the increasing economic deprivation and the provocations of a regime that does democracy through rigged ballots, there were questions regarding the political sustainability of the status quo. A week before the 'Tunisia trigger', a group of men and women of all ages in Egypt took to the street to protest the torture of one of their own young men by a state security investigations officer in a local police station.

The army and the inheritance of the presidency

One of the least explored and most opaque dimensions of the breakdown of the corporatist-pluralist governance system is the army's position on the inheritance of power from President Mubarak to Gamal Mubarak. The censorship around the army's affairs has generally been far greater than on other politically sensitive actors such as the state security apparatus. The public knew very little about the size or scope of the commercial enterprises owned and managed by the army, nor about internal governance, power relations or the nuanced dimensions of relations with the ruling regime. Rumours circulated prior and after the ousting of Mubarak that Gamal Mubarak and Field Marshall Tantawi, minister of defence, were battling out a power struggle seeking to eliminate each other. Tantawi did not approve of the president's plan to pass on the presidency to Gamal, a fact that Mubarak seemed to be aware of. The latter took some highly significant political steps to extricate powerful institutions from under the army's authority and bring them under his direct tutelage. For example, historically, the presidential guard was under the army's jurisdiction but the president brought them directly under his control, indicating perhaps a deep suspicion of the allegiances of the army's leadership. By the same token, Gamal Mubarak was, it was rumoured, seeking to remove or at least contain Tantawi through collaboration with the SSI apparatus and a number of clandestine security corps.

While the power struggle between Tantawi and the Mubaraks was being played out behind the scenes, more openly articulated voices were calling upon the army to rise against the regime. Such voices came from liberal quarters as well as from the Muslim Brotherhood. For example, Gamal Heshmat, a leading Muslim Brotherhood member and MP in the 2000 parliament, criticised in an article the complicity of the army and police force with the ruling regime, and made a claim that they (the Muslim Brotherhood) will submit to them if they rise against the current powers. In the article, Heshmat called upon the army to organise a dialogue with the various political forces on the ground.

The possibility that the army may have collaborated in the unfolding scenario of organised action against Mubarak cannot be entirely dismissed. The army had its own mukhabarat (intelligence) that acted in parallel to, and independently of, the SSI apparatus that is loyal to the regime. The mounting discontent over Gamal's candidacy for president as well as the general state of political and economic affairs in the country would not have surpassed the army's intelligence scrutiny.

Further, in moments of populist uprisings, the fear of a military coup is never far. A former general, who occupied a prominent position in the SSI apparatus, recalled the mass uprisings of 17 and 18 January 1977 against the removal of subsidies on basic foodstuffs. When the central security forces failed to contain the protests President Sadat sent orders to the minister of defence asking that the SSI apparatus undertake a count of all the vehicles and tanks belonging to the armed forces and inform him immediately. The president feared that the minister of defence may engineer a military coup against him (Geneidy 2011: 154). It is telling that in a meeting with editors of Egyptian newspapers in the middle of the eighteen days of uprising, Omar Suleiman warned of the possibility of a coup should an agreement between the protestors and Mubarak not be reached. 'A coup could come from within the regime, the army, the police or intelligence services, which Suleiman used to lead, or the opposition, he warned' (Phelps and Kim 2011). While the army's collaboration with the protestors was evident during the uprisings, conclusive evidence regarding their role prior to the uprising is yet to be uncovered.

The alignment of pressures on the system

Egypt witnessed a number of protests in the past five years in which both the nature of demands became more politically contentious as well as the symbolic spaces upon which they encroached to make their demands. It is during these protests that many youth gained the knowledge and experience in how to deal with the security forces and how to outmanoeuvre them.

The Kefaya (Enough) movement, formed in 2004, openly called for the non-extension of Mubarak's presidency and expressed its opposition to his son's succession to power. The significance of Kefaya is that in so openly contesting Mubarak's regime, it shattered the taboo that no criticism can ever be launched against the president himself. A number of other movements had emerged in the mid-2000s such as the leftist 20 March movement and the 9 March movement for the autonomy of universities. In March 2007, the youth organised across the Internet, and through other mobilisational tactics, a general strike on 6 April 2008 in memory of the general strikes of the workers in the textile industry. The strike ignited mass participation from the people of el Mahalla el Kobra and continued for three days, during which citizens took to the street and destroyed pictures of Hosni Mubarak with their feet. Through this Intifada, the 6 April youth movement came into being (Shukr 2011: 29).

The establishment of the national committee for change, headed by Mohammed el Baradei also brought together a number of youth movements and groups including those belonging to political parties and forces such as the Muslim Brotherhood youth. During those years of organising, the youth gained critical skills in coordinating and liaising via the Internet, in skilfully dealing with the security apparatus and in formulating their political demands (Shukr 2011).

Concurrently, the workers' movements were engaged in sustained political action around bread-and-butter issues. Thousands of workers took to the streets in the last five years in many of Egypt's largely populated textile towns, such as Mahalla el Kobra, and openly defied the norms of public engagement with a police state by demonstrating in the streets over several consecutive days, storming factories, holding sit-ins and insisting on better pay and an end to the corruption of the state-run factory management. These protests, which in some cases involved several thousand workers and their families, were often dismissed by political analysts as lacking the potential to bring about systemic political change because they revolved around bread-and-butter issues.

The protests by various groups that materialised particularly in the six months prior to the uprisings took a highly contentious form. In January 2011, in the aftermath of the Alexandria massacre that left more than twenty people dead and 200 injured, Egyptian Christian youth in their hundreds, joined by many Muslim sympathisers, took to the streets to protest at the state failure to protect the Coptic minority. The protests were peaceful but there was an encroachment on the public spaces – the Corniche (Nile banks) and the streets in downtown Cairo – that scared the government. These youth-led protests were autonomous from the Coptic Orthodox Church or any other hegemonic powers in the country.

They were joined by hundreds of Muslim youth sympathisers. Mohammed Idris suggests that the uprisings were ignited by two important events,[5] the first being the bombing in the Alexandria church, because it sparked mass anger among the youth, both Muslim and Christian, from among a large constituency: and the object of their attack was the regime (Idris 2011: 21) and the second being the Tunisian revolution.

On 23 January, in front of the People's Assembly, more than 200 farmers from the town of Zarqaa in Damietta congregated to protest against what they argued to be the extortionate fees charged by the Agricultural Bank upon the loans they had acquired. Another 150 workers from a car production industry protested in front of another part of the People's Assembly against the ministry of trade for its prohibitive policies which had led to a standstill in their work. Meanwhile, another 100 graduates from the University of al-Azhar protested in front of the university against unemployment. In the town of Tanta, doctors protested against the delay in releasing their financial benefits for the last three months. In Al Mansoura, more than 1,500 workers on temporary contracts since 1995 demonstrated against their denial of permanent contracts. A series of worker protests against their working conditions was being ignited across the whole country (Ghallab 2011).

The constant flare-up of protests, sit-ins, demonstrations and encroachments on public space led by average citizens were all being dismissed as too small, inconsequential and narrow in scope and interest to be taken seriously. To assume that the people would not rise up showed how dismissive we had been of the power that was building up, flaring up spontaneously almost on a weekly basis. Emboldened by the successful ousting of President Ben Ali in Tunisia, many Egyptian youth were thinking – and saying out loud – if they can do it, why can't we?

2　From the Friday of Fury to the Shari'a Friday

We do not believe in regime overthrow.
(Essam el Erian, member of the Guidance Bureau of the Muslim Brotherhood, in an interview with author, 2007)

One of the people said to me 'you rode the wave' [of the Egyptian revolution]. And I said to him 'we are the sea'.
(Sheikh Mohammed Hassan, Salafi leader, in El Wazeiry 2011)

This chapter examines the political engagement of the Muslim Brotherhood from the beginning of the uprisings on 25 January 2011 up to the organisation of the mass demonstrations on 29 July 2011 calling for the application of the Shari'a. The first part of the chapter situates and contextualises the Muslim Brotherhood's position and role in the eighteen days leading to the ousting of President Mubarak. It analyses the basis for collaboration with the youth and the reasons for shifting alliances following the president's demise and the realignment with the armed forces and other Islamist forces. The chapter argues that examining who the Muslim Brotherhood works with, at what point in time, is critical for understanding how political thought, policy and practice both converge and diverge according to the power balance on the ground.

Preparing for national police force day

Up until 2011, 25 January marked 'police force day', a day that commemorated the patriotic role of the police force in resisting British colonialism and a day of remembrance of the police officers who died in battle against the British forces in battle in Ismailia in 1952. For the first time ever, the Egyptian government announced that in 2011 that police force day would be a public holiday so all Egyptians could celebrate.

But 25 January 2011 was reclaimed by the youth for a different kind of remembrance. Among the main youth groups who planned for the 25 January uprisings were the 6 April movement, National Campaign to Support Al Baradie, the youth of the Democratic Front Party (Usama Ghazali Harb), the leftist

Freedom and Justice movement and the youth belonging to the Muslim Brother-hood in coordination with the 'We are all Khaled Said' page on Facebook set up by blogger Wael Ghoneim, which at the wake of the revolution had 400,000 members. In addition to mobilising via social networking, an estimated half a million flyers were distributed in the various governorates calling upon the people to join the protests under the banner: 'I am going out on the 25th January to claim my rights'.

Some political parties and forces openly proclaimed their support for the planned protests, including the Democratic Front, the Ghad Party, the Wafd Party, the 9 March academics for freedom movement, and the textile workers' movement as well as other groups. Yet it is significant that most of the other political forces and movements officially announced their boycott of the Day of Rage (25 January). Rifaat al Said, head of the leftist Tagammu Party, announced that they would not partake in the protests because it is a day of celebrating the bravery of the Egyptian police. Secretary-general of the Nasserite Party, Ahmed Hassan, said that the country coud not stand any instability and that people could not be driven by those paid by external agents to drive them to act. Similar statements regarding the inappropriateness of protesting on the police day came from smaller parties (*Al Akhbar* 2011). The Gama'at al Islamiyya and the Sufi orders openly expressed their opposition to the planned protests, announcing that they were calls for deviating from legitimacy (Shar'iyya) and served as a call for violence and vandalism (Al Badry and Amr 2011). Pope Shenouda called upon all the bishops presiding over their dioceses to ask parishioners not to participate in protests organised by some groups and organisations that he accused of having hidden agendas. Bishop Morcos, the spokes-man for the Pope, said that Shenouda did not want the participation of Copts in events that may lead to violence and strife (Adel 2011). Sheikh Yasser Borhami, one of the most important leaders of the Salafi movement in Alexandria, called upon the youth not to participate in the protests, which could escalate into strife and serve foreign agendas (Youssef 2011).

In preparation for the anticipated protests of 25 January, the government's response was twofold: it stepped up its media campaign to vilify the organisers and it sent out stern security warnings to the major political forces of the dire consequences of their participation. The National Democratic Party sought to mobilise half a million youth to show their loyalty to Mubarak. The National Democratic Party's Facebook page praised the patriotic role of the police and celebrated their fifty-nine years of serving Egypt. Alieddin Hellal, spokesman for the party, said the day was an opportunity for reviving the memory of the role of the police in defending this country and making the youth aware of it, in protecting social stability and security (*Al Shorouk* 2011). Makram Mohammed Ahmed, the secretary-general of the journalists' syndicate chided the youth for wishing to protest on the day when they were supposed to be showing gratitude to the police force for protecting Egyptians against the threat of Al-Qaeda: 'what makes this sick thinking preside over a group of youth?' he asked (Ahmed 2011).

General Ismail El Sha'er, first deputy to the minister of interior in charge of Cairo's security, said that they warned the political forces who wished to organise the day of rage that they must obtain the necessary permits to protest, and in the event that they demonstrated illegally, they would be arrested and there would be no leniency in how the ministry engaged with them (Kamel 2011).

If some political forces had picked up on the pulse of the street rising before 25 January, the Muslim Brotherhood leadership hadn't. When asked regarding the Brotherhood's participation, Essam el Erian announced that the Brothers would not be taking part in the scheduled protests scheduled, because it is a day that 'we should all be celebrating together'. This was clearly a political stance meant to appease the government (Slackman 2011) and which may be explained by a number of caveats. One is clearly pragmatic: the uprisings may fail (as they have on many previous occasions) and the political cost for the Brotherhood would be a more insidious crackdown leading to a further weakening of the internal organisational core (and loss of members). The decision not to participate may have also been influenced by the heavy security threats that the movement received, should it become involved. The other explanation is more ideological. Gom'a Amin wrote that the Muslim Brotherhood does not believe in advocacy through acts of civil disobedience, policy change, demonstrations and hunger strikes as a means through which to elicit reform. Such tactics fail when faced with dictatorial rule, and the Muslim Brotherhood's approach instead is based on a holistic approach to deepening Islamic values in society through da'wa, Islamic pedagogy and education (Amin 2007).

In a statement issued on 19 January (Muslim Brotherhood 2011), the Brotherhood hailed the actions of the Tunisian people and stressed that the overthrow of the Tunisian regime sent clear signals to, first, the oppressed peoples that popular legitimacy is above constitutional legitimacy, and, second, to oppressive rulers that they are not safe and that they are living 'above a volcano of people's anger and the wrath of God which is stronger and fiercer'. However, their stance was clear:

> Because we, out of duty, care for *stability and social harmony* in all matters and circumstances and because we believe that the *constitutional struggle is the natural pathway to mobilize society towards the required reform in all political and economic and social areas*, the Muslim Brotherhood and they are a part not to be separated from the nation look realistically and consciously to the other party, the current regime in the country which has more than others the ability to reform and change if it has the will and desire for this.
>
> (italics mine)

Highly significant is the emphasis of the Brotherhood on its commitment to the stability of the country, which is reiterated several times in the statement and which must be read in a political context in which the youth movements were mobilising the citizenry to reject the status quo and revolt. Equally significant is the reference opting for a high-level 'constitutional struggle for reform', which is to be contrasted with a revolutionary struggle led by the people. Up to that point, the Brotherhood was cautious to emphasise that it is working within the existing system, and not striving to eject from it.

The remaining statement stipulates clearly ten demands of the Brotherhood, the first being the annulment of the Emergency Law, second, the absolution of the People's Assembly, third, constitutional amendments to articles 5, 76, 77, 88 and 179 regulating the conditions of political participation, fourth, addressing the immediate economic needs of the people, fifth, changing Egypt's foreign policy towards Israel, sixth, the immediate release of all political prisoners, seventh, responding to the partisan (self-interest) demands, eighth, establishment of political parties through official notification, ninth, holding to account those who acquired their wealth through illegitimate means and, tenth, removing the intervention of the security apparatus from universities, schools, unions, endowments, civic associations and human rights organisations. In a press statement released the same day, the Brotherhood presented these demands and affirmed that:

> working towards implementing these demands as quickly as possible may lead to quietening the internal situation and support stability in the country and prevent Egypt from having a popular revolution that will be broader and stronger than that of neighbouring Tunisia.
>
> (Muslim Brotherhood 2011)

The Muslim Brotherhood's 'official' presence in the protests on the day of rage (25 January) was restricted to a stand-in by fifty symbolic figures in front of the Supreme Court in the centre of Cairo. However, the youth belonging to the Brotherhood were among those who participated in the protests demanding freedom, dignity and bread. They participated in their individual capacities as youth rather than as representatives of the Brotherhood. They joined the 6 April movement, the National Committee for Change and other youth bodies in their demands for the absolution of the People's Assembly and the Shura Council; a transitional government; setting a minimum monthly wage of LE1,200; a commitment from Mubarak that neither himself nor his son would nominate themselves in the upcoming elections; and an end to torture and repression.

The press sought to present the protests as a ploy of the Brotherhood that was rejected by the people. While the government-controlled press such as *Ros al-Youssef*, *Al-Gomhoriyya* and *Al-Ahram* praised the police for showing restraint and dealing with the protestors in a 'civilized manner', al Jazeera and other sources were reporting on the tear gas, the beatings, the incarcerations and the severe human rights violations. When the protestors decided to stay overnight in Tahrir Square, the security response was to send 200 armoured cars and 13,000 men to break up the protestors at midnight. In response to the events of Tuesday, the ministry of interior responded by issuing a statement saying that demonstrations were prohibited.

The protests caught everyone by surprise because of their profile and scale. Youth in their thousands were being joined by ordinary people on the street. In one instance in Tahrir Square, as the public buses were passing by, the youth called out to the passengers to come down and join them, and in many instances people did just that. There was no visible organised leadership. People were congregating in a haphazard way, occupying public space and encroaching on the forbidden space: in one instance, the people gathered in front of the National Democratic Party premises and started shouting, 'These are the thieves, these are the thieves'. No political party could claim leadership. People, as one observer pointed out, did not know who Mohammed el Baradei' or Ayman Nour were but they knew very well who Mubarak and his son were, and they were out there because of them. The government accused the Muslim Brotherhood, Kefaya and the 6 April movement of inciting youth for its own political ends. The reaction to the protests on 27 January 2011 in the independent media and press sources was to claim the uprising as belonging to the youth and to the Egyptian street and not to the Muslim Brotherhood (Khateeb 2011).

On 26 January 2011, the Guidance Bureau met and announced that they would participate in the planned protests on 28 January, dubbed the Friday of Rage. Like most Egyptians, the Brotherhood leadership were also caught off guard by the full force of the Intifada. The new development, observed El Erian, was that unlike the previous protests held by Kefaya, the workers' movements and other protests, these were acts of citizens claiming their right to publicly express their rejection of the status quo (El Erian 2011). Yet even then, the ousting of the regime was not quite on the agenda, with the Brotherhood urging in a statement to the government to implement immediate reforms and release all the political detainees (Muslim Brotherhood 2011).

The Brotherhood's official position against participation in the uprising on 25 January not only came at an internal cost, but at a heavy political price as well. Political forces that had been there since day one, though not leading the youth – could at least claim to have been more in tune with the street than the Brotherhood. Simultaneously other youth groups were criticising the Brotherhood's stance, saying that they were sitting on the fence just like Mohammed el Baradei'.

The Muslim Brotherhood in Tahrir: the politics of presence

When the youth went out to protest on 25 January, they were committed to keeping the uprising non-religious and non-partisan. The Muslim Brotherhood's participation from 28 January for the most part involved few opportunities for mobilising religion to make political gains. The uprisings were in essence civil. Several informants mentioned that when a zealous youth would shout out a religious slogan, he was often met with one of three responses: silence – no response; 'madanniyya madaniyya' (civil! civil!); or someone would shout a non-religious patriotic slogan to which people would respond energetically, thus sending a very clear message where the pulse lay. At the wake of the uprisings, Ayman Nour, head of Al Ghad, announced that all the political forces agreed that no party slogans were to be made and that only unifying slogans and the Egyptian flags would feature.[1]

The Brotherhood's acquiescence to this agreement during the eighteen days of uprising may have been driven by three important factors. First, prior to 25 January, the Brotherhood often boasted of 'owning the street' and being the only force capable of mobilising masses. After 25 January, it found itself at risk of becoming disconnected from the street if it did not engage positively with the instigators of the revolution. Second, although the Muslim Brotherhood youth were not politically powerful within the central decision-making apparatus, they were still pressing the leadership to recognise the collective nature of this youth-led uprising and were an important link to the forces mobilising this mass movement. Hence at that moment in time they would have paid a high political price if they were to alienate their youth. Finally, and perhaps most importantly, the decision not to assume ownership or leadership was strategically designed to circumvent the government's ploy to represent this as a possible Islamist plot *à la* Iran. Mohammed el Beltagui, the former spokesperson for the Brotherhood in parliament, said that the Brotherhood were cautious to keep a low profile so as not to give the regime the opportunity to portray the protests as a Muslim Brotherhood–state standoff (Gaweesh 2011).

The position taken by the various political actors to downplay the role and presence of the Islamists in the eighteen days leading to the ousting of President Mubarak was intended to abate the West's fears of a Muslim Brotherhood take over along the lines of Iran. An informant mentioned that within Tahrir Square both the media and the press were given clear instructions that they should avoid covering any symbols or actions that could serve to give the impression of a strong Islamist presence. The most minute details of how to frame the uprisings to an external audience were thought out by some of the politically seasoned protestors, who negotiated with the media about who should feature on television, what images should represent their political action, etc.[2]

Ahmed Zaghloul, an activist, recalls in his daily documentation of the revolution that on 2 February at the checkpoints:

> I noticed that some of the members of the committee had beards. After I went through the inspection I said to one of the members of the committee that those brought in by the National Democratic Party say to the people that there is no one in the Square but the Brotherhood and [those belonging to] the Islamic groups and that this weakens the protests because the revolution is of a patriotic nature and represents the full national rainbow and that its strength lies in its pluralism and that the face of the checkpoint should not be predominantly of [those who don the] beard. The man accepted what I had to say and said to me he will put forward this idea and it will be implemented.
>
> (Zaghloul 2011: 38)

Essam el Erian, in his personal recollection of the days of the uprisings, recalls that one of his friends called him up and told him he had observed people praying in Tahrir Square on a Friday and reminded him of the need to keep down all Islamic manifestations to a minimum.

The alliance between the Muslim Brotherhood, the Islamists and the youth and political forces may have worked to convey the 'right image' during the 18 days protest for Mubarak's demise but once the common enemy was ousted, possibilities of collaboration over a unified vision were undermined by ideological differences.

Yet after the Brotherhood instructed their followers to join the protests and other Islamist forces such as the Salafis followed suit, their agency was not only one of participation, it was in many instances one of leadership. There are two key indicators to this: the broadcasting service, managed by the Brotherhood, and the standing of the platform/stage set up in Tahrir Square. While different youth groups set up their own broadcasting services within Tahrir Square, the first to be established, and carrying considerable influence, was that initiated by the Brotherhood. Moreover while various political forces had set up makeshift stages in Tahrir Square the largest by far was the one set up by the Brotherhood. They had the largest speakers, the grandest stage and often managed to attract the largest audiences and they controlled who was given and denied access.

In view of the Brotherhood's organisational experience, they often coordinated with other forces the regulation of the entry and exit points to Tahrir (to ward off the thugs and pro-government intruders). Moreover, their extensive experience in dealing with the security apparatus was put to use during the uprisings, particularly in 'the battle of the camel' when thugs on camels rode into Tahrir Square, injuring and killing many protestors. At that instance, it was the Muslim Brotherhood youth in conjunction with the Ultras from the Zamalek and Ahly football clubs who organised the defence mechanisms to protect the protestors. Some protestors argue that the Brotherhood's involvement was one of tactical shielding of the protestors' space against security repression, but that they did not assume political leadership of Tahrir Square. However, the lines are more blurred than appears on the surface. Shielding the protestors served to gain visibility – and legitimacy – which was translated, after the demise of Mubarak, into claims of ownership of the success of the revolution.

The success of the revolution was possible through a constellation of factors. The army certainly represented one side of the equation, and on the other, the people. But the people comprised the youth who organised the uprisings of 25 January, the hundreds of thousands of non-politically active youth who joined in, the citizenry, in particular the middle classes who joined, as well as the workers and masses more generally. At different phases of the revolution, different actors played critical roles, for example, the Ultras, the football fan associations, who played an instrumental role in withstanding the security forces.

The Safka (deal)

The Brotherhood's commitment to collective action through alliances with other political forces proved to be shaky and short-lived. During the week of 'somoud', in which the protestors called upon the people to stand their grounds until Mubarak stepped down, the government was keen to try and arrive at a settlement that would send people back home. A collective stance of non-collaboration, to which all parties agreed, was put to the test when the Brotherhood entered into behind-the-scenes negotiations with Omar Suleiman, the vice-president. On 3 February, Mohammed Bad'i, the Supreme Guide of the Brotherhood, issued a statement that the movement refused any negotiation with any of the leaders of the current regime, in compliance with the people's will that had pronounced the lack of legitimacy of the current order with all its symbols and levels. He added that there was no Brotherhood representative who was negotiating with the regime, emphasising that it was only the Guidance Bureau alone that was entitled to act on behalf of the Brotherhood (Bad'i 2011). On 4 February, Field Marshal Tantawi, the minister of defence, visited Tahrir Square. He told the protestors 'the man [Mubarak] told you he will not nominate himself for a second time'. And then he called upon the protestors to ask the Supreme Guide of the Brotherhood to enter into dialogue with Omar Suleiman (*Al-Masry Al-Youm* 2011). This is a very significant step in view of the fact that the regime had never officially entered into dialogue with them and had never referred to them as anything but the 'the outlawed'.

On 5 February, the Muslim Brotherhood had shifted their earlier position on non-negotiation with the ruling political order. In another statement from Bad'i, they announced officially their entry into dialogue with the regime with a view to 'come to know the seriousness of those responsible towards the demands of the people and the extent of their responsiveness to them, and this is compatible with our belief in a serious, sincere, constructive dialogue' (Bad'i 2011).

On 6 February the Muslim Brotherhood, together with other political forces, participated in a dialogue with Omar Suleiman, the deputy of the president at the Cabinet. Representing the Brotherhood were Mohammed Morsi and Saad al Katatny from the Guidance Bureau. Not all political parties and other parties had agreed to participate in the national dialogue. The Democratic Front, led by Osama Ghazali Harb, for example, had refused on the premise that there was no negotiation with a regime that had lost its legitimacy. The Brothers presented Suleiman with eight demands, essentially those from the ten points they had released on 26 January. Following the meeting, Mahmoud Ezzat commented that the Brotherhood expressed their participation in the dialogue being conditional upon representation from all political forces and youth forces. Ezzat said that they are awaiting deeds, not words, from the regime in response to their demands, the most important of which was the departure of President Hosni Mubarak, and the annulment of the emergency law, and the formation of a national transitional government until a democratically elected government could come to power (al Khateeb and Adeeb 2011).

But according to other sources, that is not all what happened on 6 February. Haitham Abou Khalil, formerly a Muslim Brother, presented his resignation in March 2011 after twenty-two years of membership in the movement because he was scandalised by what happened on that day. In his personal statement, he mentioned a secret meeting between the Guidance Bureau of the Brotherhood and Omar Suleiman involving negotiations over the Brotherhood's withdrawing participation in the revolution in return for the regime to officially recognise the movement and grant it the status of a political party and a civic association.[3]

I would have expected the Shura council instead of rising in anger against them upon their knowledge [of the pact] to have immediately resigned the Guidance Bureau in its entirety, and whose members had vowed never to disclose this catastrophe.

(Abou Khalil 2011)

The allegations were vehemently denied by members of the Guidance Bureau, however, Khalil urged that a fact-finding commission be set up to investigate the matter and pass its judgements.

Renowned Judge Noha el Zeiny fiercely attacked the Muslim Brotherhood for its consideration of a pact with Omar Suleiman. She argued that the pact was presented by Omar Suleiman at a critical moment in the history of the revolution in which it risked being aborted. El Zeiny writes:

The Brotherhood, as is **their habit**, swallowed the regime's bate [*sic*]... and they began to boast of the regime's recognition of their popular legitimacy ... forgetting that they went out and encouraged people to go out to bring down the legitimacy of this regime and that their continuous discourse about the collapse of the legitimacy since the 25th of January completely goes against their own feelings of being puffed up ... and it contradicts their position of not entering into dialogue with it [the authorities] even if they justify it on the premise that they are attempting to test the seriousness of the dialogue because if the fish caught the bait and fell into the hands of the fisherman it will not help it much afterwards to find out whether the fisherman is skilful or not ... it will have no option then but to adjust, nothing else.

(El Zeiny 2011; emphasis in original)

El Zeiny rebuked the Brotherhood for entering into faulty alliances which often backfire and which are negotiated with no regard for those to whom they had pledged loyalty in Tahrir Square.

Back in Tahrir Square, the news of the Brotherhood's dialogue with the regime was met with outrage. Ahmed Zaghloul recalls that on 6 February, new slogans and banners were being raised saying 'No negotiation, no representation before [Mubarak] leaving, No wisemen! No Brotherhood! The demands are in [Tahrir] Square' (Ahmed 2011: 77) with a categorical rejection of any Brotherhood member striking a deal with the regime on the people's behalf.

The Brotherhood youth revolt against the movement's leadership[4]

Prior to the 25 January uprisings, some of the youth affiliated to the Muslim Brotherhood were involved in the organisation leading up to the protests, through synchronisation with the 6 April movement and other youth groups planning for the 25 January protests. However, such political activism was not institutionally supported within the Brotherhood since there was no structure representing the youth. The closest to being youth-targeted is the university student division of the Brotherhood and they wished to send an appeal to the Guidance Bureau to allow them to participate in the 25 January protests but the head of the division, Mahmoud Abou Zeid, objected on the premise that the Brothers had already taken a decision not to participate. Outraged, the youth appealed to the Guidance Bureau directly by setting up a meeting with Essam el Erian. At that meeting, they arrived at a middle ground: the youth were given permission to participate but in their personal capacities and not as representatives of the Muslim Brotherhood. The youth group then set up a Facebook called 'word of truth' and invited others to participate in the protests, informing them of all the logistical arrangements for 25 January. They managed to strategically outmanoeuvre the security forces by meeting at a populist district away from the main squares and then move on to the main streets and into Tahrir Square.

Simultaneously, the Muslim Brotherhood leadership and the security apparatus arrived at a pact in which the youth belonging to their movement would be left to participate in the protests but would be expected to end their protests by sunset. The security apparatus, argues Khateeb (2011), effectively struck at the protesters in the evening.

On 26 and 27 January the Muslim Brotherhood's youth joined forces with other youth movements in organising a number of protests in heavily populated areas in order to mobilise support for 28 January, dubbed the 'Friday of Fury'. El Ezzabawy identifies three orientations among the youth of the Brotherhood at the time of the uprisings: the first is the leftist leaning wing who comprise the youth who joined Abdel Moneim Aboul Fotouh's presidential campaign. They include Mohammed El Gabah, Mohammed el Shaway, Mohammed Heikal, Ga'far Zafarany, Ahmed Osama, Mahmoud Farouk and others. The second group, the centre group (al wassat), include Islam Lotfy, Ahmed El Nazary and Mohammed el Kassas while the right-leaning group comprises Hassan Ezz el Din, Ahmed Moustapha, Khaled Fouad, Amar Abd el Rahman, Moustapha el Wahsh and Hossam Badawy. El Ezzabawy notes that the most notable leaders within the Brotherhood who contributed to the instigation of 25 January were the left-leaning group, while the centre group did not join in until 24 January. The centre-leaning youth group joined in full force after the meeting that took place with the leadership on 27 January in Muqattam. As for the right-leaning youth group, they joined the protests for the very first time on the Friday of Fury.

The Brotherhood youth continued to synchronise efforts with other youth initiatives throughout those first days of uprisings until 1 February when the coalition of the revolution's youth – the first youth coalition – was established – and the first appeal for a millioniyya (a one million person turnout) was made.

The Brotherhood officially announced their participation in the Friday of Fury (28 January) but many of the youth members had already broken ranks with the orders of the leadership. Islam Lotfy, one of the youth leaders of the Brotherhood who was later forced to resign over his defiance of the leadership, said that on 25 January, the Muslim Brotherhood youth went down to Tahrir Square against the orders given by the Guidance Bureau and that on 28 January, they were asked to leave Tahrir Square between 5 and 8 p.m. and they refused. On 2 February 2011 (the day known as the battle of the camel, the Guidance Bureau gave instructions that the women and children (affiliated to the Muslim Brotherhood) should vacate the Square followed by the youth, an order that they again refused to obey. Lotfy believes that had they followed the instructions of the Guidance Bureau, Mubarak would still be in power today (Kahal, *Al Shorouk*, 2011).

During the 18 days protest for Mubarak's demise, the Muslim Brotherhood youth continued to serve as the link between the youth groups and the Guidance Bureau which greatly facilitated coordination – some of the youth leaders from other movements pointed out that they found engaging with the leadership often very difficult while the Muslim Brotherhood youth were far more amenable for consensus building. On the other hand, due to the fact that the Muslim Brotherhood youth did not have decision-making power within the Brotherhood, many of these leaders pointed out that there was always a risk that the leadership would object to what the Muslim Brotherhood youth were agreeing on, raising concerns over the outcome of any negotiations (Ezzabawy 2011).

After the demise of Mubarak, the Muslim Brotherhood youth voiced their demands for greater participation and inclusion in the decision-making processes of the Brotherhood. Historically, there has been a conspicuous bias within the movement towards the older members, who are considered to be imbued with greater experience and knowledge. However, the severity of the dispute between the leadership and some of the youth over the question of participation with other non-Islamist political forces was so severe that it eventually led to the exit of some of its younger members from the movement.

When the Brotherhood leadership chose to break ranks with the revolution's youth coalitions and to refrain from participating in a number of millioniyyas, several youth members defiantly went out to Tahrir Square to join the other movements, leading to open conflict with the leadership.

In view of the strong collaboration, synchronisation and interaction between the Muslim Brotherhood and the other youth coalitions and forces, one of the critical questions was: could this experience not have a transformative impact on the Brotherhood internally? Could it not make them more open to reconsidering their perspectives on the 'non-Islamist other' and on the fundamentals driving the vision of the kind of political order being advocated? The fact is that once the power balance became skewed in their favour, the Muslim Brotherhood's engagement with the other political forces changed radically, and this would suggest not. The predicament of the youth who wished to challenge the internal mechanisms and ideas of the Brotherhood after intensely engaging with other youth groups was either to be sidelined or in some cases to resign. This supports one of the key contentions of this book that when the Brotherhood is allowed to flourish in a politically accommodating environment, this empowers the more conservative and traditional elements of the movement, not the progressives. It provides further evidence to the difficulty of challenging the power hierarchy within, as the youth do not have a leadership role (organisationally or as a source of religious knowledge/reference) their prospects of influencing the core decision-making apparatus are minimal. The Muslim Brotherhood youth played a strategically important role for the movement's leadership during the eighteen days of uprisings and the early weeks after the ouster of Mubarak when it had not consolidated its power. The Muslim Brotherhood youth presence in several coalitions simultaneously enabled the leadership to be attuned with what the other political forces were up to (Ezzabawy 2011).

The morning after

The alliances established between the Muslim Brotherhood and other political forces began to falter after the ousting of Mubarak. The Islamisation of the revolution began shortly thereafter – the Egyptian flag, the patriotic songs and the famous slogans remained for a couple of months but with a difference: the movers and shakers were now clearly the Muslim Brotherhood in collaboration with other Islamist forces. One week after Mubarak had stepped down, Friday 20 February, Sheikh Youssef El Qaradawy led the prayers and the khutba. Google executive Wael Ghoneim, who emerged as one of the leading youth figures in Egypt's uprising, was barred from the stage in Tahrir Square on Friday by security guards.[5] While influential Muslim Brotherhood members such as Essam el Erian denied that the move to shun Ghoneim was elicited by a Qaradawy associate, the photographer who witnessed the incident confirmed this fact and pointed out that the latter was angered and left the square with his face hidden by an Egyptian flag (AFP 2011). Highly significant was the profile of the entourage surrounding Sheikh Qaradawy, which included figures such as Mohammed el Kattatny, the spokesman for the Muslim Brotherhood bloc in the 2005–2010 parliament, and renowned Muslim Brotherhood preacher Safwat Hegazy.

What ensued in the forthcoming months was a battle over the soul of Tahrir. Sheikh Qaradawy's presence in Tahrir Square and his leadership of the masses in prayer was highly symbolic – his persona was as political as it was religious in view of his close association with the Muslim Brotherhood and his views on the necessity of instituting an Islamic state. On Friday 2 April, the youth coalition announced a millioniyya (an appeal to one million persons to join) in Tahrir Square, which the Brotherhood boycotted. They managed to get about half a million in turnout. The following Friday, 8 April, the Muslim Brotherhood and other Islamist movements urged all its followers to join Tahrir Square where the youth coalition and others had called for another millioniyya and the estimated turnout was around one million. While each political force claimed a 'corner' in Tahrir Square, with its own stage, speakers and flyers being distributed, by far the largest was that of the Muslim Brotherhood, which was also strategically placed in a most visible spot. Sheikh Hegazy and other Islamist preachers took centre stage. With every millioniyya in which the Brotherhood announced their participation, the same pattern of a hegemonic presence was visibly observed.

There is strong evidence of a pact being established between the Brotherhood and the Supreme Council for Armed Forces. On a symbolic level, when Essam

Musharraf went to Tahrir Square shortly after his appointment as prime minister, it was Mohammed el Beltagui who stood beside him on the stage. When the armed forces appointed an eight-member committee to develop a number of constitutional changes, they appointed Sobhi Saleh, a Muslim Brotherhood lawyer, to it, despite the fact that he stood out in the committee as the only member who has no judicial background or exceptional legal expertise. Muhammad Habib, a former deputy guide of the Brothers who has now left the group pointed out in an interview with Joshua Stacher that: 'The military realized they could not control domestic stability yet still uphold unpopular foreign policies. They are using the Brothers to serve as this domestic source of stability' (Stacher 2011). Stacher points out that in addition to the Brothers' communiqués which are full of praise for the armed forces, the Guidance Bureau have asked their constituency not to participate in some of the major millioniyyas that have been held – even if they broke ranks with the other political forces with which they have been aligned in the days of uprising.

The subtle politics of the entente between the armed forces and the Brotherhood can be gleaned in two important events, the first involving the visit of Gül, president of Turkey, to Egypt and the second during the constitutional reforms referendum. Field Marshall Mohamed Hussein Tantawi met with President Abdullah Gül during his visit, and reportedly remarked that 'the Turkish experience is the closest to us. It's an example we can really benefit from'. During his visit, President Gül met with leaders from the opposition as well as youth groups, however, the seating arrangements are highly revealing of the spatial power relations: Mohammed Bad'i sat on a chair closest to Gül, while members of the opposition were seated further away.

Perhaps the point of greatest alignment between the Muslim Brotherhood and the armed forces was over the constitutional referendum of March 2011. The Brotherhood used its full weight to push for a 'yes' vote – a stance that the army very much favoured. The Muslim Brotherhood and the Salafis used their access and full control over an overwhelming number of mosques to push for a yes vote. Religion was instrumentalised to the maximum to show that good Muslims should vote yes, only the infidels and unbelievers would vote no. The campaign was systematic and insidious: in the streets and across public space. In the process, according to Al-Ahram online accounts for the day of voting, in Marsa Matrouh, Salafists and Muslim Brotherhood members tore down posters put up by the Tagammu leftist party calling for a 'No' vote, replacing them with 'Yes' posters. In the electoral voting offices, particularly those in the more rural and remote areas of the country, members of the Muslim Brotherhood prodded citizens to mark the green spot – which in Egypt symbolises the colour of Islam. The Brothers told people that to mark the green colour is to be in favour of Islam, to mark the black colour is to take the un-Islamic path (Rashwan Al Shorouk 2011). Informants, however, said that in many circles what was specifically said was that black marked the colour of the priest's headware ('mma) and therefore whoever marks black is in favour of the Christian unbelievers.

This event, which produced a result of 77 per cent in favour of the constitution, was supposed to represent the people's will. The level of fraud was minimal and there was a 41 per cent turnout, far greater than any turnout in Egypt's history. The people, the Islamists declared, had freely made their choice in the first time in over sixty years. There were no doubts that what the constitutional referendum had shown was the strength of the Islamists' ability to mobilise 'the people' – but it can be argued that they were voting for religion, not making an informed choice of the political trajectory the country should take. It sent a clear message to the armed forces that they could count on the Islamists' power to influence the populace, and therefore serves well as a strategic ally. It also sent a clear message to the revolutionary youth: they may have instigated the revolution, but it is the Islamists who control the streets.

The alliance with the opposition parties and the revolutionary youth groups was torn but not completely ruptured until relations suffered a severe blow on 29 July.

Six months after: Shari'a Friday

By the summer of 2011, the Brotherhood had turned its back on the youth coalitions and the opposition parties and aligned itself with the other Islamist actors in a loose coalition. On 29 July the largest ever millioniyya since the ousting of President Mubarak took place in Tahrir Square, having an estimated turnout of two million people. The protests called for the establishment of an Islamic state based on the Shari'a. The most common slogan to have been shouted in Tahrir Square on that day was 'Islammiyya, Islamiyya' (Islamic, Islamic) referring to the identity and system of governance to which the country must conform. By far, the largest stage was that put up by the Muslim Brotherhood. On top of the Brotherhood's stage, there were slogans praising the armed forces and people chanting 'The people, the army, one hand!' and 'Thank you thank you to Al Mosheer, a thousand greetings from Tahrir' (El Hindy *et al.* 2011; *Al Dostor* 2011). When the Brotherhood put on a recording of the national anthem, the Salafists lashed back 'Islamiyya, Islammiyya!' in objection (*Al Dostor* 2011).

When members of the 6 April coalition appeared on the stage put up by the Muslim Brotherhood in Tahrir Square, they were shooed down. On the much smaller stage that was set up by Kefaya, when 300 of its members tried to answer back to 'Islammiyya, Islammiyya' with 'madaniyya, madaniyya' (civil, civil), the Islamists took over, and in one instance, empty water bottles were thrown at them (Deish 2011). The same demands for the establishment of the Islamic state were voiced across governorates of Egypt, through the leadership and participation from the Muslim Brotherhood and other Islamist forces in a highly organised and systematic manner.

By 3 p.m. on Friday, thirty-three political groups announced their withdrawal from Tahrir and issued a statement explaining that:

> while all civil political forces, revolutionary groups and youth coalitions have abided by the agreement in opposing the military council's divisive

plans and keeping away from points of difference, some Islamic forces have violated this agreement and chanted slogans, hung banners and spread flyers that included our points of difference. Sticking to our principle of always maintaining peacefulness, we have decided to withdraw from this Friday's demonstrations while continuing our sit-in which upholds the revolution's demands.

(Shukrallah 2011)

But some members of both the Muslim Brotherhood and the Salafi movements denied ever having reached an agreement. Safwat Hegazy, a leading preacher for the Muslim Brotherhood told Al-Jazeera Mubasher that there had been no agreement to unify demands before the Friday demonstrations. In contrast, leading Muslim Brotherhood youth Ibrahim el Hodeiby, who was involved in liaising between the different political groups, had emphasised that the Brotherhood had confirmed the statement, together with a number of other Islamist political forces.

Initially, a large number of political parties including those of the Freedom and Justice Party, the Salafi-led Nour Party, youth coalitions and movements had met in order to agree on some common grounds for voicing a set of collective demands in relation to the armed forces and the current transitional government. An agreement was arrived at, signed by the Muslim Brotherhood (movement and political party) as well as those of the Salafis and other political forces that Friday would be for a show of 'popular will and a united front'. The intention was to show the military council a joint call for justice for the families of the martyrs, speedy trial of Mubarak and his family and the setting of minimal and maximum wages. It was agreed that points of contention between the different political actors, such as the timing of the elections and the drawing of a set of overriding principles to inform the drafting of the constitution, would be put aside in these protests. What the Shariyya millioniyya showed was the exact reverse: the extent of support that the Islamist camp had for the military council and its willingness to show how distant it was from the other political forces pressing the authorities for change. In the weeks before 29 July millioniyya, the military and the government had come under fire from the youth coalitions and revolutionaries who staged a sit-in to demand that the powers-that-be deliver on their proposed changes (such as on 27 May). The Islamists and the Brotherhood were missing and continuously reinforced the message that the military council is the protector of the revolution and must be revered and respected. In came the Islamists on 29 July to assure the military they could depend on them to claim the streets.

By the same token, the armed forces were, during those months following Mubarak's ouster, full of praise for the Brotherhood. According to Robert Fisk, Major-General Mohamed al-'Assar, member of the Supreme Council was telling 'the US Institute of Peace in Washington how jolly mature and co-operative the Brotherhood have become: "Day by day, the Brotherhood are changing and getting on a more moderate track"' (Fisk 2011). Fisk commented that Tantawi, al-'Assar and 'the rest of the gold-braid brigade will do anything to avoid the real change the original revolutionaries insist upon' (Fisk 2011).

What the 29 July uprisings also revealed was the fragility of political arrangements involving the Brotherhood's joint work with non-Islamists. It illustrated that once its political survival was no longer at stake, alliances with non-Islamists became disposable. When in a position of strength, the Muslim Brotherhood has consistently allied themselves with other Islamist forces out of commitment to a common vision – namely, the establishment of an Islamic state. The same kinds of coalitions were pursued in the 1970s against the backdrop of an entente between the Islamists and the Sadat regime. By virtue of the common ideological foundation and the common goal, coalitions established between the Muslim Brotherhood and the Islamists tend to be more cohesive and enduring. The absence of an ideological lowest common denominator makes coalitions with non-Islamists far more likely to disintegrate.

The emergence of a strong Islamist bloc (despite some exceptions on the side) is due to the alliance between the Salafis and Brotherhood facilitated by three critical factors: a common ideological foundation, organisational division of labour and, finally, a number of da'wa leaders who have 'dual identities' who can serve as the bridge-builders between the two movements. Each of these factors will be discussed briefly below.

Ideological common ground: the Brotherhood is in essence a Salafi movement in terms of a belief in following Al Salaf al Saleh. This is very much evident in the convergence between the curricula of the Muslim Brotherhood and the Salafis since their inception and up to the present day. This convergence is evident on two levels: the first is the general pedagogical approach to Islamic studies and the second is the common resources that serve as the fundamental texts.

On the general pedagogical approach, both the Salafis and the Brotherhood prioritise Islamic history, the battles of Islam and its enemies, focus on the Arabic language, the history of the followers/companions (sahaba) of the Prophet. In terms of core texts that inform the fundamental education of the Salafis and Brotherhood, there are some common areas of convergence which are based on the traditional sources of Salafi teachings, for example, the biography of the Prophet Muhammed as narrated by Ibn Hesham, the work of Imam Hamed el Ghazali, and in doctrinal studies, the explanation of the Tahawiyya doctrine. On the other hand, in the tafsir (interpretation), instead of teaching the Qurtabi, Tabari, Ibn Kathir, they teach the works of Sayed Qutb. It is important to note that they do not teach Bukhari and Muslim as sources of hadiths, an area which is fundamental to Salafi teachings. On the other hand, the Muslim Brotherhood youth's education includes important works by Muslim Brotherhood thinkers/leaders from the Muslim Brotherhood's international movement, such as Fathi Yakin, the founder of the Muslim Brotherhood's movement in Lebanon, Ali Mohammed El Sallaby, one of the founders of the Muslim Brotherhood in Libya, Mounir Ghadban, one of the founders of the movement in Syria, and Mohammed Ahmed el Rashed, one of the founders of the movement in Iraq.

Sources associated with the movement in Egypt such as Youssef El Qaradawy and others who are not organisationally affiliated to the movement, but with whom there are strong links such as Mohammed Selim el Awa and Fahmy Howeidy (El Anani 2007: 81). These books written by the Muslim Brotherhood leaders are ones that would clash with the Salafi political thought and approach, on the basis that they are in conflict with authentic, traditional sources of Islamic knowledge. For example, famous Salafi preacher Abi Oubayda, known as Ibn Hassan Al Solayman, specifically criticised Mounir el Ghadban's book on the premise that it stems from a hidden agenda of promoting underground political work, and draws unsound inferences from the Prophet's life (351).

The Wahabisation of the Brotherhood from the 1970s to 2000s meant that the political thought was taking on outward manifestations of religiosity shared by the Salafis and the Muslim Brotherhood members, such as growing a beard and the adoption of the veil in particular in its most conservative forms (the niqab). Because of this blurring of lines, any claim to identify a distinct Muslim Brotherhood standpoint, as opposed to that of the Salafis or other Islamist forces, is highly artificial and distorting. In protests, it was sometimes impossible to completely distinguish between a Salafi and a Muslim Brother.

Organisationally, a more visible division of labour between the Muslim Brotherhood and other Islamist forces ensued following the ousting of Mubarak. The Brotherhood are distinguished by their highly developed organisational abilities, which they have used in the organisation of conferences, public meetings and protests. The Salafis are able to gather a large constituency in a very short time, in particular through their revered leaders and their emotional sermons. For example, at a conference organised in Cairo, 50,000 Salafis and Muslim Brotherhood members congregated on 7 May to join ranks among the groups. At the event, attended by Sheikh Mohammed Hassan and Sheikh Safwat Hegazy, representing two of the movement's icons, the slogan shouted was 'Ikhwan, Salafis, one hand!'[6] in favour of instating the Shari'a as the basis for new governance.

It is highly significant that in the millionıyya calling for the Shari'a on 29 July, a leading Islamist figure explained that the committee responsible for the synchronisation between the Gama'at Islammiyya, the Salafis and the Brotherhood delegated the Brothers with the responsibility of securing Tahrir Square in view of their experience in doing so during the eighteen days of uprisings (Adeeb and Deish 2011).

Of course it is possible that a power struggle may ensue between the Muslim Brotherhood and the Salafis over leadership, and in such case, no amount of ideological or organisational convergence will stop either force from declaring enmity with each other in order to protect their political interests.

The agency dimension of the convergence between the Brotherhood and the Salafis is critically important in facilitating processes of consensus and power-sharing. One preachers, Safwat Hegazy, was believed by the public to be a Salafi until he announced that he belonged to the Muslim Brotherhood. Many of the famous preachers who have an audience of both the Brothers and the Salafis are able to navigate both territories freely and with persuasion (Tammam 2010a).

The agency of such preachers is extremely important because it also allows the Brothers to adopt multiple discourses/positions in relation to multiple audiences. For example, while Mohammed el Beltagui and Essam el Erian gave a kind of conciliatory political discourse regarding joint work with the non-Islamist political forces, Hegazy maintained a position of assertion of Islamic identity that would appeal to the rank and file of the Brothers as well as the Salafis. This is not to suggest that all Salafi movements approve of the Brothers, in fact some consider them as equally culpable of shirk[7] as the People of the Book.[8]

In short, the pathways of political engagement and the choice of political partners taken by the Brotherhood reflects a certain historical pattern: in times of weakness, collaboration with well positioned non-Islamist political forces is pursued, in times of political empowerment, stronger coalitional work is undertaken with Islamist political forces who share the same goal: the establishment of an Islamic state. Because collaborative work with non-Islamist political forces is regarded as temporal and transitory, the prospects of genuine internal transformation in power hierarchies or ideology are minimal. This is especially so when an enabling political environment strengthens the conservative core within the movement. However, political interests will trump ideology if the Brothers or the Salafis are forced to compete between each other for power and leadership. Some of the political and ideological pointers that speak to these dynamics will be discussed at length in Chapter 4.

3 A civil state with an Islamic reference

An oxymoron?

This chapter examines the emergence of the concept of a civil state with an Islamic reference in the Muslim Brotherhood's discourse, its meanings and how it came to be adopted as their official standpoint. It then analyses the idea of an Islamic democracy as one founded on the principle of shura and the extent to which it empowers citizens to engage in the political processes of governance. The concepts of shura and the civil state with an Islamic reference are best seen as two sides of the same coin, representing what is conceived of as a distinctive political order characterised by its Islamic character. The final section explores some of the tensions between the Islamic state and democracy in the political thought of the Muslim Brotherhood and its implications for attempts to reconcile both concepts in theory and practice.

A civil state with an Islamic reference: the development of the concept

Until very recently, the concept of a civil state with an Islamic reference was not circulated in contemporary legitimacy politics (Al-Siyassa al Shar'iyya). Conventional Islamic political scholarship and policy spoke of 'Islamic government' or the 'Islamic caliphate'.[1]

The concept of a civil state with an Islamic reference emerged in the Muslim Brotherhood's literature fairly recently, and did not appear in the official statements until the late 1990s. It was certainly not the term that was used to refer to the kind of state that was vied for at the time when Hassan El Banna established the Muslim Brotherhood, which took place at a critical juncture in the history of the Islamic world and the history of Egypt. On a global level, what was regarded as the bastion of the Islamic order, the Islamic caliphate, disintegrated, leaving many Muslims believing that Islam itself is threatened. The Muslim Brotherhood narrative suggests that it is against the backdrop of the demise of the caliphate, the colonisation of Egypt and the dissemination of Western civilisational norms that Hassan El Banna believed that there was a war against Islam (El Banna 1999: 103–104). On the domestic front, liberal and secular political thought had gained strong grounds and there were powerful critiques emerging questioning the notion that Islam is a religion *and* state or that the Islamic caliphate is necessarily the optimal political system of government for Muslims. Two critical publications published in the mid-1920s played a critical role in influencing Hassan El Banna's decision to form the organisation. The first was *Islam and the Fundamentals of Authority (Hokm)* published in 1925 by Dr Ali 'Abd el Razek, an Azharite scholar who was also a court judge. In his book, 'Abd el Razek sought to show that the position of caliph is a religious and not a political one, and that it is the entangling of religion and politics that has undermined the quality of governance experienced historically by the Muslims and that the establishment of a political caliphate is neither integral to Islam nor to Muslims ('Abd el Razek 1978). 'Abd el Razek argued that Islamic caliphate system was founded on using mighty power and that this power, except in some exceptional cases, rested on the use of physical armed force (1978: 70). He argued that:

> the reality that is supported by rational thinking and which the old and contemporary history attests to, is that the practices of Almighty Allah and the manifestations of his gracious religion do not rest on the kind of government that the legists [jurists] call Caliphate nor on those whom the people title Caliphs. The reality is also that the righteousness of Muslims in their religion does not rest on any of this. We do not need this Caliphate for religious or worldly matters. And if we wanted to, we could say more than this. The Caliphate has been and continues to be a naqba for Islam and Muslims.
>
> (1978: 83)

'Abd el Razek argued that the Prophet himself had no intention of creating a political kingdom, stripped of all meanings of reign (1978: 144) and that the unity of Arabs was based on an Islamic not political one, and that the Prophet's leadership was religious, not civil and that people's submission to him was to doctrine and faith not government and rule (1978: 173–174). Through an analysis of history, Koranic injunctions and jurist traditions, 'Abd el Razek arrives at the conclusion that Islam is a religion, not a system of governance, or practised through the state.

When 'Abd el Razek published his book, there was an uproar from the sheikhs, who declared him an apostate, and demonstrated against him. His book was withdrawn and burnt and Al-Azhar University stripped him of his doctorate and he was fired as judge. On the other hand, the liberal and secular forces supported him and widely deliberated his views.

The second critical book, published in 1926 by renowned scholar Taha Hussein, was a critical examination of the Jahiliyya [Arabian pre-Islamic] poetry, in which his critique went beyond the poetic and into the fundamental grammatical rules guiding the writing of the Koran. 'Emara argues that to have Muslim scholars from Al Azhar such as Taha Hussein and 'Abd el Razek attack the fundamentals of Islam, and its governance system (the Caliphate) was a major blow to the Muslims and represents one of the twentieth century's greatest intellectual struggles afflicting the Muslim mind (2007: 18). It is against this backdrop that Hassan El Banna established his organisation in 1928: to bring the Muslims together under one project. El Banna's conception was of an Islamic state headed by a caliph who would then unify the Muslim Ummah under one rule. In 1940 in a meeting with the Muslim Brotherhood youth, El Banna set out the vision of a righteous Muslim man who would lead a righteous Muslim household and which in sum would lead to a pious Muslim society, and the establishment of an Islamic state characterised by its compliance with Islam. He declared that the Muslim Brotherhood

> do not recognize any governmental order that does not focus in its essence on Islam or derive from it, and we do not recognize these political parties or these traditional forms that the infidels, the enemies of Islam forced us to rule by ... and we will work for the revival of the Islamic order of rule in all its facets and the establishment of an Islamic government in this order.
>
> (Amin 2007: 433)

The overriding message is that the government in Islam is based on the responsibility of the ruler, the unity of the Ummah and respect for its will. Practically, two core dimensions of the state were seen as being key to bringing the system of government into compliance with Islamic Shari'a: the constitution and legislation. The Brotherhood made a distinction between the constitution as regulating the relations between ruler and governed and the laws which govern the relationship between citizens.

In principle, El Banna did not object to having a constitutional state, but insisted that it must be brought in line with the Islamic government system, and be made compatible with the teachings of the Koran (El Banna in Amin 2006j: 260). The Brotherhood's slogan continues to be 'the Koran is our constitution'. Renowned Muslim Brotherhood political figure Mohammed El Bahi put it succinctly as follows: 'There is a constitution for the Islamic Ummah, it is a sacred constitution established by an unchanging eternal creator and not a product of changing humans, it is the Book of Allah and the Sunna of his Prophet, PBUH' (El Bahi 1980: 3–4). The Brotherhood also advocated for making the Islamic Shari'a the source of legislation in the country, in all matters, including commercial, criminal and international affairs. This was argued on the premise that Muslims are being ruled according to legislation that does not emanate from their religion, despite the fact that the constitution recognises Islam as the religion of the state.

The Brotherhood resumed their advocacy for the instatement of an Islamic state in the 1970s under the leadership of Telmesany. During that decade, the main demands were for the establishment of an Islamic state, very much along the lines put forward by Hassan El Banna: bringing the constitution and laws in compliance with the Shari'a. Significant inroads were made in terms of changing the constitution to stipulate that Shari'a is the principle source of legislation, giving it supremacy, as opposed to its previous wording in which the Shari'a was 'a source' of legislation, meaning that there are other sources which were equally instructive.

The civil versus the religious?

The political debate in Egypt continued to be around an Islamic state versus a secular state up to the early 1990s, when the concept of the 'civil' began to enter Egyptian political discourse. One of the earliest incidents of the use of the term 'civil state' was at the International Book Fair, an important platform for the discussion of intellectual and political ideas. On 7 January 1992, a public debate ensued between the secularists and the Muslim Brotherhood and Islamists entitled 'Egypt between the religious state and the civil state'. Representing the secularists were Farag Foda and Mohammed Khallafallah, and the Islamists were represented by the Supreme Guide of the Muslim Brotherhood at the time, Ma'moun el Hodeiby, the famous Sheikh Mohammed el Ghazaly and renowned writer Mohammed 'Emara.

One of El Hodeiby's first interventions was to express his objection to the title of the seminar being 'Egypt between the religious state and the civil state' because it can be interpreted as a state premised on many different religions or premised on religious pluralism. This he found unacceptable since 95 per cent of the Egyptians are Muslims who believe in the Shari'a, and therefore the title of the seminar should not make reference to a religious state but an Islamic state. El Hodeiby questioned what is meant by a civil state, arguing that the purpose of referring to a civil state is to deny its Islamic nature. He argued that there are only two options: either an Islamic or non-Islamic state. The fact that El Hodeiby equated civil with un-Islamic is highly significant in that it continues to be one of the stances expressed to this day. In the remaining conversation, Farag Foda spoke about why they were calling for a civil state and that it was a term effectively used as a substitute for a secular state, a term which was not very popular within the broader circles.

Yet by the end of the discussion, El Hodeiby signalled that Islam requires that the government be civil in the sense of being chosen by the people but that it must be governed in accordance with Islamic rule (Farag in Akladious 2003). Notwithstanding El Hodeiby's statement, the main political demand voiced by the Brotherhood was an Islamic state which continued to be pitted against a secular state. From the late 1990s, the discourse began to shift. One of the key figures known to influence the movement's political stances, Sheikh Youssef El Qaradawy, began to talk about the Islamists not wanting a religious state but a civil state with an Islamic reference, a case made very strongly in his book *From the Fiqh of the State in Islam*, written in 1996 and published in 1997 (El Qaradawy 1997).

The 'civil state with an Islamic reference' framing began to be manifest in the political positions adopted by the Muslim Brotherhood, first in the manifesto of the Wasat Party, then in the 2007 draft party platform and finally in the more recent platform of the 2011 Freedom and Justice Party.

What accounts for this shift are numerous converging factors. The emergence of the concept of a civil state came against the backdrop of the diffusion of the concept of civil society in the early 1990s, partly as a consequence of the salience of the neo-liberal paradigm in Egypt and the subsequent political liberalisation adopted by Sadat, which had expressed itself through the easing of some of the restrictions on some civil society organisations. The concept was also gaining currency in political society. It is also probably more than a coincidence that Rafik Habib, who worked for the Coptic Evangelical Organisation for Social Services, one of the development NGOs to have embraced and advocated the concept of civil society, was in close contact with the Muslim Brotherhood political office and had strong relations with many of the key leaders in El Wasat Party.

According to Rafik Habib,[2] secularists have distorted the meaning of a religious state, hence it became necessary to avoid talking about the Islamic state being a religious state. What can be inferred from Habib's arguments is that the adoption of the concept of a civil state with an Islamic reference in the Muslim Brotherhood's discourse emerged in reaction to the secularists' attacks on the Islamic movements as having an agenda of seeking to instate a repressive theocratic state. By emphasising its civility as well as its Islamic reference, they could arrive at an appropriate framing. Habib suggests that the civil state is one that expresses 'society' in terms of its choice of governor and representatives and holds them accountable and such a definition is compatible with the understandings of governance of most Islamist forces. Since the nature of the state is civil and not religious, nor military however, it is based on the Islamic reference because it derives its identity and approach from Islam (Habib n.d.).

He argued that the concept of a civil state was initially used in political circles in Egypt by the secularists as a cover-up term for secularism, since the word is highly unpopular on the street. Habib does have a case, since the word civil, despite its ambiguity (or perhaps because of it), has far less a negative connotation among the Egyptian public than the word 'secular'. Rather than saying they want a secular state which would be interpreted as being anti-religion, advocating for a civil state is more palatable.

According to Habib, since a civil state is one characterised by being governed by the free will of the people who are the source of its legitimacy and one which allows its citizens to pursue its civilisation, therefore, the identity of the state could be Islamic or non-Islamic, and therefore one can have a civil state with a secular reference or a civil state with an Islamic reference.

It is important to note that the concept was deployed by the Brotherhood at a time when they were becoming increasingly active in formal politics and vying for political legitimacy. The use of the concept reached its heights in 2007 when the draft party platform was issued and in the post-Mubarak phase when they presented their application formally for the establishment of the Freedom and Justice Party. In the first incident, although the Muslim Brotherhood did not submit the platform to the political parties committee, there was an obvious obstacle to the acceptance of their application: namely, that the constitution stated that no parties based on religion can be established. The use of the 'civil state with an Islamic reference' was in 2007 a politically pragmatic way of testing whether this new framing will be also seen as clashing with the constitutional article.

More recently, in the transition phase following the demise of President Mubarak, the Muslim Brotherhood have been championing the concept of a civil state with an Islamic reference together with a number of other Islamist political parties. The use of the concept was supposed to minimise any fears that they aspired to establish an Iran-style government and to distance themselves from accusations of theocracy.

Ironically, the notion of a civil state with an Islamic reference became part of the idiom of a significant section of political society with the increasing powers of the Islamist forces more generally following the demise of Mubarak.

The meanings of the idea of 'a civil state with an Islamic reference'

Influential Muslim Brotherhood thinkers who have elucidated the meaning of a civil state with an Islamic reference almost always start by explaining *what it is not*. The civil state with an Islamic reference is framed as not being a theocratic or religious state *as was known to Europe*; as not being a military dictatorship forced upon the people and as not being a secular state. Many Muslim Brotherhood thinkers explain that an Islamic state does not have the characteristics of a religious state in medieval Europe in terms of attributing the ruler with special divine qualities and in terms of the special positioning of the clergy as mediating between people and God (El-Qaradawy 2003: 159; El Wa'i 2007: 93; 'Abd el Khalek 'Ouda, el-Bahnasawy, el Sawi, Al Shawi). This is a common feature of the work of prominent Muslim Brotherhood figures who have supported the concept of a civil state as well as in the official stances (a 2007 draft platform and 2011 Freedom and Justice Party platform). According to chapter 1 of the Freedom and Justice Party platform: 'The Islamic state by its nature is a civil state, it is not a military state governed by the army which ascends to rule via a military coup.' The civil state is also not:

> a religious state (theocracy) ruled by a clergy. In Islam there are no religious men but specialized scholars of religion ('ulama), it cannot be ruled by divine will. There are no infallible persons who monopolize the interpretation of the Koran or who specialize in the legislation for the Umma or own the right to absolute obedience and are characterized by holiness.

This is very much in tune with El Qaradawy's position that the civil state with an Islamic reference

> is not a religious state nor a theocracy that controls people or their conscience in the name of divine truth. It is not the state of priests or clergy that

claim to represent divine will in the world or the will of heaven on the people of the earth such that whatever they agree on earth is agreed in heaven and whatever they bind on earth is bound in heaven!

(El Qaradawy 1997: 30)

Mohammed el Bahi points out the following:

> The Islamic government is a human government that rules according to the Book of Allah and His Prophet PBUH, i.e. it is not a government that is immune from error, and is not like the clerical government that it is a sacred government, infallible, the church believes in the pouring of the Holy Spirit upon humans when he becomes a president and the nature of the head of church is then a Godly-human nature and the interpretation of this for its followers is the release of his human nature that is fallible.

(El Bahi 1980: 4)

The Islamic state is one where governance is not mediated through the powers of the clergy but through written legislation in accordance with the principles of the Koran and Sunna. Where matters arise that do not have clear rulings, they are settled through shura or the principles accorded in the Koran and Sunna (El Wa'i 2001: 82).

A careful analysis of the discourse of Muslim Brotherhood scholars suggests that it is not that they necessarily rejection a religious state per se, rather they reject the Western Christian model of the religious state. For example, the late Supreme Guide Omar el Telmesany refuted that in Islam there is a religious state and argued that the term refers to the Western Christian experience. He expressed his bewilderment that people would insist on describing a government that applies the Shari'a as a religious one (1977: 12). The yardstick of what constitutes a religious government is the papal government – and that is not what the Islamic state is about, because there is no special privileges for the clergy in Islam (1977: 15). The Islamic state cannot be compared to any other form of state. Although El Telmesany argues that the opponents of the Islamic state have accused it of being a religious state, it is not. Yet the criteria for what constitutes a religious state are very much based on the characteristics of medieval European theocratic states.

Two critical issues are noteworthy here with respect to the Muslim Brotherhood political thought. First, the caliph or imam[3] in an Islamic state is not a representative of God, and is not infallible, however, he is considered as a representative of the Prophet on earth.

The title of head of state is a political and religious one. This in effect undermines the civility of the state because he must comply with the sovereign-inspired Shari'a rather than the laws created by the people. The second issue is that the clergy in medieval Europe are represented as having no counterparts in an Islamic state, however, the standing of the 'ulama in an Islamic government does not suggest a disconnection from the sources of power. El Qaradawy notes that unlike the clergy in former theocratic Europe, in Islam the concept of men of religion (clergy) is non-existent and that instead there are specialised 'ulama in Islamic matters, and that their responsibility is to provide advice and direction for all Muslims and the state must create the enabling environment for them to do so (1997: 30–31) Yet the absence of a formal political position does not preclude the performance of the function that comes from their identity as the knowledge-bearers of what it is to rule in accordance with the Shari'a. This is very much evident in El Qaradawy's elaboration (El Qaradawy 1997: 31).

Renowned political philosopher Mohammed Arkoun, a secularist, argued that rather than examining whether there is a parallel figure for the priest in Islam, we should ask whether there is a parallel function performed. He argues that while there is no pyramidal hierarchy in Islam representing religious authority, nonetheless, there is an entity of jurists that maintains a system of orthodoxy and that overseas the application of religious law in cooperation with the state. The 'ulama have played in historical and contemporary political systems a similar role to that played by the priests in the Christian Church before the separation of Church and state occurred (Arkoun n.d.: 132). 'Personalities such as the Mufti, the Judge and the Imam represent a religious and civil entity at the same time' (Arkoun n.d.: 132). What can be inferred from Arkoun is that while in Islam there is no priest to mediate between the people and God, in effect, the clergy still do play a critical role in Islam.

What actually constitutes a civil state with an Islamic reference (as opposed to what it is not) is founded on the application of the principles in Islamic jurisprudence of selecting [the ruler], al bay'a, and shura and the responsibility of the ruler towards the Ummah, and the right of every individual among the subjects to advise this ruler (El Qaradawy 2003: 159). The principle of shura will be visited in a later section in the chapter. However, what is emphasised here is that the people have the right to choose their ruler, they have the right to hold him accountable if he deviates from the application of God's laws and they have the right to advise him.

This is described in the Freedom and Justice Party platform (chapter one on the state), in which a civil state with an Islamic reference is explained as follows:

> It is the Ummah where the people who have the right to elect the ruler through free popular will. The difference between an Islamic state and other states is the Islamic Shari'a reference which is based on the creed of the vast majority of the Egyptian people and the Shari'a is in its nature an addition to the worship and ethical dimensions which govern different elements of the life of the Muslims. It organizes them in general roles and comprehensive principles and then leaves the details to *ijtehad* and legislation in accordance with what is suitable for every age and for different environments and with what achieves truth, justice.

Yet the people's will, which is essential to the civility of the state, is not undermined by what they can do (nominate the leader), but by what they can't be – by virtue of the Islamic qualifier that sets the conditions of eligibility to be a ruler.

The second major conundrum with the concept of a civil state with an Islamic reference is the question of sovereignty in the crafting and application of legislation. Here it is worthy to go back to the point that the Muslim Brotherhood's political thought is that while the state is not religious, it is not secular either:

> Secularity, whether it manifests itself in the denial of religion or enmity towards it or whether secularism takes the form of separation of religion from state and its isolation from having an impact on public life and society such as in politics and economics, culture, religion etc. is considered as anathema to the Islamic state.
>
> (El Qaradawy 1997: 31)

In juxtaposing that it is not a secular state El Qaradawy notes that it is a civil state that enforces the rules/laws of heaven, protecting the application of God's commandments as per surrah al haj 41 in the Koran. The fact that it is not the will of the ruler or the people that informs governance is argued to be superiority of the Islamic model over Western democratic models because the rules were laid

> by the Lord of the people, the King of the People, and the God of the people. Neither he [ruler] nor others from among people can cancel these rulings or freeze them. No king, nor president nor parliament, nor government nor revolutionary council nor central committee nor people's conference nor any power on earth can change from the constant [non-changeable] rules of God.
>
> (2007: 159–160)

Even if inscribed in writing, it is the sovereignty of God's laws – not the sovereignty of the people – that governs. Sallah el Sawi articulates this principle more forcefully when he argues that legislation must be based on God's laws in an absolute way, and to share this sovereignty with the people is shirk and to base the law on the sovereignty of the people, as in Western democracies, is a form of *kufr*. A system of democracy is not an end solution, it is to be accepted only in the transitional phase because it is anathema to the full application of God's sovereignty (El Sawi n.d.: 265). El Sawi further argues that representative legislatures (such as parliament) that do not rule in accordance with the Shari'a should have a singular purpose: to pronounce the sovereignty of God in the drafting of legislation. Any legislation that does not comply with the Shari'a should be regarded as null and void. Resistance or opposition to the application of the Shari'a is considered a form of apostasy (*kufr*) (El Sawi n.d.: 259). Like El Qaradawy, he argues that the supremacy of the Shari'a over any human-made law makes for a superior political order.

El Qaradawy argues that because liberal democratic orders are premised on decision-making by consensus, this sometimes leads to unprincipled decisions being made. In an Islamic system, this is not possible, especially since the principle of the supremacy of Shari'a is higher than the supremacy of the law and because no law-making legislature can deviate or violate the content of the Shari'a since no institution within the state is empowered to change or delay the implementation of the laws of the Shari'a (El Qaradawy 1997: 38).

It is not just in the legislatures that the Islamic system is found incompatible with the notion of a civil state, the same applies to the judiciary.

The high constitutional court would oversee the legislation issued by the legislatures to make sure that it complies with the Shari'a while bearing in mind that non-Muslims have the right to rule according to their own Shari'a. El Qaradawy had earlier made a similar proposal:

> The Islamic state is a constitution or legitimate state that has its own constitution to which it refers for governance and a law to refer to, and its constitution is represented in the principles and laws of the Sharia as came dome in the Koran and the Sunna in terms of doctrine, *'badat*, ethics and mou'amalat.
>
> (1997: 32)

It is critical to point out that the constitution is not human-made according to what the people or the political community agree – there are no options in it because it is based on God's laws. 'The compliance by the state by the Shari'a Law is what gives it its legitimacy.' In such a case, the people own it obedience as long as it complies with God's laws, and if it violates God's laws, this is no longer so (El Qaradawy 1997: 32).

El Qaradawy compares some countries where they comply with the law and holding on to the constitution, whereas in an Islamic state, they hold on the Shari'a, which is far superior to any human-made law (1997: 33).

> And it must be established from *among them* an authority or a supreme constitutional court to which all proposals for laws and systems will be presented so that it does not issue what conflicts with Islam, and hence we do not have the separation of the Koran and sultan [rule] which is what the hadith warned about.
>
> (1997: 31; italics mine)

What this indicates is that while they are not given a formal political position through which they rule, in fact they wield the same power through the *function* of filtering through the legislation crafted.

The fact that the Shari'a is enacted through written laws, through for example a supreme constitutional court as El Qaradawy proposes, does not obliterate its religious character, it sustains a constitutional theocracy.[4] Hirschl (2008) and Lombardi and Brown (2006) convincingly show how the Supreme Constitutional Court in Egypt accommodated the principle of Islam being the principle source of legislation in article 2 of the constitution with their own liberal standpoints by drawing upon modernist approaches to legal reasoning in order to establish its progressive reading of the Shari'a. However, the agential factors that have given rise to this are unlikely to exist in the Islamic state envisioned by the Muslim Brotherhood. The men who ruled in the constitutional courts received liberal training in law, the men who are likely to be in their positions in the Islamic state envisaged by El Qaradawy and others are more likely to come from the traditional religious training backgrounds (such as Al-Azhar) and consequently are, for the most part, more likely to apply more traditional approaches to the application of the Shari'a. Such approaches tend to produce by and large conservative judgements.

Shura: the Islamic version of democracy?

The concept and practice of shura are instrumental to our understanding of the organisation of power in an Islamic state as envisioned by the Muslim Brotherhood. Shura represents one of the core values cited in Islamic jurisprudence or Al-Siyassa al Shar'iyya. The political wing of the Muslim Brotherhood have been keen on representing shura as the Islamic equivalent of democracy, but as carrying more legitimacy in Muslim-majority states because it is grounded in the Koran. Shura can be interpreted as consultation.

Prominent Muslim Brotherhood thinker Mohammed El Bahi points out that shura is practised in the realm of the family, among neighbours and in the wellaya 'amma (1980: 424–425). Here discussions will be restricted to the application of shura in governance. In the realm of governance, its central importance lies in that 'ahl al shura' are often portrayed as ahl al hel wal 'akd and are considered the equivalent of a legislative parliament. Hence questions regarding whether the decisions reached by parliament are binding or whether they can be overruled by the imam or president are very pertinent here. Islam did not specify the nature of the practical set up it should take, hence much of the attempted theorisation of what it entails.

There is a broad consensus among Muslim Brotherhood thinkers that shura is exercised in governance through the selection of the ruler by the people, the right (and duty) of the people to offer advice to the ruler, and the right of the people to hold the ruler accountable if he deviates from implementing the Shari'a. Yet within the Muslim Brotherhood the presentation of shura as the Islamic equivalent of democracy is a matter open for deliberation, conceptually and practically. At the top of the list of issues open for contestation, is whether shura is synonymous with democracy, who constitute ahl al shura, what is the system that brings them into office and what are the criteria for selection. The third debate is whether the decision-taker is obliged to comply with the opinion arrived at by the shura council.

These contestations are not only matters around which fiqh disputes occur, they inform and influence everyday practices of politics even in Egypt's post-Mubarak transition phase where various actors are contending for political power. This is no more evident than in the dispute over Abdel Moneim Aboul Fotouh's decision to run for president and whether the Brotherhood's shura council's decision not to put forward a candidate for the presidency is mandatory or whether it is instructive only, a case study that will be discussed below.

Is shura the same as democracy?

The debate regarding whether shura is the equivalent of democracy is highly charged because of divisions over whether democracy is a desirable good in the first place and, second, because in order to ensure that the Islamic nature of the state is maintained, the positioning and power of the religious scholars ('ulama) must be resolved.

In the Freedom and Justice Party's platform, shura is used synonymously with democracy. Shura is in the first mention cited as one of the main principles guiding their platform (the first being the Shari'a, the second being respect for human rights, and the fourth being the civilian nature of the state). In the party platform, shura is conflated with democracy 'in particular in political activity, and on its premises is the right to choose the governer, the MPs and their monitoring and holding them accountable'. In the first chapter of the party platform, the shura is determined to be 'the essence of democracy and it is the means to achieving the interests of the nation so that no individual or category comes to be oppressive' (Freedom and Justice Party Platform 2011).

The practical dilemmas of shura are avoided in the Freedom and Justice Party platform by mentioning the concept in very broad and general terms and without indicating how shura will be used interchangeably to signify democracy. The omission is not by virtue of its diminished importance to the ideology or vision of the Muslim Brotherhood but in order not to make themselves politically vulnerable to attacks from the opposition as was the case when they announced the previous party platform in 2007.

The enactment of the shura council in the form of a higher body for the 'ulama in the draft party platform of 2007 caused a massive stir. The draft platform indicated that:

> the legislative authorities [of the state] must ask the opinion from the authority comprised of the senior 'ulama of the Ummah having been elected through free and direct elections from 'ulama who enjoy complete and true autonomy from the executive authority in all its technical, financial and administrative matters and it is to be supported by committees and consultants who have experience and knowledge.

This applies to the president, as when he is issuing a decree he must consult with the 'ulama (as above). 'The legislative authorities on issues that do not touch on the injunction of the law (Al-Khudrawi 128)[5] or premised on definitive text [from the Koran][6] have the right to take a decision based on majority vote.' The legislative authorities still have to refer all matters to the senior 'ulama's authority for their opinion on what it sees as closest to achieving public interest. A law would be issued to determine whom among the 'ulama are entitled to elect the 'ulama authorities.

The above vision was severely criticised by non-Islamist political thinkers and commentators. Such a high standing of the 'ulama's committee could only mean the instatement of a religious state. Yet the above vision is disconcerting at a deeper level, namely that the people's agency is contained strictly within the realm of matters not covered by the Shari'a and these can be many or few depending on the powers of the 'ulama. This filtration process severely undermines the principle of people's sovereignty and the civility of the state. Yet there is a consensus among the thinkers who have informed the Brotherhood's political thought that the principle guiding the application of shura is only in matters not prescribed in Islam. For El Qaradawy and El Wa'i, the process and outcome of shura must comply with the spirit of Islamic jurisprudence (1951: 145–146). For 'Abd el Kadir 'Ouda (1951: 145) and Khaled 'Abd el Kadir 'Ouda[7] (2005: 125) the benefits of making shura qualified by the precepts of Shari'a according to its advocates are many. For 'Abd el Qadir 'Ouda, it serves to restrain people's desires in order to ensure that people hold on to their Islam ('Abd el Qadir 'Ouda 1951: 147). El Qaradawy and El Wai'i argue that it is what differentiates an Islamic democracy from a liberal democracy which can be misguided by the people's will:

> Islam does not concern itself with [the will of] the majority where there is a clear ruling in the Koran and the Sunna, as opposed to the western democratic system which gives the majority the absolute right that its opinion is the law and the law is reformed if it is in violation of its opinion.
>
> (2007: 78)

The enactment of shura in matters other than those for which there is a clear injunction in the Koran and Sunna presents some practical conundrums. First, it clearly sets a normative framework which cannot be interrogated or challenged because it is considered sacred. In that sense, citizens cannot appeal to any other normative framework or reference because none can compete, supersede or substitute for the prescripts of the Shari'a. Second, while issues that are not definitively addressed in the Koran and Sunna are open for deliberation through shura, the lines of demarcation of what is considered definitive or not is in practice open for contestation. El Wa'i (2001) argues that shura must be enacted in a society in which Islamic values have already been deeply embedded. He argues that whereas in non-Islamic systems, shura is applied through the appointment of the ruler by the majority or through electoral systems, in an Islamic system the shura is to be distinguished by being preceded by the deepening of Islamic values in society. The assumption here is that people will want to be ruled in a system where shura is in compliance with the Shari'a. This by default limits the terms of citizen engagement – there is no place for deviance from the normative framework (Shari'a), there are no possibilities of resorting to other references/ frameworks, since all are considered inauthentic and inferior to the Islamic one.

Moreover, there is a unanimous position among the main leaders of the Brotherhood that ahl al shura (or ahl al hel wal 'akd) are to play a key position in the choice of the ruler. Yet who comprises ahl al shura, how are they elected into office, are debatable matters.

Hassan El Banna's position (Amin n.d.) was that Islam did not require the knowledge of the opinion of the people on each issue, through what is known as a general census, but it is sufficient to abide by 'ahl al hel wal 'akd', who are:

1   the jurisprudence experts upon whose words we can count for fatwas and to give legal opinions on matters;
2   the experts in general issues;
3   those who have a leadership or ruling as leaders of households, families, elders of tribes and heads of groups.

MPs would be the ahl al hel wal 'akd, a principle that Hassan El Banna does not object to, however, he argues that the rules of eligibility for nomination to be an MP should comply with Islamic rules, and not be left to anyone who wants to run for election:

> the modern parliamentary system organized the means through which we acquire ahl al a hel wal 'akd through the constitutional jurists in terms of systems of elections. 'Islam does not prohibit this system as long as it leads to the selection of ahl al hel wal 'akd, and this is easy to implement in any system that lays criteria for the election of ahl al hel wal 'akd and not allowing others to put themselves forward for parliament on behalf of the Ummah.'
>
> (Amin n.d.: 328)

Very much in the same spirit is 'Abd el Qadir 'Ouda's reading of shura:

> The logic of Islam is that all of ahl al Shura (or: ahl al hel wal 'akd) or its majority are from those who have complete mastery of the Islamic Shari'a since Shura is confined by not deviating out of the precepts of Islamic Shari'a and its spirit.
>
> ('Ouda 1951: 155)

In view of the complexity of the situation today ('Ouda writing in the 1950s) and the need for specialisations, there is no objection to having specialised persons as long as no person who does not master the Shari'a is in a position to give an opinion on matters pertaining to it. A number of persons competent in the Shari'a could form a special committee or court, depending on what is suitable to the time and context.

Different authors speak of different shura authorities. In the case of the role of the religious ahl al shura (or: ahl al hel wal 'akd), there is no mention of who elects them into office, only that by virtue of being ahl al hel wal 'akd they become representations of the Ummah ('Ouda 1951: 155–156). The logic is the reversal of representative democracy whereby representatives have their powers by virtue of being elected into office by the people, in this case, the members of the shura derive their power by virtue of being knowledgeable in the Shari'a, and therefore are entitled to represent the people. In 'Ouda's logic, they are the ones who are best equipped to take decision-making positions. By default, it means that leadership positions lie exclusively the domain of the members of this strata – no others can qualify.

In Khaled 'Abd el Kader 'Ouda's proposal for an alternative governance system in accordance with the Shari'a, he proposes that the shura is what has been arrived at by the will of the majority of the members of the Ummah after it (the matter) had been tackled from the technical and jurisprudence points of view from *ahl al 'ilm wal khbera* (the experts who have the knowledge and experience). The purpose of the shura is to provide a technical opinion for consultation in political decision-making. Those selected are considered representative of the Ummah – however, it is not the people who have the right to elect them into office. Rather, they are to be voted into office through a 'restricted census' (ikter'a moukayad) from those with expertise and particular specialisations. For the technical tier of the shura council, they are to be voted in through the experts according to each one's particular specialisation (i.e. an engineer to be voted in by engineering experts, a finance person by finance experts, etc.). For the religious tier, it is unclear who nominates them into office, however, they must be specialists in the Shari'a ('ulama) and they are empowered to ensure that any proposals made by the technical committee conforms to the precepts of the Shari'a. In other words, they have the upper hand to reject or approval proposals in accordance on religious grounds (2005: 125–126). While they do not have the right to approve legislation (this will be managed through parliament via elected MPs), they hold a consultative status (2005: 147). This is very much the underlying vision of the draft party platform of 2007.

The other critical question which has been hotly debated within the Muslim Brotherhood is the question of whether the shura is binding (molzimah) or instructive only (mu'alimah). There are two dimensions to this debate, and they clearly show that the matter is complicated by the conditions under which it is binding and not. El Qaradawy, Sheikh el Ghazaly and El Wa'i are regarded as the most enthusiastic advocates of the idea that shura is binding for the ruler.

El Wa'i argues that based on his reading of the evidence from the Quran and the Sunna, the principle of Shura is compulsory and binding even if there is a possibility that the view of the majority is erroneous or harmful 'because the harm emanating from the majority is less than the harm emanating from abandoning shura' (2001: 67). El Wa'i goes even further, arguing that the principle of shura is to be applied to all systems which are affiliated to Islam, or raise its banner, be they political, social or economic (2001: 67).

Yet the matter is far from settled, with key figures, not least of whom is Hassan El Banna, adopting the opposite stance. For Hassan El Banna, the decisions arrived at through shura were not considered to be binding. The concept of shura itself was discussed under the heading of 'the unity of the Ummah', suggesting that it is the ultimate goal.

According to El Banna, if the matter around which difference has arisen is textually prescribed, there is no ijtehad. And for what is not textually covered, 'the decision is to the ruler who unifies the Ummah on it and there is nothing after that' (El Banna n.d.: 318[8]).

> It is the right of the Islamic Ummah to monitor the ruler the most meticulous of monitoring and to give him advice in what he sees good. And he has to consult it [the Ummah] and to respect its will and take what is good from its views and Allah ordered the rulers with that.
>
> (n.d.: 319)

The above text does not suggest that shura is molzimah (binding). It is required on the part of wally al amr to unify the Ummah but this could be around his will and not around what they have proposed. Further, while the ruler has to consult and respect the will, there is absolutely no obligation to comply with it, in particular since he has the right to 'take what he sees good' from such advice – and therefore, retain the right to also disregard what he does not see as good.

In the 1940s, a group of youth belonging to the Muslim Brotherhood had a dispute with Hassan El Banna over internal governance issues, at the forefront of which was the practice of shura within the movement. In the end, it was agreed that they would leave the movement, and that *Al Nazir*, a magazine in which they were active and which had served as a mouthpiece for the Brotherhood, be in their possession. The youth group, which called themselves 'Mohammed's youth', used *Al Nazir* to present their case against Hassan El Banna. The first reservation they had was on the non-binding nature of the shura as practised by El Banna:

> His Righteousness the Supreme Guide of the Muslim Brotherhood is of the view that there is no [place for] shura in da'wa and that the da'wa is pursued by one person from the group who orders and everyone obeys. We have disagreed with him on this opinion. We insisted on our position that His Righteousness' opinion is in violation of the Islamic political order and a challenge to the Book and Sunna ... many times we tried reaching an understanding with His Righteousness but he refused except that his position be decisive and if this will lead to the pushing away of faithful members of the Brotherhood. He then came back with the justification that he did not find among the Muslim Brotherhood who could be [fitting] for ahl al shura and this is something we do not accept.

In a special newsletter, Hassan El Banna responded by emphasising that:

> In the Islamic Shura, there is no majority and minority. The Imam seeks clarification [from] different opinions and he is faithful [in the process], and he takes from all of these opinions what is revealed to him [as the right one] then he implements it in accordance with the rules of Islam and he is

responsible after that for the outcome of his policies. This is the Islamic theory on shura.

(Abou Faris 1988)

In another instance in 1942, when Mustapha Nahas asked Hassan El Banna to revoke his candidature from the elections, he agreed and by doing so he had defied the decision that the Supreme Guidance Bureau had reached unanimously. The anecdote given by Sheikh Taleimah on Sheikh Hassan El Banna is highly revealing. The story as told by Abbas el Sissy (1978: 33–48), a Muslim Brotherhood member who wrote of his accounts of being in the presence of Hassan El Banna, recalled that in 1942 when Hassan El Banna put himself forward for the elections in Ismailiya, people rejoiced, campaigns were held in his support and Brotherhood members came from other governorates to join in the mass mobilisation for his support. Not so long after that Hassan El Banna invited the Brothers to a conference in which he said that Nahas Pasha summoned him to his office and asked him to withdraw his nomination, adding that the country was in a state of war and it was in the interests of the country for him to withdraw. When Hassan El Banna pointed out to him that the government has already been highly restrictive by prohibiting his travel outside Cairo except with prior permission from the Ministry of Interior, Nahas Pasha offered to allow him complete freedom of mobility for undertaking da'wa in return for his withdrawal of his application, an offer which he accepted. While El Sissy's account describes how the multitude were angered, it makes no mention of the reaction of the Guidance Bureau.

However, the Guidance Bureau did in fact object to Hassan El Banna's contempt for shura more generally. Hassan El Banna's brother, 'Abd el Rahman El Banna's account of what he termed 'the historical' meeting on Saturday 9 March 1946 at the house of Saleh Ashmway indicated that members of the Guidance Bureau expressed their misgivings at the Supreme Guide's position on shura. An excerpt of the account indicated that Dr Suleiman said he felt that the Supreme Guide was not the Hassan El Banna of old, with whom they used to sit, he would listen to them and show his appreciation. Dr Suleiman said that they now felt that the Supreme Guide had become haughty and conceited to the extent that he now felt he needed a wasta (connection) to speak to him. He then added that he could not simply obey because he was not a machine or a car.

Salem Amin Geith then said that the Bureau had to oblige the Supreme Guide and direct him and to elaborate on the Islamic jurisprudence's theory of shura in Islam 'and that it is required and binding' (El Banna 2009: 245–246).

These precedents involving Hassan El Banna's overruling of the principle of shura have cast shadows over the extent to which the shura is conclusively binding. 'Abd el Karim Zeidan, an important figure in the movement and who served as the Supreme Guide of the Brotherhood in Iraq, said that after reviewing all the jurisprudence evidence on whether the ruler is obliged to comply with the stance taken by the shura council concludes that it is not. To present advice is one thing, to implement it is another. The shura conveys to the ruler the right opinion but it is entirely up to him whether to take it or to decide otherwise (1976: 214).

The above debate is extremely important for governance on two levels: first, if the shura is enacted in modern systems through parliament, and the ruler (president or prime minister) does not have to comply with its decisions, and may choose to follow what he sees best, then there is a serious compromise on the political and civil rights of the people. This would present an affront on the concept of people's sovereignty and the civility of the state, since his right to ignore the shura on the premise that it is not binding would be religiously sanctioned.

The second conundrum relating to whether the shura is binding or instructive has to do with the internal governance of the Muslim Brotherhood and the extent to which it is seen as inclusive in the eyes of its members. This conundrum was played out when Abdel Moneim Aboul Fotouh announced his intention to nominate himself as president following the demise of President Mubarak. This was considered a flagrant violation of the decision taken by the shura council of the Muslim Brotherhood not to nominate anyone for president. In that particular dispute, Mahmoud Ghozlan wrote a powerful commentary, explaining that this was not a personal assault on Abdel Moneim Aboul Fotouh but based on the decision reached by the shura council of the Muslim Brotherhood, one around which there was consensus. The Brotherhood had their shura council for the time on 10 February 2011, before the ousting of President Mubarak, and decided not to put forward a candidate for presidency. In the second shura council meeting held on the 29–30 April 2011, the decision was again unanimously reached that the Brotherhood would not nominate any of its members who opted to present themselves for the presidency as independent candidates. The justification for such a decision is tackled in Chapters 4 and 8. However, what is important is Ghozlan's emphasis on the fact that in view of the consensual decision arrived by the shura council of the Brotherhood, Abdel Moneim Aboul Fotouh is obliged to comply with it. Ghozlan then asks a number of rhetorical questions which reveal the significance of shura through consensus:

> Here we ask, is it possible for him who swore by God to abide by the opinion of the gama'a even if it is at odds with his own, that violates the covenant with God before violating that with the gama'a, and moreover, is not abiding by the opinion of the gama'a or its majority at the essence of Shura and the heart of democracy? And if it is difficult for a person to comply with the ruling of the Shura and respect democracy and what religion, principles and values and the covenant with God requires this of him, when he is stripped of any authority, would you see him complying with its ruling once he owns authority?[9]

Ghozlan's emphasis on a decision reached unanimously by the shura council to be unequivocally binding (or molzimah) is not one around which there is consensus within the wider Muslim Brotherhood. Sheikh Essam Teleimah[10] does not consider the violation of a decision taken by the Muslim Brotherhood as so grave by referring to Hassan El Banna's decision to go against the grain of the Guidance Bureau.

What is striking here is that Ghozlan, known to be one of the old guard, is taking a position normally associated with the reformist wing of the Brotherhood while Teleimah is espousing a position normally associated with the conservative wing of the Brotherhood. The position of the reformist wing in the Brotherhood, such as Al Wa'i, have been informed by Sheikh Youssef El Qaradawy's stance in favour of recognising the decision reached by the majority of shura members, as binding on the decision-taker/ruler. El Qaradawy, El Wa'i and 'Ouda (1951: 150) argue that the opinion held by the majority of the members of ahl al shura (or: ahl al hel wal 'akd) is binding in view of the fact that the rule is that the majority are generally correct and it is a rarity when the minority's perspective is sound and in line with the Prophet's own example.

It is significant, however, that among those who argue that the view of the majority of members of the shura council is binding, there is no place for minority contestation after the matter has been open for debate. 'Abd el Qadir 'Ouda (1951)[11] and others argue that once the opinion of the majority of the shura is announced, after the matter has been given sufficient deliberation, the minority must comply with what is agreed. This he argues distinguishes it from countries which have espoused democratic orders and where the minority can continue to dispute and contest the ruling regime, holding it up for ridicule and questioning.

But the Islamic order, argues 'Abd el Qadir 'Ouda, is based on shura and cooperation and impartiality in the consultation phase and complete obedience and trust in the implementation phase.

> Its principles do not allow for inciting one category of people against another and in this way, the Islamic order has combined the benefits attributed to a democracy and the benefits attributed to a dictatorship while at the same time being free from the defects attributable to both democracy and dictatorship.
>
> (1951: 154)

This is critically important for it severely limits the place and function of political pluralism in any system, since political parties are prohibited from objecting or contesting a decision, once the authorities have taken a decision after the deliberation phase has terminated, as will be discussed in the next chapter.

The irreconcilable in theory and practice

In this chapter it was argued that whether we are talking about a civil state with an Islamic reference or whether we are talking about shura as an Islamic synonym for democracy, it is in essence an attempt to frame the Islamic state in a way that minimises opposition and resistance. It is significant that the Brotherhood have constantly referred to Western political experiences whether historically or in contemporary times as the models against which their vision of an Islamic state is compared and contrasted. The two are not the same, as El Qaradawy emphasises. El Qaradawy argued that the essence of democracy is the same as the essence of Islam. Where they converge is that the people choose their ruler, have the mechanisms to hold him accountable and, if he does not retract, to also peacefully remove him from power (2007: 175). Where Islam and democracy diverge, from El Qaradawy's view, is in its making the individual rights supersede those of the group, in giving absolute freedoms 'and in giving the majority the right to change everything, even democracy itself' (2007: 176). However, there is another importance instance where El Qaradawy concedes that they do diverge: shura (El Qaradawy 2007).

El Qaradawy arrived at the conclusion that to make the case that shura is the Islamic alternative to democracy[12] is highly problematic because there is no consensus among the jurists that the decisions of the shura are binding. (2007: 177–178). He proposes another series of policies (all emanating from his reading of fiqh) to complement the principle of shura to ensure that the system in place is better able to deliver on the essence of Islamic democracy (such as the right to depose the ruler, etc.).

El Wa'i makes a number of distinctions between what he terms 'Islamic democracy' and 'Western democracy'. The first two distinctions suggest that individuals will abide by Islamic ethics making their performance more moral and less corrupt. The third and fourth distinctions are more structural: namely that:

> Islam does not concern itself with [the will of] the majority where there is a clear ruling in the Koran and the Sunna, as opposed to the western democratic system which gives the majority the absolute right that its opinion is the law and the law is reformed if it is in violation of its opinion.
>
> (2001: 78)

The second major difference is that unlike in Western democratic systems, in their Islamic counterparts, the assumption of leadership positions must abide by the Islamic rules of wellaya (2001: 79). What has been argued here is that, in practice, the rules governing the concepts and practices tend to inhibit and constrain citizen opportunities for participation, voice and accountability.

It follows from the above that the civil state with an Islamic reference is an oxymoron because there are clear limitations as to the power that people would have in challenging the normative framework upon which the rules of governance are set. Even if it is codified and administered through religious scholars who are not endowed with divine inspiration, there is the sovereignty of God in governance, not the people. This manifests itself in theocratic constitutionalism, and pervasive powers that the 'ulama have over all matters of public and private life, even if they do not enjoy formal titles in the government. It also expresses itself in the difficulty of separating the executive, judiciary and legislative as well as in the restrictions on the practice of shura.

The argument that the Islamic democratic order is superior to its Western counterpart (El Qaradawy, El Wa'i, 'Abd el Qadir 'Ouda) rests on the idea that the Islamic order takes the best of the Western political order, but is made superior by being guided by sovereign-inspired laws. Since the Shari'a has been implemented in Sudan, governorates of Northern Nigeria, Aceh in Indonesia and elsewhere, it is interesting that the evidence for the superiority of the implementation of Islamic democracy is presented throughout by the writers in an ideal form, and not based on contemporary country case evidence.[13]

Concepts such as a civil state with Islamic reference or an Islamic democracy may have been widely publicised by the political wing of the Muslim Brotherhood as framing strategies to show their reformist credentials and alter the public image that they are advocating for a theocratic, religious state. However, within the Brotherhood and within other Islamist movements, there are those for whom such concepts have little currency, because they do see the tensions that such framing poses for their own ideological visions of political orders, governance and the relationship between the ruler and the ruled. If the non-Islamist political parties become weaker, the contestations to such concepts as civil state with an Islamic reference will become more overtly expressed from within the Brotherhood and elsewhere.

Some Islamist figures, such as Salafi leader Sheikh Mohammed 'Abd el Maqsoud, approved of the use of the term, explaining:

> if someone says I want a sports state with an Islamic reference – and we ask what do you mean, and he says I want healthy bodies but that we go back to religion for everything, then that's fine, that's all we want. There is no disagreement between the concept of a civil state with an Islamic reference and a religious state, since the meaning is the same and since the essence is the same but the name is different, that is fine.[14]

Yet the idea of the civility of the state (even with an Islamic reference) has not been persuasive either to their own constituency or to the wider public. This is no more evident than in Egypt's transition phase. On 29 July in the Islamist-led millioniyya (see Chapter 2) some of the crowd had raised the banner in Tahrir Square 'Islammiyya Islammiyya mish madaniyya' (Islamic Islamic not civil). Underlying the message is the fundamental belief that there is a power struggle between instating the Islamic and the civil, and that the latter continues to be associated with those who are resistant to the Islamisation of politics. Similarly, during the eighteen days of protest leading to the ousting of President Mubarak, when the Islamists shouted Islamic slogans, there were many instances in which they were quietened by members of the crowd shouting back 'madaniyya, madaniyya' (civil, civil). In the discussions that ensued so far, it is possible to note that while a political stance has been adopted in favour of a civil state through various political platforms, the *political thought* of the Muslim Brotherhood characterised in the writings of the authoritative figures in the movement does not engage at length with the civility of the state, El Qaradawy excepted. Much of the literature speaks of an Islamic state, distinguished from the religious state of medieval Europe. This is important because it shows that the concept does not have root in political thought, nor has it been engaged with deeply from a fiqh point of view.

4 Political pluralism with an Islamic reference

This chapter will engage with two questions integral to our understanding of the Islamic marja'iyya (reference) in politics: first, what does it mean for the Brotherhood as a movement to exercise its agency via a political party and, second, in a state run in accordance with the Shari'a, will political pluralism be tolerated? The first question is pertinent in view of deliberations as to whether the Brotherhood will commit to engaging politically exclusively through the newly formed Freedom and Justice Party, or whether the movement will continue to serve as the powerhouse, with the party representing one of its political arms. The second question presents the Muslim Brotherhood thinking around the status of oppositional political parties in an Islamic government. The Muslim Brotherhood have repeatedly insisted that they are fully committed to the principle of political pluralism that takes the form of a multiparty system. They have argued that such a system enriches the political life of the nation and that it is an element of their vision of a civil state with an Islamic reference. There is an overwhelming consensus among the thinkers and scholars of the Muslim Brotherhood around the feasibility of having political parties in an Islamic state. Yet which political parties, espousing what kind of ideologies, engaged in what kind of spaces needs to be analysed carefully. As with the principles of shura, the civility of the state and all other governance matters, political parties are also expected to abide by the Islamic ethos of the political order. The political thought informing this and the practicalities of application are discussed here.

Engaging politically: through what?

When Hassan El Banna established the Brotherhood, it was initially a religious civic association whose charter, written in 1930, specifically said in article 2 that 'it will not broach political affairs, whatever they be' (El Nimnim 2011: 26). Around five years later, the charter was revised again and the prohibition of engaging in politics was removed altogether. The word civic association was replaced with gama' (society). In 1945, the charter was revised again, and the Muslim Brotherhood described as 'a universal Islamic entity/authority [that] works to achieve the aims that Islam came for' (El Nimnim 2011). By the 1940s, Hassan El Banna was representing the movement as a political entity (hay'a siyassiya).

Islamic political thought, argued El Masry, did not historically concern itself with the concept of the political party until the demise of the caliphate which had led to the disconnect from applying the Islamic Shari'a in governance and which prompted the Ulama, loyalists and leaders to form political parties in order to reinstate Islamic rule (El Masry 2006: 128).

It is important to note, argued El Masry, that while the non-Islamic definition of a political party is to arrive at power to achieve the principles of the party and implement its political programme, on the other hand, a political party in Islam is 'an organized group that came together according to what Allah and his prophet ordered, to participate in political life with the aim of instating truth and justice and to care for the interests of the Ummah' (El Masry 2006: 121).

There has been a radical shift in the official stance of the Muslim Brotherhood from rejecting the formation of a political party to one in which it has become one of the principle pathways through which the movement advances its mission.

Hassan El Banna is famous for his categorical rejection of political parties. On 20 February 1938, the first conference for the Muslim Brotherhood student federation was held, in which El Banna delivered a speech on politics and Islam, and again specifically attacked political parties. He argued that the permissibility of the existence of political parties must be linked to the circumstances of each country. In view of the weakness and partisan nature of political parties in Egypt, their presence is not welcome. They cause divisions which undermine the unity of the Ummah and consequently make it vulnerable to attacks from the foreign colonialist power. 'I believe that the current Egyptian political parties are artificial parties more than being true, and the personal element in them is more than the patriotic' (2006: 244). He sought to further substantiate his position by making reference to Koranic verses to show that Islam is a religion of unity and does not allow for a party system and does not approve of it. He clearly set his alternative vision: 'It is now time to raise the voices to eliminate the party system in Egypt and to replace it with a system united by the word, and through which the efforts of the Ummah are united around a patriotic *Islamic* righteous one' (2006: 245; my italics). The elimination of political parties represented such a priority for El Banna that it featured in the second and third recommendations of the conference, as follows: to demand the liquidation of all existing political parties and to substitute it with a unified entity that has an Islamist reformist programme addressing all aspects of the renaissance (2006: 246). The recommendation that follows emphasises: 'the need for every student who belongs to the Muslim Brotherhood to do away with any party colour [shade] while simultaneously being fully imbued with the idea that is based on the policy of the Koran and its teachings' (Bakarra 138).

On 2 February 1939, at the Muslim Brotherhood's fifth conference, El Banna addressed the members of the movement, reminding them of all the reasons why the Muslim Brotherhood called for the liquidation of political party system in Egypt: that they were partisan, had no party platform, strove for power through whatever means, and were undermining the nation's unity. In his speech, he indicated that the Brotherhood had actively advocated and striven for the elimination of political parties and had asked the king to liquidate them and had appealed to Prince Muhammed Ali and Prince Omar Tousan to do likewise (Collection of Hassan el banna's rasa'el 2006: 369). He added:

> and I would like to say to our brethren who support political parties: the day that the Muslim Brotherhood use any political thought other than their Islamic thought did not come and will not come and the Brotherhood have no particular issues with any party among the parties, but they deeply believe that Egypt will not be reformed or saved except through the withdrawal of all the parties and a national entity is established to lead the Ummah to victory according to the teachings of the Koran.
>
> (2006: 370)

In October 1939, in an impassioned article 'Towards the light' in *Al Nazir* magazine, at the top of the list of reforms he proposed in the political, judicial and administrative domain was 'the elimination of political party system and the direction of the Ummah's power to one front and one rank' (El Torki 2006: 175).

In the Muslim Brotherhood's daily magazine of 1947 Hassan El Banna again criticised the divisive impact of the existing political party system on the unity of the country and appealed to 'the decision-takers in this country, the head of the government, the men of Al-Azhar, the leaders of the political parties, authorities and universities and those who are jealous for this country' to find a solution for the ills of the existing system through the Islamic order (El Torki 2006: 671–672).

His position on political parties remained constant throughout his leadership of the Muslim Brotherhood. It is ironic that while the Brotherhood are defined as a political entity, and engage like a political party in terms of aspiring to be in power, to win office in parliament, yet it is only their political engagement that is seen to be legitimate. It is also significant that his appeal for the liquidation of political parties and the establishment of a higher Islamic entity did not address how leftist and secular forces would fit within such an entity, leaving the impression that they were excluded from the political equation altogether.

There are three key factors that influenced El Banna's opposition to political parties. First, El Banna referred to Koranic injunctions that sanctioned the establishment of political parties and it is based on this fiqh standpoint that many members of the Brotherhood rejected the idea of the movement becoming a political party. Second, the state of political parties in Egypt at the time was one of widespread corruption and much internal factionalism. Third, El Banna wanted to assume supremacy for the Brotherhood as an all-encompassing political entity that went far beyond the limited scope of a political party.

The position of the Muslim Brotherhood's leadership on establishing a political party and recognising other parties happened around 1986 against the backdrop of a revived movement seeking to find its political standing in a more acquiescent political environment. These were the views of two former leading political figures of the Muslim Brotherhood, Abu El Ela Mady who recounts that El Telmesany sought to establish a political party in 1984 in order to run in that year's parliamentary elections and the Muslim Brotherhood were shocked by the idea and vehemently opposed it. El Telmesany kept silent about it until 1986 when he wrote a draft for the Shura Party, but he did the same year. Abdel Moneim Aboul Fotouh sought to revive the idea and it failed and in another attempt Mohammed el Samman sought to establish the party but, again, it never materialised until the fifth try by Abou el Ella Mady which led to the establishment of the El Wasat Party in 1996.[1]

Yet the quest for political legitimacy had commenced in the preceding decade. As was widely documented, Sadat sought to obliterate the influence of the leftist and Nasserite forces in Egypt through empowering the Islamists to counter them. An entente was establishment between Omar el Telmesany and Sadat which saw the rebirth of the Muslim Brotherhood once again starting with the release of the Muslim Brotherhood members from prison in 1971 and ending with the famous meeting between the Supreme Guide and the president in 1979. The Brotherhood enjoyed once again the freedom to infiltrate, occupy and claim new and old political spaces, and exercise their political agency in full as a political party while, legally, their status as a liquidated NGO remained unchanged.

During the 1970s and 1980s, many of the Brotherhood gained extensive experience and expertise in political mobilisation. Omar el Telmesany, the Supreme Guide at the time, had himself a long history of political engagement, as a Brotherhood member who put himself forward for parliamentary elections under the Wafd Party's list of nominated candidates. In 1985, El Telmesany published his memoirs in which he stated that

> the Muslim Brotherhood believe that if a political party is the ideal means to achieve their principles, *and its enactment*, they will never hesitate ever in the establishment of a Muslim Brotherhood party, and struggle through it to establish a Muslim society that complies with God's Shari'a.
>
> (El Telmesany 1985: 183)

This, he explained, is in light of the fact that they need a channel through which to further their mission. He later concluded that if it will not be feasible to establish a political party, then at least a return to their original state as 'A general comprehensive Muslim authority will be better' (1985: 186). Yet according to Hisham al 'Awadi's account of this historical phase, the Muslim Brotherhood refused

> to accept Sadat's offer to participate in his newly-formed political platforms (manabir) or to register as a charity organisation under the supervision of the Ministry of Social Affairs, or be appointed (in the person of their Murshid Umar El Telmesany) to the Consultative Council (or majlis al-shura).
>
> (al 'Awadi 2004: 14–15)

The Brotherhood's toying with the idea of establishing a political party did not mean, under any circumstance, that there was an intention of replacing the movement itself.

Throughout the 1970s, El Telmesany continued to criticise the party system in Egypt, while seeking to negotiate a deal with Sadat to secure a legal umbrella for the movement (al 'Awadi 2004: 39). Negotiations never reached an outcome involving registration of the party. Legally, the constitution prohibited discrimination along the basis of religion, gender, ethnicity, etc., yet on the other hand, the Shari'a was recognised as the principle source of legislation. The three Supreme Guides that followed, Mohammed Hamed Abou el Nasr (who assumed leadership in 1986), Mustapha Mashour (who assumed leadership in 1996) and Ma'moun el Hodeiby (Supreme Guide from 2002) refused the idea of establishing a political party. There is a notable shift, a softening of position towards the question of the establishment of a political party from the 1980s to the 1990s. For example Supreme Guide Mustapha Mashour wrote in 1981 in *Al Da'wa* magazine (issue 64) that the Muslim Brotherhood are concerned with the establishment of an Islamic state and the revival of the Islamic caliphate, and in pursuing this vision, their activism is not to be reduced to a political party or civic association. The Brothers reject the separation of religion and politics which they find to be artificial and anathema to Islamic fiqh. Almost ten years later, writing for *Al-Shaab* newspaper in April 1990, however, Mashour was presenting justifications for why the Muslim Brotherhood would consider establishing a party. 'When the Brothers think of establishing a political party, the impetus would be to overcome the obstacles that were imposed to their exercise of their political right' (Mashour in Ezzat el Gazzar 2004: 119). Mashour pointed to the legal environment as being inhibitive to their exercise of their rights to political activism. He warned that the government's prohibition on the Brotherhood on the establishment of a political party on the pretext that their Islamic platform was going to cause sectarianism was likely to have the contrary effect, it would only encourage activism through unregulated underground movements. It is important to note that this softening of the position is not out of seeing the benefits of engaging through a political party but out of political necessity.

In 1992, Ma'moun el Hodeiby, who was then the spokesperson for the Muslim Brotherhood, indicated that the movement was considering forming a political party but that they had not yet decided when they would present their application ('Abd el Sami' 1992: 82–83). He did admit that there were some differences in viewpoints among the Brotherhood on this matter, and that what they rejected was the kind of political party system that was in its old form, which means characterised by 'fanaticism towards an individual or a particular thing and deviation from Islam' ('Abd el Sami' 1992: 83) and that the kind of political party system they support is holding on to beliefs, morals, good character ('Abd el Sami' 1992: 83).

El Hodeiby, who then became the Supreme Guide of the Brotherhood, spearheaded the movement to reconcile El Banna's antipathy towards political parties with the new realities of their positioning in Egyptian society. He made two principle arguments, first, that El Banna's position was informed by the political context of the time, namely one in which party squabbling was undermining the jihad or struggle against colonialism, thus, acting in a way incompatible with the Islamic Shari'a. Hodeiby argued that El Banna did not reject the idea of political parties itself, but rejected their actions and practices. In other words, El Banna's position may have been different had the political parties been performing differently. Finally, 'the Brothers may have a viewpoint at one time then circumstances change around it, and this [leads to] a change from this opinion to another and this is evidence of the flexibility of the Brothers and lack of rigidity' (El Hodeiby in conversation with El Ansary, 1999). Other Muslim Brother leaders who favoured the party system also suggested that had El Banna lived in these contemporary times he would have changed his opinion especially since fatwas change with them (El Qaradawy fiqh al dawla) and that El Banna was expressing his personal opinion which is not binding for the movement (El Masry 2006). Finally El Masry points out that he is of the view that when El Banna banned political partyism he did not include Islamic parties (El Masry 2006: 140).

Yet the political moment for aspiring for formal political legitimacy had not come in view of the highly turbulent relationship the movement had with the government during that decade. In the mid-2000s, the situation changed somewhat as the Brotherhood gained eighty-eight seats in the 444-seat parliament, running as independents using the Brotherhood's slogan and platform, despite the movement being technically banned. They acquired the largest representation in parliament they had ever gained in their history. Against this backdrop, a short phase of a more relaxed political environment, the idea of developing a full political platform evolved.

In 2004, the Brotherhood under the leadership of Mahdi Akef issued the Moubadara which was intended to present the movement's position on the reforms needed in the political, economic, social and religious arenas. With respect to its position on political pluralism, its content was not different from that of the 2007 draft party platform or the Freedom and Justice Party platform issued in 2011.

Throughout these last two decades of deepened participation in formal political life, the stance on its appropriateness and legitimacy was not unified within the movement. After all, the shift from the position that Hassan El Banna took was radical and was not convincing for all members.

The shift towards a political party is by no means supported by all members of the Muslim Brotherhood. Hossam Tammam argues that views are essentially polarised between the members of the political office of the movement and those involved in da'wa (Tammam 2008). Those who endorse work through a political party tend to be from the generation who became politically active in the 1970s through the universities and who were deeply involved in bringing the Brotherhood as an actor to the formal political sphere. They believe that a natural development of the Brotherhood is to become a legal entity as a party, while continuing to expand its outreach and offer a new model of how to engage politically.

Opponents to transforming the Muslim Brotherhood into a party argue that while they do not object to the movement acquiring a legal umbrella to render them legitimate, their *raison d'être* and mission goes far beyond that of a political party. They see that a political party compromises the status of the movement as a religious authority mandated with spreading the da'wa to all. Tammam argues that many of these opponents come from a background where they have been deeply involved in the pedagogical activities of the Brotherhood and have no presence on the political scene.

But the demise of Mubarak and the new political scene made matters more complicated. Some argued that the Brotherhood should not even consider having its own political party anymore, but its members should be free to establish their own parties. Abdel Moneim Aboul Fotouh, a member of the political wing of the Brotherhood and former member of the Guidance Bureau expressed the view that the movement should not become a political party (before the Freedom and Justice Party had been established):[2]

> After the revolution there is no longer a need for the Brotherhood to become a party or to establish a party.... I have told the Brothers it is not right that there be a party but has to remain an Islamic da'wa movement and a civil organization undertaking its da'wa and activist work through legitimate means and these are the means that the Brotherhood used from 1970s to the January revolution ... it is not permissible for the Brotherhood to have a party that it says represents or speaks on its behalf. we are against this, not from an organization angle but from a question of principle.

In essence what is being debated is the power base of the Brotherhood. If the Brothers establish their own party, they will continue to politically direct the membership, power hierarchies and how members of the party engage. If they do not establish their own party, but render their support to whoever wants to establish a party from among its members, then the political power will be transmitted to a series of new nodes (members heading their own parties) rather than continue to be focused at the centre (the Brotherhood's movement). The stakes of engaging politically through offshoot political parties while the movement concentrates on da'wa represents high risks for a diffusion of its power base – to use its constituency for influencing political processes and to have to negotiate with whoever comes to power their own standing.

When the Brothers established their own Freedom and Justice Party, they set a number of conditions. First, that the members who will assume political leadership positions in the party will have to leave their official positions in the Brotherhood (such as in the Guidance Bureau). Second, that the Freedom and Justice Party be the sole political party through which its members can engage. They are not to join any other party.

Third, that those who violate these rules by joining other parties or forming their own will be held accountable for violating the Brotherhood's rules.

However, if the Brotherhood could deploy 'the unity at all costs argument' to elicit the obedience of its members when they were subject to Mubarak's assaults, the context following his demise made the use of such a strategy less successful. Members created parties that are offshoots from the Brotherhood and did not comply with the Brotherhood's decision that the Freedom and Justice Party be the only political party through which members can engage politically. Mahmoud Hussein, the secretary-general of the Muslim Brotherhood, sternly warned members and the youth that have violated the general shura's decision not to join any other political party other than that of Freedom and Justice should either resign voluntarily or that the Brothers will expel them.[3] According to the Supreme Guide, there were four parties that were offshoots of the Brotherhood: the Renaissance (Ennahda) Party led by renowned Brotherhood leader in Alexandria, Ibrahim el Za'afarany, who has close connections with Abdel Moneim Aboul Fotouh; the Reyada Party founded by some figures close to el Za'afarany such as Khaled Dawood and Hatham Abou Khalid; the Reform and Development Party led by Hamed el Dafrawy; and the el Tayar al Misri Party led by Islam Lotfy and Mohammed el Kassas Badi'e (25 January e-newspaper, 9 June 2011).

Bad'i comments that many of these leaders either resigned or were expelled. Yet upon further attention, it appears that the leaders mentioned above had all resigned. This presented a number of immediate challenges to do with the relationship between the political party and the movement. There were two issues at stake: first, contesting the centralised power base – and its potential implications for the allegiances of the movement's constituency; second, a litmus test as to the challenges of dealing with internal dissidence within the Muslim Brotherhood raised questions as to the fate of political pluralism in a state run in accordance with the Shari'a.

Question of political pluralism in an Islamic state

The stance of the Freedom and Justice Party on political parties in an Islamic state was not updated to reflect the situation post-Mubarak. It is almost a word-by-word copy of the stance that they adopted in the draft party platform of 2007. The position adopted is that of the right to parties being formed by notification without intervention from the authorities, as long as they are not military or paramilitary in nature and their programmes do not discriminate between citizens. This may have reflected the Muslim Brotherhood's stance on the permissibility of political parties in a phase of authoritarian rule. Once the context and historical juncture changes, the position on political party system changes accordingly. The permissibility of a multiparty system in an Islamic state is a matter around which there is much contention.

Within the Brothers, there is a group, including key thinkers such as Fathi Yakin, who reject political partyism as haram (religiously prohibited) on the basis that it undermines 'the necessity of the unity of Islamic action'. Yakin's main argument is that this kind of fragmented action does not cumulatively amount to a small fraction of what he calls the 'first organization' (1997: 70) (which he does not define but presumably means the early years of Islamic rule at the time of, or immediately after, the Prophet).

Yakin emphasises that political partyism discourages Muslims from being involved as members in political forces because they have a variety of parties to choose from, it weakens the Islamic forces because it fragments efforts and it enables the enemies of Islam to attack Islamic work by attacking each separately. It creates competition between the different Islamic factions. Further, the existence of political pluralism replaces Muslims' loyalty to God with allegiance to parties (Yakin 1997: 70–71).

One of the benefits of a multiparty system is that it allows a group to collectively hold the ruling regime accountable. Yet many influential Muslim Brotherhood thinkers such as Mohammed el Bahi (1980: 442) insist that in an Islamic system when the caliph deviates from the truth, it is on an individual, rather than collective, level that action should be initiated to advise him on the truth. This is also the view of Qumeihy, another Muslim Brotherhood thinker.

It was not possible to identify any political thinker belonging to the Muslim Brotherhood in Egypt who advocates for the right of non-Islamist political parties to be allowed to freely exist even if they do not purport to the Islamic marja'iyya. The only case of an Islamic political force cited in Muslim Brotherhood literature as permitting the existence of any political party, irrespective of its ideological orientation, is the Ennahda (Renaissance) Party led by Rachid el Ghanoushy in Tunisia. Their position in favour of unrestricted political partyism rests on the fact that the Islamic system allowed the Magous (here referring to the fire worshippers), Christians and Jews to abide within its system and secured all their rights – and the Prophet himself made a covenant with the Jews in Madina allowing them to live under an Islamic system. The logic is if the Islamic system was able to accommodate the Jews, Nazarenes (Christians) and Magous, would it not be sufficiently flexible to accommodate the communists and secularists who could not be greater infidels than the Jews, Christians and Magous? (El Ghanoushy in El Sawi 1992: 101). El Sawi rejects such a position and its religious justification on the premise that it runs against the consensus arrived at by the majority of Islamic thinkers. He further points out that the interpretation of the Prophet's covenant with the Jews is misguided since it was never intended to allow non-Muslims to assume authority over Muslims but it was intended to allow People of the Book to make a home in an Islamic state and allow them to govern in their own affairs such as in family matters (El Sawi 1992: 101–103).

What El Sawi finds highly problematic is the idea that in a politically pluralist system non-believers would be entitled to mobilise support for their platforms and through a majority vote come to power and implement non-Islamic programmes over a Muslim people. He rejects the possibility that 'an atheist or Budhist or Christian' assume political leadership of a Muslim nation (1992: 103), insisting that there is a consensus among the Muslim scholars that one of the principle conditions of the Grand Imamate is that whoever deviates from Islam is immediately excluded from governing and that there is no authority of a kafir (apostate) over a Muslim (1992: 103). He emphasises that allowing non-Muslims to reside in Dar el Islam is one thing and allowing them to assume sovereignty over Muslims is another. He describes the problematique as follows vis-à-vis non-Islamist political parties and groups:

> Accepting pluralism means a preliminary acceptance of their right to rule/ govern (wellaya) and of their programmes [for all those allowed to particip-ate in the political system] because rotation of power is a basis of pluralism. Does [not] the Islamic doctrine allow the magous and atheists and others from the infidels to rule and to apply their programmes on the Muslims? If the Islamic doctrine does not allow this then why this political hypocrisy that has gripped the Ummah and faked the truth and made the Islamic project equivalent to the atheist and worldly projects?
>
> (El Sawi 1992: 105)

El Sawi argues that the equality of opportunity guaranteed under a politically plural system does not in practice comply with the fundamentals of Islamic Shari'a in Dar el Islam. Allowing all parties, irrespective of their belief system, the right to use the media to propagate their platform even when it is incompat-ible with Islamic beliefs is unacceptable in an Islamic system. Moreover, a polit-ically plural system may allow them accession to power to occupy the positions of leadership and membership in Ahl Al 'Akd wal Rabt which goes against the fundamentals of Islam (1992: 106). Ahl 'Akd wal Rabt, as defined by El Sawi, are the MPs elected to parliament.

The overwhelming majority of Muslim Brotherhood thinkers (El Sawi, El Wa'i, El Masry) insist that all political parties must conform to the precepts of the Islamic Shari'a and not deviate, question or challenge it in any way. It is both the normative framework that regulates all processes and policies and against which ideas are assessed as being legitimate or not. In 1994, the Islamic Centre for Studies and Research of the Muslim Brotherhood issued a document on 'the Muslim woman in Muslim society, Shura, and multipartyism', pronounced that they believe in a multiparty system in a Muslim society and that each political party or society is left for each party to decide,

> as long as the Islamic Shari'a is the principle constitution and this law is applied by an independent judiciary that is qualified from an intellectual, technical and jurisprudence point of view, this is enough to guarantee the safety of society and its abidance by the true path.
>
> (1994: 38)

As will be discussed below, the freedom of political parties to develop their own programmes is negated by the Islamic Shari'a qualifier.

Khaled 'Abd el Kader 'Ouda succinctly summarises this position:

> political parties that are founded on principles or adopt programmes in contradiction with the fundamental principles and/or overall rules upon

which the Shari'a is founded or those that deny a given[4] in religion, there is no place for them in an Islamic society because they will be a catalyst for destruction of the social foundation and this view is one upon which there is consensus (ijma') among all the jurists including those who permit political pluralism.

(2005: 63)

El Qaradawy suggested that a multiparty system is possible under an Islamic state but is conditional upon the fulfilment of two critieria: the first is that political parties must acknowledge/recognise Islam 'as *a faith* and a Shari'a' and must not oppose it or deny it; the second is that it does not work for an entity that is antagonistic towards Islam or the Islamic Ummah, irrespective of where its premises are based or what name it assumes. Qaradawy then makes it more explicit that atheist political parties are not allowed in an Islamic state nor those who are opposed to the application to Islam (including the application of the Islamic Shari'a) (El Qaradawy 2007: 148).

Mosheer Amr El Masry[5] (2006: 191–193) contended that for political pluralism to advance the interests of the public, it has to be provisional upon the fulfilment of certain conditions, including the following:

1   that political pluralism is built upon a complete belief in the Islamic doctrine, and the Islamic Shari'a from which it stems;
2   abidance by truth and public interests over party allegiance such as that which secular political parties demand;
3   obedience to waly al amr (the ruler) on the basis that he represents the whole Ummah (Islamic nation) without contesting him or defying him unless he defies God's decrees;
4   to acknowledge *Hakemmeyat Allah* in all aspects of life;
5   to fight uncompromisingly those who wish to separate the Islamic Shari'a from governance;
6   adopting the moderate (wasat) approach in bringing closer the ranks of Islamic movements.

However, El Wa'i proposed that the only condition for political parties be that their platforms are in compliance with Islam as the principle source of legislation, a position that he argued was espoused by the international movement of the Muslim Brotherhood (2001: 125) on the basis that it was not expected at the time of the Prophet that the Jews who entered into a pact with him recognise Islam as a faith.

Abdel Moneim Aboul Fotouh, whose views stand at the most liberal end of the spectrum, within the Muslim Brotherhood argued:

I cannot imagine any party, even if it were a leftist or communist party not to be based on the Islamic civilization and here I distinguish between civilization and religion. Religion is about [being] a Muslim, Christian, Shia or

Sunni. As to the Islamic civilization, it is one that all Egyptians have contributed to its making, and therefore it has to be the reference for all parties, a chosen and not imposed reference.

(Abdel Moneim Aboul Fotouh 2011)

Whether the political order adopts Qaradawy's or al Masry's or El Wa'i's or Abou el Fotouh's criteria for the presence of political parties in an Islamic state, the outcome is the same: there can be no political party functioning which does not conform to the Islamic framework and law. Its very existence is anathema to Islamic governance. Mustapha Mashour stipulated clearly that with respect to the existing political parties that are present in Islamic countries 'the Muslim Brotherhood reject these kinds of political parties that are founded on worldly principles' (Mashour in El Gazar 2004: 111).

The conditions laid are full of loopholes that enable the authorities in an Islamic state to crack down on the opposition, on the premise that they are defending Islam and its Shari'a from its enemies. It is a pluralism within a highly contained political framework. In essence, it also makes it very inhibitive even for Islamic political parties to contest the status quo.

Khaled ''Abd el Kader 'Ouda argued that in addition to the principle above political parties should avoid political disputes, which fragments rather than unites. This kind of political division is corruption itself and is the basis for all the Ummah's ills and 'we have to avoid it and to strive to bury it alive'. He emphasised that political thinkers who object to political pluralism in Islam arrived at this conviction because of their fear of sectarianism and disintegration deriving from different political parties. Islam by its nature leads to unity of thought although variation is permissible in terms of interpretation within the Shari'a (such as the four schools Hanbali, Hanafi, Shafi' and Malki). Consequently, political parties can be established along the four different mazaheb (jurisprudence schools) as long as they do not become fanatic to their school.

The major difference between a liberal democratic system and an Islamic one, suggested Khaled 'Ouda 'Abd el Qader, is that in the former, the minority (political party or voices of deviance) are allowed to debate and contest the decision of the majority to the point of non-enforcement. This means, he argues, that those in power can sometimes be a source of constant challenge and ridicule. On the other hand, in an Islamic system, he argues, the minority who have objected in the phase of consultation would assume a different position once the majority's will has been confirmed. Once decided, the minority has no right to question it (based on his jurisprudence interpretations). Critique of the decisions after they have been arrived at is in contradiction with the principles of shura, the people govern according to what the majority decide and from a jurisprudence point of view, the stance taken by the majority is one that has to be obeyed. He summarised it as such: the Islamic political order

pushes everyone to think and be objective during discussion and to listen and obey at the time of implementation and therefore, the understanding of political opposition in states which apply the principle of political pluralism is not feasible for application in an Islamic society even if the majority and minority agree on the principle and differ on the means.

(2005: 67)

This is justified on the basis that from an Islamic jurisprudence point of view, the majority rule is correct, and minority being correct is a rarity. In order to protect the political order from unnecessary political disunity at the implementation phase, if during the period of deliberation, for some reason, a group or party were not represented, and they were from the minority, once a decision has been arrived at, there is no place for them to discuss or question the decision taken (2005: 68).

Khaled ''Abd el Kader 'Ouda's point reflects that of the majority of writers cited here, and is commensurate with the conditions prescribed as to when shura is desirable and possible in an Islamic system (see Chapter 3).

El Masry argues that it is possible from a fiqh point of view to reconcile the differing viewpoints on the standing of non-Islamic political parties. He argued that it is acceptable to accept non-Islamic political parties and establish coalitions with them in the phase when the movement is weak, according to Islamic political legitimacy (Al-Siyassa al Shar'iyya) which calls for the application of the jurisprudence of balancing interests (masaleh) with harm/ills (mafasid) (El Masry 2006: 187). In other words, the gains made by creating coalitions with these non-Islamic political parties outweigh the harms from blocking the opportunity of changing an unfavourable reality. The situation changes once the Islamists reach a phase of political empowerment (tamkeen) and then 'preventing the violators from spreading the thought of their parties, secular or communist and inciting people against them represents a fundamental issue in Islamic Shari'a' (El Masry 2006: 187). Evidence quoted, including from Mustapha Mashour, also points to a change of policy depending on whether Islamic parties are at the da'wa stage or at the stage of instituting an Islamic state (Mashour in El Masry 2006: 188).

In short, from the examination of the Muslim Brotherhood's own political thought and political trajectory from inception to the post-Mubarak period, it seems that calls to separate the da'wa 'wing' from the political party fail to note, first, that the movement sees its political agency greater and broader than that of a political party; second, that such a separation would undermine the positioning of the Muslim Brotherhood members who work through the political party because the politicised da'wa is considered as the powerhouse of the movement. With respect to the question of the permissibility of having a multiparty system in Islam, there is an overwhelming consensus among Muslim Brotherhood thinkers that political parties will be tolerated so long as they comply with the Islamic framework (Shari'a+) This '+' may vary from one thinker to another in terms of what the political party needs to show as a manifestation of its commitment to the Islamic system, yet overall, the space for contestation is quite limited.

The application of fiqh al masaleh and mafasid shows that it is highly deceptive to base one's analysis of the position of the Muslim Brotherhood on political parties based on their phase of pre-consolidation of political power, when it is likely to change if they reach the tamkeen stage. Based on fiqh al masaleh/ mafasid, it is also possible to understand the instrumentalisation of alliances with non-Islamist political parties at times when the movement is politically weak and the erosion of such alliances when the standing of the movement changes. The differential position that Islamist forces have in the political thought of the Muslim Brotherhood also explains why such coalitions tend to be stronger: despite the power struggle between the different political groups, the fact that they are bound by a similar vision of the fundamentals of Islamic governance makes a significant difference. It is also probably why despite the standoffish position that the Muslim Brotherhood has taken in relation to 'deviant' members, their agency would be far more politically tolerated in an Islamic state than a non-Islamic political actor.

5   The Copts and the Brothers from El Banna to Bad'i

Following the ouster of Mubarak, there was a new optimism that Muslim–Christian relations would experience a new era of social harmony. Tensions in the relations were blamed on the Mubarak regime's adoption of divide and rule strategies that were intended to deter the formation of a unified front among the people against him. The first part of this chapter examines whether there was a positive transformation in relations between Muslims and Copts, Egypt's largest non-Muslim minority (amounting to about 10 per cent of the population) and whether, accordingly, the rapport between the Muslim Brotherhood and the Copts changed in the light of the new political configurations. The second part of the chapter traces the historical and political relations between the Brotherhood and the Copts from the time of El Banna up to the present leadership by high-lighting key events, actors and relationships.

Post-Mubarak Egypt: unresolved conflict out in the open

It is important to note that the new political configurations following the ousting of President Mubarak empowered the Muslim Brotherhood, by virtue of their new pact with the armed forces and influence within the transition government (see Chapter 2). Concurrently, there was an alienation of the Coptic Church leadership from the centres of power as the rapport between the Church leaders and the previous ruling regime came to an end. In the months following the ouster of Mubarak, Egypt witnessed a number of attacks against non-Muslims, most notably Christians but also including the Baha'is.

After the demise of the Mubaraks and the rise of the Islamist movements, the leaders of the Muslim Brotherhood have consistently argued that Copts (not non-Muslims) have nothing to fear from the rise of the Brotherhood because it was the regime that sought to create rifts between them, putting the Copts in a state of undue alarm.

Certainly many leading public figures have urged the Copts to turn a new leaf in relation to the Muslim Brotherhood pointing out that during Mubarak's regime the movement was repressed and could not be held accountable for its relationships, which have often been obstructed by the government. Advocates also reminded Copts of the need to maintain the united front shown in Tahrir

Square and to keep its spirit alive. The eighteen days that came to characterise the '25 January revolution' were days in which sectarian tensions were visibly absent, whether at the sites of protests in Tahrir Square or at a community level where vigilante groups comprised of Muslims and Christians were standing guard against thugs and criminals. Despite the withdrawal of security forces from guarding churches, and their notable absence from the streets of Egypt, there were no reported cases of attacks on Christian sites. The slogan 'Muslims and Christians: one hand' was frequently reiterated in Tahrir Square by the Brotherhood-led group as well as by others. Tahrir Square, however, came to represent a distinct space- and time-sensitive moral economy of its own.

However, the spirit of Tahrir was not sustained for long. This is no more evident than on the millioniyya of 29 July when the Brotherhood and the other Islamist forces occupied Tahrir Square (see Chapter 1). The famous revolutionary slogan of 'Raise your head high, you are an Egyptian!' was replaced with 'Raise your head high, you are a Muslim!'. The slogan of 'Muslims, Christians, we are all Egyptians' was replaced with 'Muslims, Muslims, we are all believers' (Watany 2011). The flexing of the Islamists' muscles that day was not only intended to convey a number of political demands, but to reassert Egypt's Islamic identity. The message implicitly relayed to the Copts is one of conformity to the Islamist normative values to which *the majority* subscribes.

The most significant incident that occurred immediately after the 25 January revolution which heightened tensions between the Muslim Brotherhood and the Copts was over the constitutional referendum of March 2011. Accounts of the constitutional referendum indicate that the Muslim Brotherhood implemented a comprehensive outreach strategy to encourage people to say 'yes', using the mosque as a platform to argue that if you are for Islam, you vote yes, if you are against Islam, you vote no. They argued that voting yes for the constitutional amendments was about choosing to go to paradise because it was about choosing your Muslim identity, while to vote no would be to lose your hereafter. The basis of such an argument is that if they did not vote yes to the constitutional amendments, there was a risk that article 2 of the constitution that recognises Islam as the religion of the state and the Shar'ia as the principle source of legislation be abrogated. The Brotherhood widely circulated that only apostates (such as Christians) would vote 'no'.

In reaction, the Coptic Orthodox Church instigated a massive campaign across all its churches nationwide to press its parishioners to say no to the constitutional amendments. It invited experts, both Muslim and Christian, to talk about why voting 'yes' would stall the democratic process. No doubt, the idea that to vote 'yes' would be to help bring the Muslim Brotherhood to power was one of the central arguments – if not the central argument – advanced to encourage Christians to reject the constitutional amendments. The Ahram online updates for what was happening at the polling stations that day are highly illustrative:

17:03 p.m. A monitor for the NGO Egyptian Organization for Human Rights tells one of our correspondents that 'there is a psychological war between Islamists and Copts' being witnessed at polling stations across Egypt.

18:12 p.m. Hussein Osman Ismail, secretary of the Tagammu party, has filed an official complaint against the Muslim Brotherhood. In it, he accuses the group of entering polling stations where they tell people to vote 'yes' and that Copts are voting against the amendments with the intention of removing Article 2 from any new constitution.

The Muslim Brotherhood was also involved in playing a leading role in the sectarian campaign against the appointment of a Coptic governor in Qena in April 2011. Massive protests sustained over ten days brought Qena to a standstill. What happened in Qena involved a complex constellation of actors: the tribal leaders, the Salafis, the Muslim Brotherhood, leaders from the now dismantled former ruling party, the NDP (National Democratic Party) with critical interjections at various points in time from the Sufis and the officers from the dismantled state security investigations apparatus (*mabaheth amn al dawla*) who, according to some reports, actively helped block the railways which halted rail travel in Qena, Sohag and Aswan. The common objective was not a demand for a civil governor, but a Muslim one. It was the religion of the governor that served to unify all the different parties into one alliance, not the demand for a civil, democratically-elected governor.

This is the second time that Qena was appointed a Christian governor, Magdy Ayoub being the first and having served as its previous governor. Ayoub was loathed by the Christian Qenawis who argued that in his attempt to give the image of being non-partisan, he discriminated against Christians. It was during his time in office that Egypt witnessed one of its bloodiest sectarian attacks (in Nagi Hammadi on parishioners leaving church following Christmas Eve mass in 2010). Qenawi Muslims also complained that his fear of antagonising different political forces locally made him a weak leader. While the rule of Mubarak's generals as governors over Egypt often created tensions with local constituencies, some of the complaints that Ayoub received were specifically on the basis of his religion, namely, that he could not participate in the Friday prayers when in office.[1]

A statement produced by the 'intellectuals of Qena' said that a person by the name of 'Abd el Aziz from the Muslim Brotherhood reached an agreement with the director of general security of Qena (modeer al amn) to delay the trains leaving the railways for two hours only but later admitted that the matter (halting rail transport) got out of his hands. The statement suggests that it was the Muslim Brotherhood and the Salafis who led the protests but later the former retreated, leaving the space for other actors to occupy and lead it. According to several press reports, the mosques of Qena were transformed into platforms for the Muslim Brotherhood and Salafis to call upon the people of Qena to reject the appointment of a Christian governor because there is no wellaya (authority/governance) of a non-Muslim over a Muslim.[2] Among the most popular slogans

raised in the public protests of Qena were: 'Islamiyya, Islammiyya, not Christian, not Jewish', and 'There is no God but God, Mikhail is the enemy of God.
We want a Muslim governor' and 'There is no God but God, the Nazarene [the
Christian] is the enemy of God' and 'Salafis and Brotherhood one hand against
the Nazarene governor!'.

Fahmy Howeidy warned against ignoring the differences within and among
Islamist political forces, but the Qena crisis showed that in particular political
moments coalition building occurs quickly, efficiently and with a high level of
synchronisation. The Muslim Brotherhood, Gama'at al Islamiyya and the Salafis
set up speakers in front of the governorate's premises, threatening to pick up
arms and collectively achieve their aims if the Cabinet and the armed forces did
not respond to their demands to have a Muslim governor.

After the government retracted with a freeze on Mikhail's assumption of
responsibilities in Qena, the protestors released a statement saying that they were
not thugs and had blocked the railway for legitimate demands, namely that they
did not want Qena *to be the quota for* Copts.[3] The statement represents the greatest evidence that the primary objection was his religious – and not security –
identity. By virtue of the Muslim Brotherhood's involvement in initiating and
supporting the 'no Nazarene for governor' campaign, their role in deepening
religious divides and undermining the principle of equal citizenship cannot be
overlooked.

Relations between the Muslim Brotherhood and the Coptic Orthodox Church
took a turn for the worse in May 2011 when Mahmoud Ezzat, the deputy
Supreme Guide of the Brotherhood, stated at a public conference that they aimed
to implement the Islamic Shar'ia and after the preconditions for its implementation had been secured (economic prosperity, a faithful Muslim community, etc.)
they intended to apply the *huddud*. The Coptic Orthodox Church reacted by can-
celling scheduled meetings with the Brotherhood.[4] When the Brothers sought to
open a channel of communication with the Coptic youth directly the attempt
created further tensions with the Church, which saw this as an attempt to side-
step its authority. The youth responded that should the Brothers wish to engage
with them, it should be in their capacity as Egyptian citizens not religious
subjects.

At another occasion, Sobhi Saleh announced that 'If Copts knew their rights
in Islam they would seek the application of Islamic law'. This statement reflects
the representation of the Copts' opposition to their vision of the Brotherhood's
governance in accordance with the Shar'ia as an attack on Islam itself. In the
deeply religious context of Egypt, it effectively served to politically mobilise
support for the Brotherhood as the defenders of Islam.

The Brotherhood's statements following anti-Christian attacks never recognised that they were driven by religious bigotry or were driven by Islamist
forces. On 11 May 2011, in response to the burning of two churches in Imbaba,
the Muslim Brotherhood released a statement calling upon the government to
hold accountable the former officers from the state security investigations
apparatus for inciting sectarian strife. They reiterated their rejection of any

pleas made by internal actors for international intervention for the protection of churches. Such a statement is significant in that while it rightly points to the involvement of remnants of the former regime in inciting violence, it does not acknowledge the Islamists' agency. A crowd of some 2,000 Salafis (and unknown others) had formed to 'liberate' 'Abir, a Christian woman who had allegedly converted to Islam, married a Muslim but was then abducted by Copts in a building belonging to the Mari Mina church. The allegations proved to be untrue but in a context of heightened fears of an assault on the church and lax security, clashes erupted with neighbourhood Copts, including an exchange of gunfire. Property belonging to Copts was burned and looted, and the mob proceeded to set St Mary's church ablaze as well. A fact-finding mission from the National Council for Human Rights attributed the violence to the deficient response of security forces and accused NDP remnants of instigating social strife to abort the revolution. The council's report also pointed to extremists trying to reconfigure Egyptian society so that Copts have no rights except as Ahl al Dhimma.[5]

The Brotherhood's refusal to acknowledge a power-over relationship being exercised against Copts reflects an unwillingness to recognise the idea of a group that is not only numerically a minority, but politically as well. This is very much consistent with their historical and contemporary viewpoint that Copts' political and economic powers exceed their numerical representation in society.

The Brotherhood have not only consistently refused to acknowledge that sectarianism is inspired by religious biased values and beliefs held by Muslims towards Christians but have often held the latter responsible for any attacks generated against them. During Mubarak's era, the Brotherhood was keen to emphasise that all Egyptians suffer discrimination, and when it comes to oppression, the government's iron hand weighs far more heavily on them than the Copts. El Shamach (2008: 119) contended that while Copts may face some problems, so does the rest of the Egyptian population – hence, any injustice they are exposed to is a manifestation of the repressive rule of the state. Closely linked to this is that if the Copts suffer, the Muslim Brotherhood suffer twofold. Essam el Erian's argument is that the entire population suffers from discrimination, and the Muslim Brotherhood has suffered from more discrimination than some Copts – and victims of discrimination should positively empathise with each other (*Al Osboa*, 28 November 2005).

Amer el Shamach argued that Copts do not only enjoy the full rights of citizenship as equal, but even more, they have become a privileged section among the people, for despite the claim that their percentage does not exceed 5 per cent of the population they own almost a quarter of the country's economy and monopolize other privileges not enjoyed by Muslims. They own '20% of the Contracting Companies, represent 29% of businessmen, occupy 20% of managerial positions in the economic sector, and comprise 20% of investors in the industrial cities … etc.' (2008: 119). El Shamach does not indicate how he arrived at the statistic of Copts comprising 5 per cent nor at any of the other numbers cited.

From Bad'i back to El Banna: the Brotherhood and non-Muslim relations historicised

There are two intertwined battles that are at the heart of the political animosity between the Muslim Brotherhood and the Copts. The first is associated with the categorical rejection of the majority of Copts of the establishment of an Islamic state premised on the full implementation of the Shar'ia. The second source of tension is associated with the historical relationship between Copts, the Church leadership, Brotherhood rank and file, and leadership. On its part, the Brotherhood is highly critical of the Coptic Church's political stance, which it argues is anathema to its spiritual leadership role.

Akef, Shenouda and open warfare

Relations between the then Brotherhood's Supreme Guide, Mahdi Akef and Pope Shenouda were strained, and occasionally openly in conflict. The Brotherhood argued that the Church supported the regime, which it should not do, while various Church leaders accused the movement of using religion for its own political ends. This was no better epitomised than in the 2005 presidential and parliamentary elections. Mahdi Akef was openly critical (as were other parties) of Pope Shenouda's public support for the regime and the NDP candidates (although the same stance was taken by Sheikh al Azhar). Pope Shenouda openly called upon the bishops and archbishops to appeal to parishioners to vote for Mubarak. Mohammed Habib criticised what he called the Church's meddling in politics, arguing that when the Muslim Brotherhood engage in politics, it is because Islam is a comprehensive system that does not recognise the separation of religion and politics, whereas in Christianity, there is such a separation, and it is one that the Church should respect and adhere to by not professing its allegiance to any one particular candidate. Habib announced that the Church's support for the president was a political act that transformed the Copts into a political bloc, which was unacceptable.

On the other hand, the mobilisation of religion for political purposes by many Muslim Brotherhood candidates in the 2005 elections only served to increase the suspicion held by many that the Brotherhood could not engage with Copts in their capacity as Egyptian citizens, and not as religious subjects. The mobilisation of religion to win supporters in the 2005 elections was apparent in many forms: first, many of the Brotherhood (as well as NDP candidates) in various electoral districts appealed to the citizenry not to vote for their contender if he was a non-Muslim. In Minya, the leftist Tagammu Party candidate Wagih Shoukry (a Copt) ran for office, competing with the NDP candidates Faiza el Tahtawy and Ahmed Senousy, with the Muslim Brotherhood candidate, Mohammed el Kattatny, running as an independent. The latter's rallying cry was 'do not give your vote to the church candidate, give it to the mosque candidate' (the position of the Church was in support of the NDP candidates despite the fact that one of them, Faiza el Tahtawy, was also using anti-Christian slogans). After the first round, the NDP candidates were out of the race, with Wagih Shoukry winning 7,498 votes and Mohammed el Kattatny, the Muslim Brotherhood candidate, winning 13,928 votes. During the campaigning, El Kattatny's supporters put up speakers on top volume, close to where Shoukry was holding his campaign meeting, calling people to prayers and used slogans about not voting for a kafir (apostate).

The second way in which religion was used for mobilisational purposes by the Brotherhood during the elections was in appealing to the Copts as Ahl al Dhimma. In electoral circles with a large Coptic constituency, where Muslim Brotherhood candidates were running, the candidate in the electoral district of Masr el Gedeeda and Madinet Nasr did not only use the conventional slogan of 'Islam is the solution'. Rather, they used another interesting slogan: 'We protect the covenant and ahl el Dhimma ... the Copts are sons of the Ummah' (Labib, *Roz el Youssef*, 15 November 2005). The use of 'Ahl al Dhimma' is, despite its abandonment in official high ranking Muslim Brotherhood discourse, still very much prevalent among the rank and file.

In response to the Brotherhood gaining eighty-eight seats in the 2005 elections, Milad Hanna, a prominent Copt and former MP, publicly announced that if the Brotherhood reached power, he would pack up his bags and leave Egypt.[6] 'Good Riddance', lashed back Akef, the Supreme Guide, adding in an interview that that the Muslim Brotherhood are persecuted a hundredfold more than the Copts, and that the 'Copts enjoy more freedoms than the Muslims'.[7] Akef was renowned for his brusque commentaries, many of which were direct assaults on the Pope, and which served to create deeper rifts between the two.

Mashour, the infamous 'jizya' comment, and its aftermaths

If the 2000s were known for the souring relationship between the leader of the Muslim Brotherhood and the Coptic Church, and Copts more generally, the 1990s did not witness a significantly more conciliatory relationship between the Copts and the Muslim Brotherhood leadership. Relations turned sour after an infamous statement made by Supreme Guide Mustapha Mashour in *Al-Ahram Weekly* newspaper in 2007. Asked whether Copts should be allowed in the army, Mashour replied in the negative, but argued that that in return for not fighting, they must pay the jizya. The institution of modern citizenship in the 1920s had led to the abandonment of the notion of non-Muslim citizens paying a special tax (jizya). Mashour's statement was interpreted as a direct assault on the concept of equal citizenship and was fiercely attacked by liberals as well as some members of the Muslim Brotherhood who felt that the statement caused the movement much undue public embarrassment. The timing of the statement was significant too, since it was pronounced in April 1997, days after forty Coptic citizens were killed by members of the Gama'at islammiya for refusal to pay *attawa* (protection money).

A committee within the Brotherhood drafted an official statement which was sent in Mashour's name to all the newspapers to 'clarify his position'. The issuance of a public statement in the name of the Muslim Brotherhood was a clear indicator of the gravity of the situation – the Muslim Brotherhood's apologetic statements, historically, are few. Although he did not (could not) deny the statement (the journalist had recorded the interview), he nevertheless explained that there was a 'confusion/misunderstanding'. He indicated that it had been established that the interpretation of the Koranic ayat (verse) in Surat el Touba pertaining to the payment of jizya, relates to those who fought Islam and Muslims. This would not apply to Coptic citizens, he argued, since they have fought the enemies of this nation.

In the statement which was published in *al Shaab* newspaper, the Islamist mouthpiece, Mustapha Mashour also reiterated the famous slogan used by Hassan El Banna: 'they [the Copts] are entitled to what we are entitled to and they owe what we owe [obliged to]'. A similar message was sent to Pope Shenouda personally (*Al Osboa*, 21 April 1997). The official position of the Coptic Church was to keep a low profile and not respond with any public statement. A high official delegation from members of the Muslim Brotherhood and the Islamist Labour Party visited the Pope as a gesture of reconciliation and to pledge the Brotherhood's friendly relations with the Church. In the meeting, the Pope also emphasised the 'good relations between the Copts and the Muslim Brotherhood' (*Al Hayat*, 28 April 1997). Mashour's statement was commensurate with stances he had adopted on the subject in his writings (see for example *Al Da'wa*, Issue 60, 1981).

Under the leadership of El Hodeiby, there was an attempted rapprochement between the Brotherhood and lay Copts (as opposed to the Church leadership). In December 1991, a group of Coptic intellectuals and some leading members of the Muslim Brotherhood began to meet at the Muslim Brotherhood headquarters in el Tawfeqiyya on a regular basis. The Copts included a former member of parliament and one time minister of housing, Milad Hanna, the famous writer and judge at the Cabinet Suleiman Qelada, renowned writer Maged Attia, and member of el Wafd Party and businessman Amin Fakhry 'Abd el Nour. Representing the Muslim Brotherhood were El Hodeiby, Salah 'Abd el Mo'atal, Mohammed 'Emara, Sayed Dessouky and Salah 'Abd el Maksoud (a journalist). It is claimed that Ahmed Seif El Banna (son of Hassan El Banna) and the former Mufti Mohammed Mahdi Akef also attended. There were several purposes to the meetings reported in the press. One explanation was that the dialogue sought to find common grounds for addressing the heightened sectarian (fitna) tensions in Egypt. Others suggested that the purpose was to see whether there were possibilities for attracting Copts to become founding members for a proposed establishment of a political party, which would minimise the prospects of accusing it of establishing a religious party (*al-Hayat*, 23 April 1992).

The dialogue faltered. According to Milad Hanna:

> after five sessions they presented us with the Islamic cultural project to rule Egypt in the face of the Western civilization project ... we were expected to give our thumb of approval (tobsom) on it but we refused and I told them let

us examine the Egyptian cultural project which recognizes religious pluralism and the right to citizenship, Copts and Muslims on the basis of equality.

(*Roz el Youssef*, 12 October 1992)

According to another press source (*Sabah el Kheir*, 8 May 1997) one of the main
sticking points in the meetings that took place was the Copts' abject refusal of
the idea of accepting to live under Shar'ia law.

The Islamist awakening, the rise of sectarianism and the rise of Omar el Telmesany and Shenouda

The 1970s and 1980s were characterised by a notable increase in sectarian attack
and violence against Copts by Islamist jihadist groups, in particular al Gama'at
al Islamiyya. Many authors have conceded that the increase in anti-Christian
assaults was a deliberate outcome of Sadat's policy of empowering the Islamists
in a bid to quell the leftists and Nasserites – his prime political enemies. The
Islamisation of state and society and increasing tolerance towards militant Islamist groups had its toll on national social cohesion at a community level.

One of the effects of the entente was to deepen the religious lines of demarcation between Muslims and Christians. The government-sponsored Islamisation
of Egypt was fervently opposed by the newly ordained Patriarch of the Coptic
Orthodox Church, Pope Shenouda, who had also replaced Pope Kyrollos in
1971.

In the political battle that ensued between Sadat and Pope Shenouda, the
Brotherhood took an overt policy of supporting the president against the Patriarch. This was evident from the statements made by *Al Da'wa* magazine – the
Brotherhood's mouthpiece which was used as a platform to propagate highly
inflammatory material against the Copts. *Al Da'wa*'s editor-in-chief was no other
than el Telmesany himself. For example, an opinion article published in *Al
Da'wa* (*Al Da'wa*, Issue 64, August 1981) by a leading Muslim Brotherhood
figure, Rashad Mehana, under the heading 'Sincere advice to the Nazarenes of
Egypt', attributed the rise in sectarianism to the appointment of Pope Shenouda,
and 'his provocative speech and action'. Mehana pointed to Shenouda's opposition to being governed by the Sunna and Koran as being an assault to Muslims
and accused him of inciting the Coptic Diaspora to protest. He expressed his
sympathy with the president of Egypt who was met in a most unwelcoming
manner by the Copts in the US Diaspora upon an official visit.

The Brotherhood aligned itself with the president, blaming much of the anti-
Coptic attacks on Christians and on the Pope. The events in Al Zawwya al
Hamra, a poor quarter in Cairo, present an illustrative vignette to this. In June
1981 a dispute erupted between a Copt and a Muslim over the ownership of a
small plot of land. Rumours spread that the Copts wanted to build a church on it,
which prompted the Muslims in the neighbourhood to claim ownership of it and
to put up a sign that a mosque would be built on the grounds. A fight broke out
and bullets were fired. A group believed to belong to Gama'at al Islamiyya went

around marking all Christian homes, children were thrown from balconies and many were killed. Property belonging to Christians and a nearby church were also burnt after being looted. The security forces allowed the fighting and the attacks on Christians to continue with no intervention for three days. Eighty people, including some Muslims, died in the incident.[8]

The Brotherhood blamed the Copt who claimed ownership of the plot of land for the violence that escalated. They argued that he shot several bullets in the air which caused the deaths of many Muslims and which provoked the latter to retaliate. Another cause behind the sectarian strife, according to *Al Da'wa*, was the Copts' unlawful attempt to seize a piece of land which belonged to the Muslims. The Brothers openly blamed Pope Shenouda for sectarian events such as that of al Zawya: 'the events of Zawya al Hamra are a consequence of the policy pursued by Shenouda the Patriarch and which the President of the Republic of Egypt made reference to last May'.

Accompanying their account of the events was an 'appeal' unclear to whom it was addressed, in which it was explained that the Muslims and Nazarenes have lived in the shadow of Islam in harmony, with dignity for citizens of different creeds assured. Since Islam secured the rights for all citizens, the appeal insists, it would be a major mistake for some to try and replace it with another system.

What was especially worrisome about the statement (read threat), was its warning that while Islam is tolerant and makes no distinction between people on the basis of creed, the Christians 'should be careful' because their livelihood is dependent on their economic transactions with Muslims. The matter was put more bluntly in the issue that followed (Editorial, 'Truths we present to the decision-makers with respect to the events of Zawya al Hamra', *Al Da'wa*, Issue 63, July 1981, pp. 20–21) in which there was an open threat of a Muslim boycott of Coptic services and goods should they continue to act in an inappropriate manner. The Muslim and non-Muslim populations in Egypt are (for the most part) not geographically segregated. To suggest that Muslims will boycott services provided by Christians would be to spark an intensive reconfiguration of Egyptian society along religious lines, where Christians would have to relocate in order to develop all-Coptic communities for the purpose of sustaining livelihoods. Since they are a minority, it would mean the ghettoisation of the Coptic community.

The last four issues of *Al Da'wa* all addressed various dimensions of sectarianism, and served to deepen Muslim–Christian conflict. The articles evoked the impression of danger from a Christian assault on Muslims. In the August issue of *Al Da'wa*, Mohammed 'Abd el Qodous thanked Al Azhar for donating 50,000 dollars for the construction of the Zawya al Hamra mosque 'which the Christians' attempt to seize its land was the cause behind the sectarian incident that took place'. In the same column, he requests information on what is being said about some of the churches being like armed citadels, used for storing arms ('Abd el Qodous 1981: 48).The spread of such rumours of alleged possession of arms would have inflamed the feelings of many of *Al Da'wa*'s readers of the need to protect Islam and the Muslims from the Christian threat.

In yet another article on the causes behind sectarianism, Mohammed 'Abd el Qodous, a close associate of the Muslim Brotherhood (1981: 48), attributes sectarian tensions to the Copts' violation of the rules of engagement for them as a non-Muslim minority in an Islamic state. The general gist of the argument is that in an Islamic state, there is a covenant established between Muslims and non-Muslims which entails the former providing protection for them and the latter to be submissive to the Islamic authority. 'Abd el Qodous cites ways in which submissiveness should be demonstrated – including being respectful of the Islamic creed and the payment of jizya, kharaj (taxes) and alms, within the context of the dhimmi agreement. It is significant that there is a justification for the payment of jizya, defending it on the basis that it does not touch on the principle of equality because the Muslim has to pay with his blood to protect the dhimmi. In addition, the Muslim has to pay the zakat, which the dhimmi would have to pay the kharaj for. The timing of such postulations was critical. For Muslim Brotherhood followers, this would have been part and parcel of the move towards the application of the Islamic Shar'ia in all aspects of governance. For the Copts, this would have been interpreted as testament to the legitimacy of its fears that the Islamisation of politics is anathema to the concept of equal citizenship rooted in Egyptian nationalism.

While the position of the Muslim Brotherhood was in strong animosity to the West and its policies in support of Israel, in many of these articles in *Al Da'wa*, Western foreign policy was conveyed as a reflection of a new crusade led by Christians against the Muslims, of which local Christians were not free from blame. A reading of *Al Da'wa* throughout the 1970s and up to its closure in 1981 highlights reference to Copts as Nazarenes, and as the Crusaders.[9]

In an article in *Al Da'wa*, Sheikh Mohammed El Khattib responds to what he claims to be efforts on the part of the 'crusaders' infiltration manifested in the prosletization cancer' (1981: 46). While the content of the article mainly addresses issues of creed (comparing the position of Islam on various prophets to that of Christianity), the concluding paragraph offers Christians advice that reflects what the author believes to be appropriate behaviour for a minority living in a Muslim country: after warning that Christians must pay attention to the feelings of Muslims and to respect the tenets of those in whose shadows they live, he adds that they should never openly claim a creed or an idea that is contrary to the creed of the state and its religion. Sheikh El Khattib observes that the full implementation of the Shar'ia is being stalled by the Christians or proselytisers and 'these serpents go around spreading poison among the youth'. He called upon teachers and pedagogists to protect youth from these thoughts and ideas (Mohammed Khattib, fatwa section of *Al Da'wa*, Issue 61, May 1981, p. 46).

Hassan El Banna, Coptic civil activism and the rise of the Muslim Brotherhood

There is very little to say regarding relations between the Copts and the Muslim Brotherhood during the 1950s and 1960s, when the movement had gone underground as a consequence of the government's crackdown. On 4 January 1952, prior to the military coup that brought the Free Officers to power, a church was burnt in Suez. There were different accounts of who was responsible. Some say the Muslim Brotherhood, a claim that Father Sargious himself implicitly referred to in *al-Manara* (21 January 1952, Issue 3, p. 2). The Muslim Brotherhood accused the British. The burning of the church and the incurring deaths of several Copts heightened tensions between the Wafdist government and the Church leadership who accused the authorities of complicity. In a bid to contain the crisis, efforts were made to emphasise national unity. Makram Ebeid convinced Hassan el Hodeiby, the then Supreme Guide, to pay a visit to the Patriarch. Some have argued that the aim of the meeting was for El Hodeiby to apologise on behalf of El Banna for the Suez burning. The Muslim Brotherhood's account of the events was different: Hodeiby went to meet with the Patriarch in order to mitigate any accusations that the Muslim Brotherhood were responsible for the event, for which the Patriarch expressed his confidence in the Muslim Brotherhood (see for example 'Abd el Halim 1994).

The Muslim Brotherhood's engagement with the question of non-Muslims during the 1930s–1940s can be examined from the point of view of Hassan El Banna's personal relationship with non-Muslims, that of the Muslim Brotherhood's engagement with non-Muslims more generally or the political thought of the movement on non-Muslim positioning. The latter will be dealt with in the chapter that follows. On a personal level, Hassan El Banna's ability to build a vast social capital also incorporated non-Muslims. Some of the stories cited about El Banna's positive relationship with Copts are included in his own biography (*mouzakerat al Da'wa wal da'eya*). For instance, while he was living in Ismailiya and teaching at a school, a Christian of anonymous identity submitted a complaint to the administration that El Banna was a fanatic teacher leading a fanatic association (the Muslim Brotherhood). Once this complaint reached the headmaster, it was met with complete rejection from the Christian community in Ismailiya, who sent a delegation to the school to refute such claims (El Banna 1986: 102).

It was also largely publicised that the only Egyptian to have broken the government cordon and attended El Banna's funeral was the renowned Coptic politician, Makram Ebeid. The Muslim Brotherhood pointed to the Christians that served as councillors as evidence of the absence of fanaticism. Tawfik Doss was the legal councillor to the Guidance Bureau and together with Akhnoukh Labib Akhnoukh and Karim Thabet, the three Copts represented on the Higher Council of the Muslim Brotherhood. Despite the prominence of these names, the Higher Council had no authority or influence on the internal decision-making apparatus, being a consultative, non-binding committee.

In terms of the movement's wider engagement with the Coptic citizenry, relations were not always characterised by the collegiality found between El Banna and some Coptic figures. The Brethren were implicated in the burning of a church in 1949 and 'they were also involved in a number of minor incidents like removing crosses from the tops of churches' (Carter 1986: 277). Copts who lived in Shubra also shared anecdotes of members of the Brotherhood painting crosses on their houses, to 'single them out' from among the Muslim population. Incidents of strain in Muslim–Christian relations as a consequence of Brotherhood instigation were also reported in several villages.[10]

It is, however, on an ideological level, in relation to El Banna's revival of the Islamic caliphate project, that tensions between Coptic leaders and the Muslim Brotherhood were most conspicuous. Hassan El Banna's project sought to reaffirm the country's Islamic identity whereas it was the Egyptian identity that offered Copts the greatest prospects of inclusion and full integration as citizens in the country's affairs. It was the banner of Egyptian nationalism, not that of being part of an Islamic Ummah, that had united Egyptians together. In 1936, he drew a list of fifty demands that he submitted to Muslim leaders, heads of religious institutions, agencies and universities, which represented an agenda for the political, social and economic development of the country. Some demands entailed the Islamisation of society and government which would have directly undermined the possibility of non-Muslims' full participation in the life of the nation. For example, the bid to strengthen the army by 'increasing the youth contingents and inspiring them on the basis of Islamic Jihad' would have been problematic as a mobilising call for the Copts. The fourth demand in the list to strengthen 'the Islamic bonds between all the Islamic regions and especially the Arab one, in preparation for the establishment of the worldwide Islamic Caliphate' would have clashed with the idea of an Egyptian nation-state. The fifth demand, the infusion of the Islamic spirit in all government offices so that all citizens feel that they are required to abide by the teachings of Islam would lead to the alienation of non-Muslim civil servants. The same applies to the twenty-second demand, which is the 'encouragement of Koran learning in public and private offices and making its learning a mandatory requirement for work permits associated with a linguistic or religious element and making it mandatory to learn some of it at school' which would have meant the exclusion of non-Muslims from employment in the workforce (1986: 256 257).

Another demand put forward by El Banna which would have also been regarded by default as being exclusionary is the 'allocation of some of the military and administrative positions [in the government] to Al Azhar graduates' (1986: 206) in view of the prohibition upon non-Muslims to enroll at Al-Azhar University.

In the liberal era (1920–1940), the Coptic elite and middle classes were very active in political and civil society and many members were vocal in their objections to El Banna's Islamist project. In October 1948 a nationalist priest, Father Sargious, who was famous for his participation in the 1919 revolution against the British with Muslim religious leaders, drew a petition calling for the dissolution of all organisations which combined religion and politics and were detrimental to equality (Carter 1986: 276–277). Father Sargious' magazine *al Manara al Masriyya* was a platform for launching a scathing critique of Hassan El Banna and his political thought to which the latter responded by accusing him of being an agent of British colonialism. Nevertheless, El Banna sought to assure the Coptic citizenry that the Islamic project would not detract from their rights, resting his case on the fiqh principle of 'lahum ma lana wa 'aleihum ma 'aleina' (they have the rights that we have and the duties that we have). As will be discussed in the next chapter, this fiqh principle is found inadequate on many grounds.

Conclusions

To conclude, the Brotherhood's use of Islam for mobilisational purposes has consistently led to the reinforcement of divisions along religious lines. Historically, it is under the ideological banner of Egyptian nationalism that non-Muslims have been able to take part fully in a national political project: yet Egyptian nationalism is in conflict with the Brotherhood's ideological project of adherence to an Islamic Ummah, where all identities are subsumed under an Islamic one. A historical reading of the relationship between the Brotherhood and the Copts suggests that it is one of a political struggle over many levels. On one level, there is the relationship between the Pope and the Supreme Guide of the Brotherhood, which has varied according to who was in power in both institutions, the government in power, the configuration of political forces in that particular historical moment and the dynamics of communal relations on the ground. The political struggle, however, also played out on the level of micropolitics. In many instances, the actions of the rank and file of the Brotherhood on a neighbourhood mosque, university or work level have been more influential in determining the nature of relationships between them and the wider non-Muslim citizenry.

The ousting of President Mubarak after eighteen days of unified Muslim–Christian activism in Tahrir Square was, many expected, going to herald a new age in social cohesion and solidarity that would cross religious divides. It was expected too, in view of the new political configurations in Egyptian political society, that new possibilities of a rapprochement between the Brotherhood and the Copts might emerge.

The Brotherhood has rightly argued that Mubarak's regime played on the Copts' fear of an Islamist-led state to elicit support for the ruling party. However, it is argued here that the deepening of hostility between the two parties following the demise of Mubarak suggests that soured relations cannot be reduced to regime manipulation.

The increase in sectarian tensions in the period following the ousting of President Mubarak and in which the Brotherhood were implicated (such as in Qena) challenges the notion that if it were not for the authoritarian regime's divide and rule strategies, there would be no points of conflict. The Brotherhood has deployed a religious discourse that polarised Muslims in relation to Christians in the constitutional referendum campaign. Such mobilisation of religious for political ends has contributed to the intensification of an 'us' versus 'them' normative framework that deepens divisions along religious lines, and which ultimately increases Copts' sense of being a religious minority threatened by the resurgence of Muslim Brotherhood power.

It is methodologically useful when examining political relations between the Muslim Brotherhood and the Copts not only to examine the official stance of the movement's leadership but also the coalitions and alliances in which they have taken part. The participation of Muslim Brotherhood members in alliances and coalitions with other Islamist forces who have taken highly antagonistic stances on Muslim–non-Muslim matters (such as on the Camillia case and Qena conundrum) means that they cannot be read as adopting an autonomous, more moderate stance than for example the Salafis.

Against the backdrop of the overthrow of Mubarak's regime and the continued spike in attacks against Christians, the Brotherhood could no longer resort to a discourse universalising and equalising discrimination, in particular since the new political configurations empowered them to assume full political agency.

The question of the application of the Shar'ia is one which has historically and to this day represented a real contentious issue for the Brotherhood. Sheikh el Ghazali is correct to point out that the fundamental problem between Christians and Muslims in Egypt lies in the Copts' resistance to the notion of an Islamic government (1989: 349). According to many authors (El Qaradawy, El Wa'i, El Bahi), since the majority of the citizens are Muslim, any protest by a minority against the application of the Shar'ia would be a violation of the principle of the right of the majority to rule according to their belief system. In other words, it is a case of respecting democracy conceptualised as the will of the majority (as was the argument put forward in the Qena conundrum). This particular brand of democracy promotes a highly tyrannical political order because your status and rights are bestowed depending on which side of the religious fence you stand.

6 Islamic citizenship and its qualifiers

This chapter examines the Brotherhood's perspectives on the concept and practice of religious pluralism in Muslim majority contexts such as that of Egypt and in a scenario in which the Shari'a is more fully and comprehensively implemented. The Brotherhood have consistently proclaimed from the time of El Banna to this day that they believe in full equality for all citizens, Muslims and non-Muslims, in accordance with the principle of 'lahum ma lana wa 'aleihum ma 'aleina' or 'they have the same rights as us and the same duties as us'.[1] Here, the doctrinal basis for such a position, its nuances and its implications for Muslim–non-Muslim relations is explored at length. In a context in which Islamic scholarship is well established (Al-Azhar University, many of the scholars belonging to the Salafi and other Islamic movements), the fiqh basis of such a position is extremely important in determining the extent of its legitimacy and credibility as a policy vis-à-vis the non-Muslim other.

The concept and practice of an Islamic citizenship from the point of view of identity, the basis for membership in a political community, and the exercise of rights and duties are explored at length. What is argued here is that the nature of the conflict is as much ideological as it is political; in essence it is not only about a political struggle over recognition and resources, but also about whether the vision of the Brotherhood of Islamic citizenship is in conformity with the Shari'a guarantees full equality. The outcome is a compromise on the very principle of religious choice. People must fit within one of two categories: a Sunni Muslim or a member of the 'People of the Book', whose status qualifies them for a differential set of rights. Those who espouse a secular ideology, calling for the separation of religion and state (be they Muslim or otherwise), those who belong to any other religion other than the People of the Book and atheists are not welcome in an Islamic state because the Muslim's Brotherhood normative framework is one in which non-conformity to the Shari'a is seen as deviance that cannot be tolerated.

The Muslim–non-Muslim contract: the parameters of citizenships, rights and duties

The Muslim Brotherhood have consistently spoken of a contractual relationship between Muslims and non-Muslims in an Islamic state in accordance with the

Shari'a. The Brotherhood's political thought on non-Muslims did not undergo significant reform since the conception of the movement. This is not to suggest a complete uniformity within the movement on every matter, there are different positions on jurisprudence. At one end of the spectrum is Salem el-Bahnasawy, representing the most liberal perspective and on the other end of the spectrum, representing the most conservative standpoint is Al Gabry, and Sheikh Mohammed el Khattib. Somewhere close to the conservative end of the spectrum is Sheikh El Qaradawy. Let us take the example of a Muslim man marrying a woman from the People of the Book as an example. El-Bahnasawy allows the marriage from People of the Book (2004: 89), Al Gabry prohibits it. El Qaradawy allows a marriage to a woman from the People of the Book, but forbids her inheriting from her husband. On the subject of sharing burial sites with non-Muslims, El-Bahnasawy believes that in dire circumstances it is permissible to bury a Muslim in a non-Muslim graveyard, while El Khattib prohibits it on the basis that this would mean a Muslim would share in the eternal suffering (punishment) of a non-Muslim in his graveyard. The difference in opinions can be explained in terms of agential and structural factors. Salem el-Bahnasawy is part of the international Muslim Brotherhood, based in London, and his primary audience has often been Muslim Diaspora and non-Muslims living in the West. It is no surprise that the tone is often more conciliatory. On the other hand, El Khattib as the Mufti of the Brotherhood speaks to a majority audience of Muslim Brotherhood followers and rank and file in Egypt who tend to be very conservative. El Qaradawy presents himself as a follower of the moderate school in Islam and therefore to qualify the negation with exceptions or qualify the acceptance with restrictions.

It is also important to note that whether one is examining the views of leaders at whatever end of the spectrum, they all relate specifically to the position of non-Muslims in Dar el Islam, and in some cases specifically to the position of non-Muslims in Egypt. They do not apply to contexts categorised as belonging to Dar al Harb. Also, it is pertinent to note that for the Muslim Brotherhood, not all non-Muslims can be put in the same basket. The rights of non-Muslims are qualified according to whether they belong to the People of the Book or not, and whether they have deviated from Islam or were born into another religion. In the qualification of rights, there is no room for atheists, they simply do not exist as a category. Below is a discussion of the one unified stance taken by virtually all members of the Brotherhood, the doctrinal principle of lahum ma lana wa 'aleihum wa 'aleina followed by a discussion of the concept and practice of Islamic citizenship as an identity, and as a set of rights and duties.

Lahum ma lana wa 'aleihum ma 'aleina

The Muslim Brotherhood has a very popular adage, 'lahum ma lana wa 'aleihum ma 'aleina' (they have the same rights as us and have the same duties as us) which has come to represent the official stance of the movement on the rights of the Copts in an Islamic state. The phrase is believed to be a fiqh principle first pronounced by Hassan El Banna. Gom'a Amin notes that in 1945 (Amin 2006a). Hassan El Banna responded to the accusation that the Muslim Brotherhood is divisive in its impact on the nation, by insisting that there is no fanaticism in Islam, and that the Prophet supported the idea of unity among the different sects of the Ummah on the basis of national interest. He then pronounced that the position of Islam in relation to non-Muslims is: 'lahum ma lana wa 'aleihum ma 'aleina' (2006: 257–258). All of El Banna's successors who have served as Supreme Guides that have adopted the same adage as representing the position of the Muslim Brotherhood and of Islam on the matter (including Mustapha Mashour who made the infamous statement on the payment of jizya, see Chapter 5).

In all the political platforms that the Muslim Brotherhood have issued, the principle of lahum ma lana wa 'aleihum ma 'aleina has been declared as their position on the Copts' right to equal citizenship. The 1994 *moubadara* (initiative) (published 30 April 1995) stipulates:

> our position regarding our Christian brothers in Egypt and the Arab world is clear, old, and known: lahum ma lana wa 'aleihum ma 'aleina, they are brothers in the long national struggle, they have all the rights of a citizen, the material and moral aspects of them, the civil and the political, and treating them well and cooperating with them in doing good are all Islamic ordinances (fara'ed) that a muslim cannot take lightly ... and whoever says or does contrary to this we absolve ourselves from him, of what he says and does.

This is the same stance taken in Akef's moubadara of 2000, the election platform of 2005, the draft party platform of 2007 and more recently, the Freedom and Justice Party's charter. The third chapter of the Freedom and Justice Party charter declares that all other matters aside from doctrinal matters will be regulated by the Islamic principle of *'lahum ma lel moslemeen wa aleyhum ma 'aleihum* which represents the principles of justice and equality between all citizens with no exception' (my italics).

Further, this is the position taken by political thinkers who have shaped the Muslim Brotherhood's position on this matter, such as Youssef El Qaradawy who also stipulated that with respect to the People of Dhimma,

> these are in the modern expression 'citizens' an Islamic state. The Muslims reached ijmaa (consensus) from the very first day that they have the same rights and duties as the Muslims 'lahum ma lil Muslimeen wa 'aleihum ma 'aleihum' except in matters relating to religion and doctrine which Islam lets them follow what they believe.

> (El Qaradawy 1973: 353)

The fact that this political stance reflects the Muslim Brotherhood's understanding of fiqh was confirmed to me by Mahmoud Ghozlan, Mohammed Habib,

Abdel Moneim Aboul Fotouh, Essam el Erian and others, however, none of them could offer guidance on its jurisprudence source. Ghozlan mentioned that he recalls it was articulated by the Prophet but could not remember the details.

Most agreed that this has always been the stance taken by Hassan El Banna in relation to the People of the Book. But where did Hassan El Banna get it from? None of the leading members of the Brothers were quite sure. Upon further probing, it appears that the source of 'lahum ma lana wa 'aleihum ma 'aleina' appeared in two hadiths considered authentic[2] – however, with a very different meaning.

The first hadith is present in five credible sources of hadiths collection: Abu Dawud (2641) Al Tormozi (2–100), Al-Nissa'I (2–161), Ibn Haban (7–557) and Imam Ahmad (3–199).

In Abu Dawud (2641) it says:

> I am commanded to fight with men till they testify that there is no God but Allah, and that Muhammad is his Servant and His Apostle, face our qiblah, eat what we slaughter, and pray like us. *When they do that, their life and property are unlawful for us except what is due to them. They will have the same rights as the Muslims have, and have the same responsibilities[3] as the Muslims have.*

> (my italics and underlining)

Al Albany comments that this hadith is evidence of the voidness of the hadith which is widely circulated by public speakers and writers that the Prophet said to the People of Dhimma 'They have the same rights as us and the same responsibilities as us'. The latter, he argues, 'has no basis in Islamic fiqh, because the authentic hadith shows that the Prophet made this statement in relation those who converted to Islam from the infidels and the People of the Book' (Al Albany 1995: 613).

The second authentic hadith present in the authentic hadiths accounts of Imam Ahmad (5–259), Mousnad al Rawyani (30–220) states that:

> *whosoever converts to Islam from the People of the Book* has two-fold reward and has the same rights as us and the same duties as us, and whoever converts to Islam from the infidels will have his reward has the same rights as us and the same duties as us.

> (my italics)

'Lahum ma lana wa 'aleihum ma 'aleina' (without the conditionality of conversion) is also cited in the compilation of weak or inauthentic hadiths. Al Albany comments that while some people attribute this hadith to Al-Hedaya[4] there is a consensus among all the scholars that this is a weak hadith because its origin cannot be attributed to the Prophet. As Al Albany comments: 'void, it has no origin[5] for it' (Al Albany 1988: 222–223). Al Albany further comments with respect to this weak hadith:

we have heard from many public speakers and Guides reiterated in their sermons, bragging and claim that Islam made equal the Dhimmis and the Muslims in rights and they do not know that this hadith does not have its origin with the Prophet of Allah.

(1988: 224)

The second hadith considered of weak origin (2176), 'They have the same rights and the same duties, meaning the People of Dhimma', is also attributed to Al-Hedaya. Al Albany comments that the circulation of this hadith is an example of the negative impact it has on the Ummah (Al Albany 2005: 196). Al Albany believes that it is Hassan El Banna who circulated this inauthentic hadith among the youth of the Brothers and others. He attacks the way in which laws and rules were built upon this weak hadith when it has no grounding among Islamic scholars and notes that both Sheikh Mohammed el Ghazaly and Sayed Qutb espoused this line of argument when it has no basis.

The principle of lahum ma lana wa 'aleihum ma 'aleina also has no basis in fiqh references.

If we turn to the books that explain Al Hedaya, such as Nasb al Raya le'ahadeeth el hedaya, Hafez Gamal el Din Al Zaylaa' states: 'I do not know the aforementioned hadith and this meaning is not present in Islamic fiqh' (Vol 4, p. 55).

This allegedly fiqh principle is also not to be found in the history of Islam, whether at the time of the Prophet or his successors. Despite the many covenants that were signed between the Prophet and the People of the Book, we do not find reference to this principle. For example, the famous covenant regulating the relations between the Prophet and the Jews in Madina makes no such reference and the agreement with the Jews living in Madina after the conquest of Mecca makes no such reference. The letter sent to the bishops of Nagran and the Covenant with the Christians of Nagran makes no such reference (174–179).[6]

There are two pertinent questions here: why would the Muslim Brotherhood support an adage that is supposed to be grounded in fiqh when it is a fake hadith? The second question is: does it matter? With respect to the first question, the use of this hadith, even though it has no basis, could be premised on the fundamental ideas of fiqh al maslaha (weighing the benefits and their relative weight in comparison to the harm) or it could be that some members are not so well grounded in fiqh. This leaves, however, the perplexing question of what about world-renowned scholars such as Sheikh Youssef El Qaradawy and Sheikh Mohammed el Ghazaly?

As to the question: does it matter? It matters on two levels: the first has to do with its credibility among the other Islamist groups, the second has to do with its future application. Learned and well versed members of the other Islamist movements will find the usage of this adage a distortion of Islamic fiqh and it will never have any legitimacy among them as a policy to be pursued when considered a weak hadith. Moreover, if this is pronounced at the time of establishment of an Islamic state, it may be challenged on the basis of its invalidity, with severe ramifications on the kind of policies that will be pursued afterwards.

Islamic citizenship as an identity

An Islamic citizenship is one that seeks to reconcile the concept of citizenship which is originally nation-bound with the Shari'a. In the very first pages of the Freedom and Justice Party platform, the issue of the application of the Shari'a and its implications for non-Muslims is tackled (2011). The Shari'a, argued the party charter, emphasises national unity since it acknowledges the right to belief, the right to worship and the right of non-Muslims 'to rule according to their legislation in their personal matters and provides equal rights and duties to all people' (which is then enforced in chapter one, Principles and Premises, point one). The Freedom and Justice Party also explicitly sets out the Islamic Ummah as the common identifier for all Egyptians (2011).

The previous Muslim Brotherhood draft party platform has also made the case for Egyptians' allegiance towards the re-establishment of the Islamic Ummah, given that all share in the Islamic heritage, regardless of their personal religious faith.

> First, the state will strive towards the establishment of Arab and Islamic unity. Since there are no boundaries separating Muslims joined in faith. Since the Egyptian state is a guardian over the Egyptian political community, it must work towards first reaching Arab unity, then Islamic unity. In this quest for the greater Islamic Ummah, the MB point out that the Egyptian gama'a has religious and civilizational loyalties to this Ummah, and that irrespective of their religious loyalties, they are still bound by a collective conscious to the realization of this Islamic unity.
>
> (Draft Party Platform 2008: 16)

There are pertinent points here. First, is the instrumentality of the Egyptian nation-state for building the larger Islamic Ummah. This idea of the instrumentality of the nation-state is reminiscent of Hassan El Banna's writings where he speaks of a series of 'circles', the first of which is the Egyptian one. He contests those who see the Islamic allegiance as incompatible with the allegiance to the Egyptian nation state, arguing:

> how can we not defend Egypt with all that is possible?... We consider ourselves faithful to this beloved nation, working for it, struggling for its prosperity, and we will remain so as long as we live, believing that this is the first circle in the chain of aspired for renaissance, and that it is part of the Arab nation, and that when we strive for Egypt, we strive for Arabism, Occidentalism and Islam.
>
> (El Banna in Amin 2006: 485)

The Islamic civilisational project leaves no room for genuine cultural or religious pluralism. Non-Muslims may have a personal faith practised in places of worship and a separate family law, otherwise, their religious identity is subsumed under an Islamic one. While the party platform's section on cultural revival and development argues that there is no intention to dissolve the attributes of Christian culture or refute the role of Christianity in Egyptian history, there is no evidence to suggest that religious pluralism is celebrated or appreciated. Indeed the platform is clear in stressing that 'the Islamic civilization is the unifying framework for bringing together all the elements of the Ummah' (2007). The homogenising, all-embracing, all-encompassing vision of Islamising identity, society and governance is also manifest in the discussion of the political system which urges making the constitution reflective of the identity of the Ummah with its Islamic, civilisational and Arab dimensions (P18). There is no mention of the Coptic dimension of the nation's identity.

Affiliation to Islam must be the supreme identity marker, with all identity markers in subservience to it, including identity based on an affiliation to a territorial nation-state. Egyptian nationalism founded upon 'religion for God and the nation for all' is vehemently rejected by Youssef El Qaradawy and all other influential writers to have informed the Muslim Brotherhood's viewpoint. El Qaradawy argues that what binds the political community is not an allegiance to a territorial state but allegiance to Islam:

> the truth without doubt is that Islam affirms the religious bond above all other bonds, be they patrilienal, or regional or ethnic or class, a Muslim is a brother to a Muslim.... And a Muslim is closer to a Muslim than a kafir (apostate), even if he were his father or son or brother.
>
> (El Qaradawy 2005: 75)

And Copts? Qaradawy argues that Christianity does not require an allegiance to the territorial state: 'religion for God, nation for God' (El Qaradawy 2005: 88).

The assumed allegiance of non-Muslims to an Islamic Ummah represents the greatest disconnect between the Muslim Brotherhood's political project on the one hand and, on the other, the Copts' experience of citizenship. The widely publicised notion of Coptic allegiance to an Islamic Ummah is premised on a number of assumptions which can be summarized as follows:

1   the common struggle against Western colonialism;
2   the elevated position of Copts under an Islamic state; and
3   the Copts' identification with an Islamic civilisation, having been part of the fabric of a community whose majority belong to the Islamic faith.

Common struggle against Western colonialism to defend Islam?

Mohammed Moro, editor-in-chief of the Muslim Brotherhood magazine *Al Mokhtar al Islami* and one of the leading activists in the movement, argues that Copts' allegiance to an Islamic identity is part and parcel of their allegiance to the Egyptian nation. This is to be contrasted with those whose loyalty is to the

Western civilisation, and who are consequently traitors to the nation (Moro 2007: 301). This is very much in line with Huntington's clash of civilisations theory in which Islamic civilisation is pitted against Western civilisation. Copts who reject the Islamic Shari'a as a premise for statehood are traitors because such a position would signify they are supporters of the Western project. Egyptian nationalism cannot but be Islamic because the alternative is the Western 'other'.

Copts faithful to their homeland Egypt would by default be faithful to their Islamic heritage by virtue of their common history against Western colonialism. The historical nationalist struggle against colonialism is framed as about defending Islam: 'Copts have a sense of belonging to Islam as a culture, civilization and nation and they are partners with Muslims in the struggle against the European civilization and European culture and against European political, military and economic intervention' (Moro 2007: 302).

Historical narratives in question

Closely associated with the above argument is that the history of the Copts who were treated as People of the Book abiding in Dar el Islam boasts of equality and full respect for their rights (El Qaradawy, el Ghazaly, El Wa'i, El Kholy). Proponents of this stand argue that the People of the Book (Ahl al Dhimma) enjoyed a level of freedom and tolerance not witnessed in other civilisations or historical phases. For El Qaradawy, with the exception of a few 'unrepresentative moments in history', Islamic rule secured the right of non-Muslims' freedom of worship and belief. El Qaradawy expresses his surprise that non-Muslims are offended by a term (Ahl al Dhimma) which is supposed to carry such positive connotations from their historical experiences. He argues that if Ahl al Dhimma is an offensive term for non-Muslims, then it can be replaced with the term 'Citizenship in Dar el Islam' (the same proposition put forward by El Wa'i 2007: 26). It is significant, however, that in many cases, the replacement of the concept of dhimmi with citizenship is qualified, i.e. in Dar el Islam, or bearing the 'Islamic nationality' (Al Ghazaly, Abd al Khaleq 'Ouda). The people of Dar el Islam have one nationality, the Islamic nationality, whether they be Muslims or Dhimmis, and, regardless of how an Egyptian is distinguished from a Syrian or an Iraqi or a Moroccan, this distinction is based on locality, and is not the basis for the application of any judicial rule nor for any distinction. The notion of an Islamic nationality enjoined by all the people who belong to an Islamic Ummah is an attempt to render positive connotations to the revival of the old caliphate system, one which for many is seen as more particularistic than universalistic in its essence.

Common Islamic civilisation?

The third argument regarding non-Muslims' allegiance to an Islamic state is their commitment to a common civilisational foundation, the Islamic civilisation. In the third chapter, the Freedom and Justice Party platform declares:

the Islamic Shari'a represents the governing policy in determining the priorities, strategies and these ends represent the cornerstone in our *civilizational* values and which the Muslim belongs to through belief and civilization and which the non-Muslim belongs to through civilization.

The assumption is that both Muslims and their non-Muslim counterparts identify with an Islamic civilisation, the same ethos that unites both under a common Islamic nationality banner:

> and the basis of nationality in Dar al Islam is espousal of Islam or abidance by its rulings, he who espoused Islam is a Muslim and who abided by the rulings of Islam and did not become a Muslim is a Dhimmi, and both Muslim and Dhimmi are re'aya (subjects) of the Islamic state and the nationality of both is the Islamic nationality.
>
> (Abd el Khalek 'Ouda 1951: 308)

Yet the above arguments have not been convincing enough to deal with the citizenship conundrum. If anything, they reveal a disconnect (whether deliberate or otherwise) with Copts' own reading of their history and experiences of citizenship. With the exception of a few Coptic writers with strong Islamist tendencies and who wrote in their personal capacities, the majority of historians have pointed to two important realities: that Copts' experience of full citizenship materialised only when they were liberated from the status of Ahl al Dhimma and, second, that it is in moments when the Egyptian identity is elevated above religious identity that social cohesion and inclusion are achieved. Conversely, whenever there is an intensification of the Islamisation of politics and society, its impact is an increase in Copts' social exclusion, political marginalisation and rise in identity politics. Such a disconnect does only feature in intellectual debates but in day to day politics – as is evident in the strong resistance and opposition displayed towards the Muslim Brotherhood for naming Copts 'the People of the Book' or 'the People of Dhimma' (see Chapter 5).

Islamic citizenship as a set of rights

In Dar el Islam, citizens would enjoy belonging to an Islamic state in which they would enjoy the rights and duties of Islamic citizenship. Below, the 'qualifiers' that come with these rights in relation to non-Muslim citizens are problematised.

Equal as long as there is no wellaya of a non-Muslim over a Muslim

Politically, the rights to which non-Muslims are entitled to in Muslim Brotherhood scholarship relate to the right to occupy certain positions of public office and be represented in representative councils (such as parliament). The Freedom and Justice Party platform makes no mention of the qualifications for assuming the position of president. Various leading political figures of the Muslim Brotherhood (Sobhi Saleh and others) have, however, commented that while any persons are entitled to nominate themselves as president, the Brotherhood will ask their members not to vote for them if they are Christian or a woman. This is very much the stance that is shared by the rank and file (see El Anani 2007). The draft Muslim Brotherhood Party platform made a clear position on the prohibition of non-Muslims from occupying the position of head of state, on the basis that this is a position of wellaya or authority, and in Islam, it is not permissible for a non-Muslim to have authority over a Muslim. This draft party platform explained the premise of such a position as follows:

> The state has some principle religious functions, it is responsible for the protecting and guarding religion, and the Islamic state also must protection non-Muslims in their creed and worship and their places of worship, and it [the state] will be responsible for guarding Islam and protection of its affairs and ensuring against what would be in opposition to its worship, Da'wa, pilgrimage and other [issues]. Such religious functions/roles are represented in the head of the state or the prime minister depending on the political system in place. Accordingly, we are of the view that the president of the state or the prime minister has duties which conflict with the creed of the non-Muslim, thus sparing the non-Muslim of this mission in accordance with Islamic Shari'a, which does not oblige a non-Muslim with duty in conflict with his belief system.
>
> (Party Platform 2008: 15)

The wording suggests that rather than being deprived of a citizen right, the non-Muslim is being granted a favour, namely, being spared the ordeal of ruling according to a creed that is not his/hers. To further substantiate the reason for the 'exemption' of non-Muslims, the draft platform argues that as one of the roles of the head of state involves taking the decision of when to go to war, any leader's decision will have to be bound by the Shari'a laws (2008: 15).

According to Mohammed Habib, the decision to prohibit a non-Muslim from occupying the position of head of state is one on which there is a consensus among the Brotherhood, and although the platform was in draft form, this particular stance is irreversible. This was confirmed by Ghozlan who considered it as one of the thawabet in religion. Despite the massive outcry that erupted when the platform was announced on account of its implications for equal citizenship, it is important to note that this has consistently been the position espoused by the movement. The famous document written by Mahmoud Ghozlan, *Yes Islam is the Solution* (2005) which bore the Muslim Brotherhood stamp of approval as representating the movement's position, also confirmed this idea. Ghozlan briefly cited the MB's recognition of a wide array of rights which they believe Copts are entitled to in the frame of 'all the rights of citizenship' such as the right to freedom of belief and worship, right to human dignity, right to choose their professions, right of mobility, right to be governed according to their

Shari'a in personal status matters, right to consume and trade in alcohol which is banned for Muslims, etc. It also includes political rights of nomination and election in political life and occupation of all public positions in the state except the position of the General Imamate (head of the state) (2005: 25–26). The same applies for the position stated in the 1994 *moubadra* and the 2004 *moubadra*. Such a stance is not new.

The Muslim Brotherhood's stance on which positions non-Muslims will be allowed or prohibited from occupying is largely determined according to the interpretation of wellaya. In the case of the presidency, the Muslim Brotherhood chose a judicial interpretation in which the president is considered as presiding over al wellaya al 'uzmah. Other judicial options would include considering the presidency as wellaya sughra rather than wellaya qubra/uzmah, which would leave space to consider the different jurists' position on the matter.

However, the concept of wellaya still poses limitations on citizenship in actual practice. It is not only the Grand Imamate that is considered a 'religious position' and therefore non-Muslims cannot lead, all positions in the judiciary which involve the application of the Shari'a are also prohibited by the same token: that it involves a wellaya of a non-Muslim over a Muslim. The same would apply to the military (since the leadership of the military is not a strictly civil position since jihad is one of the highest forms of worship in Islam) and the administration of charity (sadaka) (El Qaradawy 2005: 24).

While the official position of the Muslim Brotherhood indicates that Copts are allowed all leadership positions except the Grand Imamate, the Brotherhood's political thought and practice suggest a broader set of occupations which would be prohibitive because they would involve the wellaya of a non-Muslim over a Muslim. El Sawi for example argued that ministries that involve policy-making (wezarat tafweed) would require that the conditions of wellaya uzma apply (i.e. be Muslim, male, etc.) (El Sawi 1992). Non-Muslims would be allowed to occupy implementative positions such as ambassadors since these would be considered the equivalent of wezarat tanfeez.

El Wa'i also notes that the non-Muslims' right to public office excludes those positions that involve 'working according to Islamic Shari'a since they do not believe in it' (2007: 27). He does not highlight what they are, however his position has the most explanatory power in making sense of the strong opposition shown by members of the Muslim Brotherhood to a Copt occupying the position of a governor in Qena (see Chapter 5).

This leaves the dilemma of how to justify the representation of non-Muslims in parliament. The matter is widely debated among Muslim Brotherhood scholars. El Qaradawy's position is that there is no objection according to Islamic jurisprudence to their participation in the representative councils (i.e. parliament) but they are 'to be represented according to a certain percentage' as long as the council is majority Muslim. He quotes the Koranic verse (al momtahena 8) and says that this would be evidence of justice that they are represented in the majalis 'so that they express the demands of their group as women would represent the demands of their sex', 'and so that they do not feel excluded from among the people of their nation and this be exploited by the enemies of Islam' (2007: 195).

Equal in access to personal status jurisprudence but not the rest

The Brotherhood have consistently pointed to the right of People of the Book to rule according to their own jurisprudence as evidence of their commitment to the concept of equal citizenship. Yet in cases where non-Muslims' jurisprudence does not make reference to a matter, such as in the punishment of adultery or theft, then they would abide by Islamic jurisprudence, for example, through the universal application of huddud ordinances.

El Qaradawy argued that non-Muslims are obliged to abide by the rulings of Islamic law, which are enforced on Muslims 'because by virtue of the dhimma, they have become bearers of the Islamic state nationality and so have to abide by the laws that do not touch on their creed or religious freedom' (2005: 43) El Qaradawy argues: 'I do not know what would make a Christian or Jew anxious about cutting the hand of a thief, be he muslim or Christian or the flogging the adulterer or the drunk and other huddud verdicts?' (2005: 87). The Muslim, he argues, receives these verdicts as part of his religion, and the non-Muslim as part of the state law which has been espoused by the majority.

Abd el Khalek 'Ouda explained the logic of equality: since Islam recognises previous prophets, it can allow non-Muslims (although he is specifically talking about People of the Book) allowed them to follow their own jurisprudence and applied Islamic ruling only when it was not covered in the realm of their belief system. Equality therefore is that each party complies with its own religious jurisprudence and does not comply with what violates it and this is true equality' (196–197). Such a rule would only apply to the People of the Book, namely Christians and Jews. Atheists, Baha'is and others whose jurisprudence is not recognised, cannot but comply with Islamic Shari'a.

Equal rights to worship but must be tied to the minority status of the People of the Book

The official Muslim Brotherhood line is that they believe in the principle that 'freedom of belief and worship is respected for all' (2011, *moubadra* of 2004, 1994). However, some critics have questioned whether this position when tested on the ground still stands. At the heart of the controversy lies one particular infamous fatwa issued by the late Sheikh El Khattib in response to a question regarding the permissibility of the construction of churches in Dar el Islam (*Al-Daw'a*, Issue 56, December 1981, p. 40). Sheikh Abd el Khattib's fatwa is that in the instance that territories were established and built by Muslims such as Maadi, Helwan, 10th of Ramadan City, these and other territories, it is prohibited for churches to be constructed on such territories or the establishment of congregations (of People of the Book). In the second instance, if the lands which were conquered by the Muslims such as Cairo and Alexandria and Constantine in Turkey, and it is prohibited to construct churches on these lands as well and adds that some scholars allow for their destruction because they are now lands owned by Muslims. The third instance are the lands that became under Islamic rule after an agreement with its inhabitants, and in such a case, it is possible that the churches that were present at the time of seizure remain as they are, without restoring those that were destroyed or the construction of new ones. He concludes that it is therefore prohibited to construct churches in Dar el Islam.

The fatwa received much infamous press coverage from both Coptic writers such as Samir Morcos and journalists such as Abd el Rehim Ali who both urged the Muslim Brotherhood to take a clear stance as to whether they support or condemn this fatwa. In an interview with the former Supreme Guide, he said that this fatwa represents the opinion of the Sheikh Khattib personally and he is to account for it, rather than the Muslim Brotherhood. El Erian made a similar point at a seminar held at Sawassiya (p. 39). El Khattib never apologised or retracted his fatwa. Yet the argument that the fatwa reflects El Khattib's personal opinion and not that of the Muslim Brotherhood is problematic since it was published in the organisation's mouthpiece, *Al Daw'a*, and its author is a respected source of knowledge and learning to many generations of the Brothers. While most of the members of the Muslim Brotherhood interviewed said that they condemn these fatwas, nevertheless, no official statement declaring a reformed position was ever made.

At the heart of the Muslim Brotherhood's reluctance to allow for the construction of churches as mosques is a fear that this would undermine the Islamic identity of Egypt. Muslim Brotherhood writer Amer Shamach (2008: 115) argued that:

> what the Muslim Brotherhood fear are the thoughts of some Copts who call upon expansion in the construction of churches to change the face of Egypt to a Coptic face – all they care about is the construction of churches in prominent places, on public roads, in squares and at the gates of towns and in reality these churches are not built for worship but it is to push the line of demands further.

It is the same viewpoint of Mahmoud Ghozlan who commented that the issue of church construction should not be about the implanting of churches everywhere as an indicator of the size of the Copts,

> meaning that if I as a church am receiving a billion dollar annually and it is very easy for me to build a church here and there without people needed it just to give the Christian face to the outside [world].
>
> (Interview with Ghozlan, July 2007)

In short, the right to have places of worship for non-Muslims is not the same as that of Muslims. Being a minority in a Muslim country, places of worship for non-Muslims are to be commensurate with their numbers.

Equal as long as you belong to the People of the Book

The above discussions regarding wellaya, right to worship, right to be ruled according to parallel system of jurisprudence have been consistently used to refer to People of the Book living in Dar el Islam. This may be because Christians and Jews were the two groups who have historically lived in Muslim territory and which are mentioned in the Koran. However, the failure to mention other non-Muslims is not only due to contextual factors, but ideology as well.

Followers of denominations like the Baha'is do not have either the right to freedom of belief or worship. In an interview with Mahmoud Ghozlan, when asked whether non-Muslims who are not from the People of the Book have the right to worship in an Islamic state, he answered categorically 'they do not have the right, meaning that the principle is not freedom of belief but freedom of the belief of the [people of the] book'. Ghozlan then argued that while they may continue to live, they may neither congregate nor proselytise their faith. Historically, the Muslim Brotherhood have championed the uprooting of the Baha'is and Ahmadis in defense of Islam. The Brotherhood took it upon themselves to 'purify' society of all the denominations that they believed posed a threat to Islam. They used their magazine *Al-Ikhwan* to combat what they saw as these dangerous ideas (Amin 2003: 102–104).

The Brotherhood members also sought to publicly deter Muslims from joining the Baha'is or Ahmadis by refusing to allow their dead to be buried in Muslim cemeteries. Goma'a's historical account praises incidents such as that which took place in Ismailiya in 1938 in which a Baha'i died and the Muslim Brotherhood stood united in preventing his burial in Muslim burial sites to teach a lesson to all Muslims who may consider following their way. In 1939, the Brotherhood issued a statement in which they recounted how the minute they found out that a Baha'i, an infidel, had passed away in Port Said, they immediately pronounced the prohibition of his burial in a Muslim cemetery, and mobilised the people in the village to rise. Soldiers were sent to protect the household where the deceased lived from being attacked from the mob that had congregated outside and, at the end of the day, the deceased's family had no option but to go bury him on the Ismailiya Road, fifty miles from Port Said. The Brotherhood's statement concluded: 'This was a stern lesson that the Brotherhood gave to the Baha'is, the atheists and all those who have deviated from religion. It was also a victory for the Muslims that made their eyes water and their hearts rejoice' (Amin 2006a: 302). Goma'a also recounts that when the Muslim Brotherhood discovered that two of the students who had enrolled at Al-Azhar University were Ahmadis, the Guidance Bureau immediately wrote to Sheikh Al Azhar who called for an investigation into their affiliation to this denomination. As a consequence of the Brotherhood's uproar, notes Goma'a proudly, the two students reverted 'to the true doctrine of Islam' (Amin 2006a: 304–305).

More recently, the Baha'is won a court case entitling them to have their denomination recognised in their religious ID, a move that was widely rejected by the Brotherhood. The level of intolerance towards *their right to existence is not specific to the Muslim Brotherhood but accounts for a significant proportion of the population*. 'Abd el Kadir Al Seba'i, a renowned member of the Muslim Brotherhood, in his book on the Baha'is explains that since they have deviated from the path of Islam and are to be considered apostates, the state should take every measure to prohibit their existence in a Muslim country like Egypt, where they threaten its stability and creed (Al Seba'i 2006). The ID indicating one's religion is also bound by what type of religion is permissible or prohibited under Islamic rule. There are only three acceptable religions permitted in the ID: Muslim, Christian, Jew. Since the Baha'is are considered apostates, the Muslim Brotherhood insist that it is prohibited to recognise a Baha'i on the ID. The same applies to an atheist.

People of the Book equal as long as they are mindful of Muslim sensibilities

Some of the most influential thinkers to have informed the Muslim Brotherhood's engagement with the nature of the position of People of the Book in Dar el Islam have argued that one of the markers of the non-Muslim's respect and loyalty for the Islamic order under whose mantra they live is to be mindful not to offend Muslims' sensibilities in any way. Sheikh Al Ghazaly considered the objection by Copts to the implementation of the Shari'a as one manifestation of the disrespect-ful behaviour of non-Muslims towards Islam. What will be considered offensive to the sensibilities of Muslims is very much open for contestation and debate, and is very much based on the normative values that are espoused by society. It is import-ant to note too that in view of the heightened sensitivities towards possible offences from non-Muslims, there is often the application of a double standard: what an average Muslim can get away with may be considered a major crime against Islam when emanating from a non-Muslim.

Ironically, the threat of using a Muslim-led boycott as a weapon for discipli-nary purposes against deviant Copts for showing disrespect towards Islam was made in two incidents in which the Brotherhood's power and that of the Islam-ists was at its peak in contemporary Egyptian history. The first time, in 1981, following the Zawya al Hamra incident, and the second time in July 2011, when the head of the Muslim Brotherhood's Freedom and Justice Party, Morsi, called in a public conference on Muslims to boycott all companies belonging to Egyp-tian Coptic tycoon Naguib Sawiris. Naguib Sawiris, whose party is also compet-ing against the Muslim Brotherhood's Freedom and Justice Party, had posted on his Twitter account a picture of Disney cartoon characters Mickey with an Islamic beard and Minnie donning a niqab. The picture, which was posted on several Saudi sites, was intended to be humorous, but when it appeared on Sawiris' Twitter it was interpreted by the Brotherhood and other Islamists as blasphemous, and a lawsuit was filed against him. Sawiris apologised and emphasised that he intended no harm, and filed a lawsuit against the Brother-hood for insulting him and damaging the national economy.

Conclusions

This chapter argued that the vision and practice of the Brotherhood falls short of ensuring religious pluralism because all rights are tied to a number of qualifiers which undermine their essence. By representing themselves as the guardians of Islam, the Muslim Brotherhood have effectively warded off criticisms by representing the movement as synonymous with Islam. What this chapter has proposed is the Brotherhood's vision of citizenship accorded by an Islamic nationality does not secure the full rights of citizenship or secure religious pluralism. The Brotherhood's much lauded 'lahum ma lana wa 'aleihum ma 'aleina' is, by the nature of its framing, indicative of an 'us' versus 'them' principle. Its doctrinal basis does not endorse equality, but the conditional guarantee of rights, subject to affiliation to Islam. It symbolises assimilation based on the negation of religious identity.

What is particularly worrying is that while the Brotherhood have made hundreds of statements assuring the Coptic citizenry that their rights as citizens will be fully protected and respected under an Islamic system, they have actively sought to block making full and equal citizenship central to the Egyptian constitution. In the discussion of the constitutional amendments put forward by the government in 2007, an additional article was drafted, stating that the Egyptian state is based on citizenship.[7] Muslim Brotherhood MP Ragab Abou Zeid (Sabry 2007) refused the proposed amendment saying that this statement suggests a division between religion and the state. In effect, what he was implicitly objecting to is the fact that there is an absence of mention of the Shari'a as mediating the rights of citizenship. Another vignette is from 2008 when deputy speaker for parliament Zeinab Radwan put forward a proposal to allow a woman from the People of the Book to inherit from her Muslim husband (and vice versa, for him to inherit from her) and another proposal suggesting a change in existing law to allow for a Christian's testimony in matters pertaining to Personal Status affairs to be accepted (*Al-Masry Al-Youm*, 11 March 2008, front page). Zeinab Radwan, a professor in the Fundamentals of Religion (Usul al Din), argued that there is nothing in the Koran or Sunna to prohibit women who belong to the People of the Book to inherit from their Muslim husbands. Radwan argued that since Islam allows a Muslim man to marry a woman from the People of the Book, hence she should enjoy the same rights and duties as a Muslim wife, and should be able to inherit from her husband and he should be able to inherit from her. Her proposal was supported by some of the most well established Islamic scholars including the Grand Mufti of Al-Azhar Ali Gom'a, and Mahmoud Zaqzouk, the minister of endowments, yet some critiques may contest the validity of their testimony because of their relationship to the government. Yet it was rejected in the People's Assembly: the Muslim Brotherhood sided with the Islamic Research Council in rejecting it.

The foundation of an Islamic citizenship is one in which religion mediates all aspects of private and public lives of all citizens in all spheres and it cannot but lead to subtle inequalities that are framed as being 'fair'. For example, when asked whether once in power the Muslim Brotherhood will require of Copts to pay the zakat, former deputy Supreme Guide of the Brotherhood, Mohammed Habib, answered in the negative but said that it will impose double the taxes on them instead (Mouawfy Nahdet Misr 2007).

On an identity level, the Muslim Broterhood's vision that all non-Muslims can have a sense of belonging to an Islamic Ummah run in accordance with the Shari'a on account of a common Islamic civilisational foundation is founded on a number of highly problematic historical inferences. The first is that non-Muslims subjects enjoyed full rights under an Islamic state and this should give them an assurance that they will be protected under a system with an Islamic reference point. The second is that non-Muslims' struggle against Western colonialism was part and parcel of their struggle to protect Islamic civilisation. The third is that they are a numerical but not political minority and therefore religious status in a Muslim majority context is not an issue in the first place. Such a historical reading is at odds with that of the Copts' own perceptions of their historical experience, in which it is only when freed from ahl al dimma status and the assumption of an Egyptian citizenship identity that they secured full citizenship, and in which the struggle against Western colonialism was one driven by an Egyptian nationalism, one not imbued with an Islamic identity. Third, that their experiences of religious discrimination have been intrinsically associated with the rise in power of political Islam, whether in the 1970s or in the post-Mubarak transition phase.

However, the vision of a political community whose membership is based on a religious identity is problematic for religious freedoms more broadly because it does not recognise atheism or non-affiliation to a religious community. There are ultimately two groups: the Muslims and the People of the Book, two sources of jurisprudence: Islamic or that espoused by the Christian or Jewish religions. This categorisation undermines people's free exercise of agency in choosing not to be affiliated to a religious group.

The application of an Islamic references produces an Orwellian reality in which all citizens are equal, but some are more equal than others by virtue of their religious identity as Sunni Muslims. This is manifest in the prohibition of non-Muslims of assuming wellaya over Muslims. In practice, the Brotherhood's strong opposition to the appointment of a Coptic governor in Qena shows that the concept of wellaya applies to a wider set of leadership positions than the officially announced stance of its reference to the position of president only. The position of a duality of systems of jurisprudence also fails to secure full equality since the parallel systems are not imbued with equivalent power, they are positioned in a hierarchy in which Islamic jurisprudence trumps all other sources of jurisprudence. It is important to note that allowing the People of the Book to have their own system of jurisprudence does not secure religious pluralism because other religions are not bestowed with the same rights. There are no universal rights for non-Muslims living in Muslim countries and their very right to live according to their faith (or in the case of atheists without a faith in God) is threatened because the terms of religious pluralism have already been set through the Brotherhood's Islamic marja'iyya.

7 The Sisters of the Brotherhood and the woman question

This chapter is about the Muslim Sisters section of the Muslim Brotherhood. It looks at the way in which structural and agential factors have interacted to undermine the full flourishing of a Muslim Sisterhood. Structurally, the organisational and political nuances of being a section, whose prerogatives are far more limited than other sections, like that of the university students, has meant that they were consistently contained. Agentially, the fact that the Muslim Sisters were consistently led by a male leadership (to this very post-Mubarak day) has meant that the possibilities for the development of an autonomous female leadership capable of mobilising a constituency for political influence within the movement has been severely restricted. This is not to make the simplistic suggestion that a female leadership would have necessarily been any more empowering. As will be argued below, the Muslim Sisters have been mostly followers of the dogma rather than Muslim women reformers. However, it is to say that the Muslim Sisters section was completely subsumed to the agenda of the leadership of the Muslim Brotherhood, with very limited space for contestation.

The chapter traces how the Muslim Sisters and the Muslim Brotherhood more widely sought to influence and reacted to the gender matters arising within the movement and in the broader socio-political context of Egypt during three historical stages: from the time of its inception to its dissolution in 1948, from 1954 to 2010 and finally in the six months since the instigation of the Intifada calling for Mubarak's ousting.

The rise and fall of the Muslim Sisters (1930s–1950s)

Despite the wealth of literature on the Muslim Brotherhood, women's agency in the movement is one of the least explored dimensions of the movement even though they played a pivotal role in its survival at stages when they were subject to extreme repression. Zeinab el Ghazali has come to be an icon representing the Muslim Sisters however she was never a member of the Muslim Sisters division at the time of Hassan El Banna and in many ways reflects a unique pathway into the movement, a theme we will return to later.

Shortly following Hassan El Banna's establishment of the first branch of the Muslim Brotherhood in Ismailiya in 1928, he established a club, a mosque, and a school for boys followed by a school for girls named 'Umahat al Mo'meneen' (the mothers of believers). The school was designated with teaching the wives, daughters and relatives of the Muslim Brotherhood members, combining Islamic teaching with subjects that are seen to be pertinent to women's domestic role (Khayal and El Gohary 1993: 231–232). The female staff entrusted with teaching the students were given the title of 'the Muslim Sisters group' (Khayal and El Gohary 1993: 232). Hassan El Banna envisioned a role for the Muslim Sisters that would extend beyond the classroom and encompass da'wa (proselytisation) among women in the households of Muslim Brotherhood members and society more widely. Hassan El Banna drew internal by-laws for the organisational structure of the group in which he established modes of communication between the leader of the Sisters division and the Brotherhood leadership to be through a trusted Muslim Brother. Hassan El Banna appointed Mahmoud el Gohary as secretary general of the Sisters Division. Mahmoud el Gohary recounts that when he wrote a request to Hassan El Banna that he be exempt from his responsibility as secretary-general of the sisters in order for him to dedicate himself to the work of the Brotherhood, the latter smiled and on the spot wrote: 'Mahmoud el Gohary secretary general of the Muslim Sisterhood until death', signed it and gave it to him (Khayal and El Gohary 1993: 236).

The internal by-laws of the Muslim Sisters division (la'ehat qism Al Akhwat al Muslimat) stated that the purpose of the division was to raise women's awareness of the decrees of their own religion, spread Islamic culture and the Muslim Brotherhood's da'wa among women and act as a countermovement against other destructive ideologies that find appeal among women (presumably referring to feminism). Each branch[1] would promote the establishment of a Muslim Sisters' division to be supervised by a righteous Brother of good repute. The Brother would organise lectures and lessons at a time when the mosques of Muslim Brotherhood premises were vacant. The Brother would select the preachers (men and women) for the lessons. Mitchell notes that despite the development of its organisational structure, 'there never developed among the ladies' auxiliary anything resembling the growth of the male organization. In the early years, whatever Banna thought, there was simple resistance from the male members of the Society' (Mitchell 1969: 175).

In 1932, after the central premises of the Muslim Brotherhood was transferred to Cairo, the Muslim Sisterhood division also moved. Once in the capital, a female leader was appointed to oversee the activities of both branches, Labiba Ahmed (Khayal and El Gohary 1993: 233), Labiba Ahmed was the editor-in-chief of the *Women's Renaissance* magazine, a publication that was specifically aimed at propagating Islamic values in society and towards women in particular. Hassan El Banna chose her on account of her piety, her role in Islamic da'wa, in particular through her writings and because, given that she donned the proper Islamic attire (fully veiled, but revealing face), he thought he would serve as a role model for Muslim women and published her photo in the Brothers' own weekly publication, *Al Ikhwan al Muslimoon* (Amin 2003: 212–214). Her departure to Saudi Arabia, however, led to the inactivity of the group.

Yet in the early 1940s, the Muslim Sisters' section was resurrected, thanks in large part to the efforts of a small core group of six women, led by Amal Al 'Ashmawy, the daughter of Mohammed Al 'Ashmawy Pasha, the Minister of Ma'aref. Farid Abd el Khalek (Abd el Khalek 2011), recounts that Amal 'Ashmawy had converted her home into a venue for the lessons and activities of the Muslim Sisters and she capitalised on her social and financial status to support the Muslim Sisters and the movement at large.

A section of the Brotherhood, not a Sisterhood!

According to Gom'a Amin, the Muslim Sisters reached the apex of their activism in Cairo between 1943 and 1945. He recounts that as women became more active, the branches of the Brothers supported the Muslim Sisters' initiatives to form their own NGOs. At that time, the division was headed by Sheikh Al Latif Al Al Sho'she'i, and supervising the division from the Guidance Bureau was Saleh Al 'Ashmawy. As the activities of the Sisters grew, an (all-male) implementing committee was formed in 1944. A general guidance committee emerged out of the implementing committee comprised of twelve women with Amal 'Ashmawy serving as president and Fatma 'Abd el Hady as her deputy.

At that time, some internal incident happened that led the Muslim Brotherhood leadership to decide to annul the general guidance committee. Regrettably, we only have one version of the happenings, that of Amin, which is told very much from the perspective of the power centres in the Brotherhood:

> The establishment of this [general guidance] committee with the spread of the Muslim Sisters' NGOs led to the emergence of some conflict over the presidency of the Sisters and it led to their separation from the branches and the districts in some places, which prompted Imam Al Banna to form a committee from the brothers Saleh 'Ashmawy, Helmy Nour el Din and Mohammed El Houlagy to rethink the rules upon which the division is run.
>
> (Amin 2005: 189)

The new committee drew new a by-law which annulled the general guidance committee as well as delegated all leadership positions to men (Nour el Din as its president, and 'Ashmawy as its deputy). The new structure blocked any possibility for women assuming leadership positions. In effect, other than the leader, his deputy and one woman who would serve as the liaison between the leader and the women members, the new Muslim Sisters division had no positions, committees, taskforces, or any other organisational mechanism for delegating responsibilities and authorities.

Article 3(g) of the by-laws states:

> *the establishment of independent administrative entities for women is completely forbidden* so that they do not occupy themselves with structures and

titles from which no benefit results, but they should free themselves fully to benefit from the lessons and their application in their homes with their children, their sisters and brothers and services and disseminate them outside their homes among their friends and relatives.

(Amin 2005: 359; my italics)

The absence of an internal structural can be contrasted with other divisions, like for example the students' division, which at that same period had a head, a deputy and a secretariat which was elected from among the students. In 1944, the student division had six committees and representation on a local and regional level.

Moreover, the new by-laws destroyed the organic formation of an autonomous Muslim Sisterhood which had began to emerge when women had began to coalesce together to form NGOs and other institutional umbrellas that brought them together. The new by-laws prohibited women's coalescing into a collective agency that cuts across geographical divides. Instead the by-laws forced them to go back to working strictly under the different geographical branches, thus fragmenting them and bringing them into subservience to local branches led by male leaders.

Further, while in other divisions, the membership could nominate a representative on their behalf, in the Muslim Sisters' division, the line of command was entirely vertical, with no space for the Muslim Sisters to even choose their meetings convenor. This limited the Muslim Sisters' ability to influence the power hierarchy, for there was always a Brother representing them at the Guidance Bureau. If his agenda was not aligned with theirs, it was very difficult institutionally for them to circumvent him.

El Banna's insistence that the Muslim Sisters Division be represented through male voice and leadership, and be heavily controlled from within meant that women's autonomous agency was in fact prohibited. It is perhaps why Zeinab el Ghazali refused to come under the wings of the Muslim Brotherhood. Zeinab el Ghazali joined the first Egyptian feminist organisation, the Egyptian Feminist Union (EFU) at the age of eighteen. In 1936, she left the EFU to form her own organisation, the Muslim Women's Society, because she wanted to establish an organisation whose value system would be more concomitant with her own beliefs in Islam, and the possibilities for obtaining justice for women and men within that frame, rather than through a Western one (Badran 1995). Six months after Zeinab el Ghazali established her organisation, she was invited to give a lecture to the Sisters at the premises of the Muslim Brotherhood and afterwards Hassan El Banna invited her to join her organisation with his. She told him she would discuss it with the general assembly. She never joined forces and her organisation continued to thrive autonomously from the Muslim Brotherhood with her as leader until its dissolution.

From the beginning, al-Ghazali conceived of the Muslim Ladies Association as equal and equivalent to, yet deliberately separate from, that of the Muslim

Brothers. When Hasan al Banna, the leader of the Muslim Brotherhood, invited her to incorporate her organization into his, she refused.

(Cooke 2001: 88)

This is further corroborated by one of the leading founders of the Muslim Sisters in Cairo, Fatma 'Abd el Hady,[2] in her own account:

> Sister Zeinab el Ghazali had her own activism in the Islamic Da'wa among women but it was autonomous of the Muslim Brotherhood and she did not join it [the Muslim Brotherhood] except later after the death of Hassan el Banna. I remember that upon joining the Brothers in 1942 Sister Zeinab had already established the Muslim Women's Society and her activitiy was great so at that time I said to Sheikh Hassan el Banna: why is there division in the Da'wa? And why does not Sister Zeinab El Ghazaly join us? And he said to me: we proposed this to her sister Fatma and we proposed that she be responsible for the Sisters division but she insisted that we call it the Muslim Sisterhood and we said to her: we are the Muslim Brotherhood and the society will remain as such and there will be a division for the Sisters and you will be its head or responsible for it and she refused and she did not join the Brothers except in 1965.

('Abd el Hady 2011: 23)

It is important to note that when Zeinab el Ghazali joined the Brothers formally in 1965, it was not to dissolve her organisation into the Brotherhood. She was tried by the Nasserite regime on charges of planning to overthrow the regime and was subjected to the most inhumane forms of torture while imprisoned. She re-emerged later as the spiritual mentor of the Muslim Sisters in the 1970s.

The Muslim Sisters in action

During the 1940s, the Muslim Sisters were engaged in a number of different activities, ranging from attendance at religious lessons and lectures, da'wa, charity, education and fundraising. Farid Abd el Khalek recounts how El Bahi el Kholy,[3] who was responsible for the education/pedagogy section, used to give the lectures to the Muslim Sisters on doctrine, worship and spreading awareness of the true Islam. In addition to belief and ethics, the lectures also focused on building the right foundations for the family and for society at large, and on social dimensions of Islamic practice such as helping the poor, the collection of zakat and its legitimate means of distribution (Abd el Khalek 2011). The choice of curriculum material for the Muslim Sisters was clearly marked by a gendered perspective underpinned by a deep belief in patriarchal gender roles and division of labour. This is particularly so if compared with the curricula delivered to the Brothers, which tended to provide them with a much deeper engagement with Islamic jurisprudence (see Chapter 2). For such a rigorous Islamic education, the Muslim Sisters would have to, in the 1970s, turn to Al-Azhar University.

The Muslim Sisters began to spread the da'wa among women, travelling from one governorate to another to establish new branches for the Muslim Sisters. In 1948, they established and oversaw a school for girl orphans called the Islamic Education Institute for Girls and pursued other activities such as nurseries, outpatient clinics, extension of charity to poor families, etc. (Khayal and El Gohary 1993: 234). Within the Brotherhood, gender segregation was observed and premises were vacated for the Muslim Sisters during their activities. Internally, the Muslim Sisters division played another critically important role: helping the Muslim Brothers find partners among the Muslim Sisters. Fatma 'Abd el Hady recounts the following:

> The Brothers used to approach Mahmoud el Gohary asking him to find him the suitable wife from among the Muslim Sisters division. I would ask Mr Gohary for information about this Brother and I would nominate the right sister for him.
>
> ('Abd el Hady 2011: 39)

At its peak in 1948 the Muslim Sisters had 150 branches across the country and an estimated membership of 5,000 members (Khayal and Gohary 1993; Zaki 1990).

Through their da'wa, the Muslim Sisters called upon women to don the proper Islamic attire. 'Abd el Hady recounts the following da'wa strategy:

> We in the Muslim Sisters division gave much importance to resisting the wave of nakedness[4] that had struck some sections of the Egyptian society especially in the city. This wave had led to the spread of the fashion of dressing in short clothes among girls and women and the performance of 'badat such as prayer was not of the common matters in this young generation, only the elders observed it. I remember one of the memorable stories from this period was that I used to advise the Sisters to take a pin with them and if they were taking [public] transport and they saw a girl or lady exposed[5] they would prick her in her exposed [part of] body then apologize to her and take the opportunity to open conversation through which they would relay a message about modesty and wearing the Islamic attire and many times this was the first step along the path of attracting them to the Muslim Sisters' Da'wa.
>
> ('Abd el Hady 2011: 37)

The attire of the Muslim Sisters was a plain headscarf, covering the hair, and tied around the neck and long loose clothing, often distinguished by a long jacket (or coat). Despite the fact that it was not a full veil, even then in a context in which women in the towns and cities were not covering their hair at all and wearing clothes at or above the knees, the Muslim Sisters 'stuck out'. Farid Abd el Khalek recounts that back in the 1940s there was not such a fuss about the length of the veil, or the extent to which it hid or exposed strands of hair nor any of the highly superficial debates around veiling in contemporary Egypt today. El Banna however was clear that in terms of revealing the face and the hands, 'if she felt safe from causing sedition, this is permissible for her and if not, then it is religiously prohibited (haram)' (Ashour 1999: 336).

The Muslim Brotherhood shaping the nation's gender agenda in the liberal era (1930s–1940s)

From the 1930s onwards, the Muslin Brotherhood used *Al Nazir* and *Al Muslimun* as a platform to promote women's veiling in particular in the 1940s when many women were removing the head cover, a trend that the Brotherhood characterised as a conspicuous form of *tabarojj* and *sofour*. At that time, the debate about whether veiling is necessarily required by Islam was alive, and it was particularly distressing for Muslim Brotherhood members such as Sheikh ali Tantawi at the time to find themselves in a situation where they do have to draw evidence in support of their arguments about the necessity of veiling (*Al Ikhwan al muslimeen*, Issue 58, 3 May 1945, pp. 5–6, in Amin 2006b: 190). In the light of the appearance of more and more women in public space unveiled, the Muslim Brotherhood advocated a more active role for the Morals Police against what they saw as conspicuous manifestations of public immodesty (Amin 2006a: 191) Moreover, they stood behind Mohammed Korany, an MP who advocated the issuance of legislation for the regulation of women's attire, and sent many letters of support to the constitutional committee in parliament in favour of this proposal (Amin 2006a: 153–154; Amin 2005d: 189). They urged the newly established ministry of social affairs to take measures to preserve social mores and values by playing a more active role in fighting these displays of immorality (Amin 2006a: 192).

The Brotherhood initiated many campaigns against co-ed education. Education they argued should be limited to what is compatible with their nature and their future roles as mothers and wives, and education which involved gender mixing was seen as a source of moral decadence. They openly supported Mohammed Al 'Ashmawy Pasha's demand for the establishment of a private university for women, rather than to allow them access to that of men (*Al Ikhwan al muslimeen*, Issue 37, 17 June 1944, p. 2, in 'Abd el Aziz 2006: 211). One of the strategies adopted in the campaign against gender mixing was to shame public leaders, politicians, officers and members of the Islamic religious establishment who attended parties where mixing of the sexes took place. Consequently when one of the sheikhs of Al-Azhar and Sheikh Mustapha 'Abd al Razik, minister of endowments, attended a party hosted by famous feminist Huda Sharawi, a party where 'there was a mixing of Muslim girls and women with their non-Muslim counterparts, foreigners with non-foreigners, unveiled women mixing with men' (Abd al aziz 2006: 204), the Brotherhood wrote to the king to condemn the actions of Islamic scholars, and called for the preservation of their dignity, and that of Islam and the Ummah. In the Muslim Brotherhood's sixth conference in 1941, the recommendations tackled several measures associated with social reform. One of the recommendations was to 'resist immodesty (al tabarojj) and mixing between the sexes in education and in public societies, and to raise awareness to the extreme danger of this, and its deviance from the teachings of Islam and its corruption of society' (sixth conference, in 'Abd el Aziz 2006: 471). Moreover, they fiercely condemned women's entry into the workforce, deeming it as compromising their femininity, undermining their sacred domestic mission and competing with men for employment opportunities (Amin 2003a; Amin 2006a).

The decades of the 1920s, 1930s and 1940s were characterised by feminist activism to reform the Personal Status Law. The Muslim Brotherhood expressed their vehement opposition to a proposal to restrict polygamy on the premise that it would encourage men to engage in illicit sexual relations. They rejected a proposal by Mohammed Ali Alouba Pasha, minister of social affairs, that the ma'zoun not proceed with marrying a man already married except through court order and to allow a first wife to initiate divorce if the husband take on another wife. They also opposed any restriction on a man's right to divorce through registration in court. The argument given was that mediating divorce in courts would undermine women's dignity, marriages are best publicly proclaimed and celebrated, divorces are best discreetly and quietly initiated in order not to hurt women's feelings (*Al Ikhwan al muslimeen*, Issue 56, 4 April 1945, p. 20, in 'Abd el Aziz 2006: 155).

In 1948, the Muslim Brotherhood was dissolved as well as the Muslim Sisterhood. The next phase of the Muslim Sisters' agency in the 1950s and 1960s proved to be far more politically contentious than the earlier da'wa and charity work.

The Muslim Sisters: the power (and limitation) of backstage agency (1954–2011)

The Sisterhood rose to the task of distributing food to the malnourished Brothers in prison as well as being the lines of communication through which important messages and information were relayed. They collected money and distributed it to the female-headed households of the Brothers who were in prison or who had fled to Saudi Arabia and other countries. They were in one sense the powerhouse of the movement that prevented the members and their families from completely collapsing. Their activism was so essential for the survival of the movement that the Nasserite government imprisoned fifty Muslim Sisters. Fatma 'Abd el Hady herself was incarcerated on charges of collecting funds for the Muslim Brotherhood. The dissolution of the Muslim Sisters division in 1954 signified the death of the Sisterhood organisationally. The Muslim Sisters division never regained the same organisational strength and ambitious public role. When interviewed in 2006, members of the Muslim Brotherhood said they did not feel they needed a 'sisterhood' to represent their interests.

The Brothers who were released from prison bore great gratitude to the Muslim Sisters division for their role in sustaining their families during the great ordeal. There was great esteem for the women who were involved, but as the Brothers worked to revive the organisational structure of the movement, Zeinab el Ghazali, according to one account (Ahmed 2008), emerged as the new spiritual mother of the Muslim Sisters. El Ghazali thought to create a new cadre of women activists who would comprise the Muslim Sisters. However, towards the late 1980s, she began to retreat from extensive public engagement and she passed away in 1995. Except for some visible faces who are engaging in the political arena, there is no sense of the profile of the Muslim Sisters. Those who are politically active are usually the wives of key political actors in the movement, however they certainly do not represent the broad spectrum of Muslim Sisters.

In addition to her central importance to the Muslim Sisters, Zeinab el Ghazali had substantial power even if she was not given a formal leading position in the Guidance Bureau, for example. For many years, she wrote extensively in *Al Da'wa* on gender-related as well as governance issues. Moreover, while El Ghazali in and of herself was revered, her personal history epitomises the disconnect between professed ideology and individual agency. She divorced her first husband for 'interfering with her religious work, and agreed to remarry only under the condition that her second husband, an older man who was already married and therefore less demanding, recognize that her da'wa supersedes her marriage' (Cooke 2001: 101). Yet throughout her writings in *Al Da'wa* and elsewhere, El Ghazali called upon devout Muslim women to dedicate themselves first and foremost to the service of their husbands and children. She warns that it is only when women's first and most important mission towards raising children in accordance with proper Islamic values and when they have fulfilled all obligations towards their husbands that they can then consider da'wa (Cooke 2001: 91).

During the 1970s, Sadat's entente with the Islamists directly and indirectly increased the political influence of Wahabi-Salafi movements' impact on the Muslim Sisters. In the 1970s, the veil emerged as a symbol of Islamic identity in universities among women affiliated to the Muslim Brotherhood and other Islamist movements. It is highly significant that the Muslim Brotherhood led – and won – a campaign demanding that Sheikh al Azhar make Islamic attire (at that time deemed as a veil and long loose clothing) as mandatory dress for all the faculty and students studying at the University of Al-Azhar. The Brotherhood believed that in view of Al-Azhar University representing the bastion of Islamic teaching, all women who entered it must abide by Islamic teachings. The Brotherhood fiercely attacked feminists who objected that veiling should be by choice and not compulsory as an assault on Islam. The Brotherhood also fully endorsed one MP's proposed law to force all women who go out to work in state institutions to done the Islamic attire (Naf'e, *Al Da'wa*, March 1981: 24–25 and 'Ashmawy 1981: 47). A more subtle but equally impassioned campaign was initiated to universalise the donning of the veil by condemning those who show their hair as lacking in morals and deviant from their religion.

While Muslim Brotherhood women advocated the adoption of the veil among Egyptian women as they had done in the 1940s, many members of the other

Islamist movements believed that the Muslim Brotherhood women were not sufficiently covered. Abd el Khalek (2011: 14–15) and Tammam (2010: 14, 27) both argue that emphasis within the Muslim Brotherhood on women's attire and the donning of many of the niqab was a direct consequence of the spread of Wahabi' ideology from Saudi Arabia.

Concurrently, the 1970s also saw increasing pressure upon the government from feminist groups to reform the family law. Aisha Ratib, the minister of social affairs, as well as Gehan el Sadat, the First Lady, pushed for a new Personal Status Law which was issued through presidential decree no. 44 in 1979. The Brotherhood launched a campaign against the law, aligning itself with Al-Azhar in its opposition to the proposed legislation.[6] *Al Da'wa*, the Brotherhood's mouthpiece in the 1970s and 1980s, was used as a platform for leading Azhar scholars and other writers to voice their reservations to the law from a fiqh point of view. They rejected the requirement that a man notify his wife of divorce via court (rather than relying only on verbal proclamation of her being divorced) on grounds that it is not mandated in the Shari'a. They rejected that a woman may apply for divorce on grounds of having incurred harm from her husband taking up another wife, again, on the premise that there is nothing in jurisprudence to suggest that taking up another wife is necessarily going to harm the first. Moreover, they rejected the idea that a woman divorced by her husband can abide in their marital home while she raises the children on account that this imposes an unnecessary economic burden on the husband with no grounding in the Shari'a.[7]

The battle for qawamah[8] and against gender empowerment

In 1994, the International Conference for Population and Development (ICPD) was held in Cairo. The Muslim Brotherhood's political forces, as well as the new generation of Muslim Sisters, established alliances with a view to forming a bloc against the proposed reproductive health policies. Camillia Helmy, an engineer by training who is also the director of the International Islamic Committee for Woman and Child which is an affiliate of the International Islamic Relief Committee, as well as other Muslim Sisters formed a lobby with the pro-family right-wing American groups. In response to their activism in building a strong movement with Islamist and non-Islamist forces in opposing the ICPD agenda, Al-Azhar set up the International Islamic Committee for Woman and Child (IIC) as one of the committees of the International Islamic Council for Da'wa and Relief[9] headed by the Grand Imam Sheikh of Al-Azhar.[10] In 2003, the IIC gained consultative status to the UN, enabling it to participate in non-governmental and international events associated with women's issues. Camillia Helmy currently heads the ICC, indicating the strong presence of the Muslim Brotherhood close to the centres of powers in Al-Azhar. Other active members of the ICC include Hoda Abd el Moneim, a lawyer who currently holds a high ranking position in the Muslim Brotherhood's Freedom and Justice Party, and Manal Abu Hassan, a professor of media who put herself forward as a candidate for the women's quota seat in the 2010 parliamentary elections. Through the ICC, the Muslim Sisters have been active on two fronts: lobbying in international events to present the Muslim perspective on proposed agendas and campaigning against the use of international women's treaties as the basis for reforming national family legislation in Egypt and other Arab countries.

Hoda Abd el Moneim is one of the strong lobbyists against the application of the CEDAW and Child Conventions, on the premise that they are part of a universalising, hegemonic agenda against Islam. She sees the reforms in family legislations in Egypt and elsewhere as one manifestation of the negative impact of Egyptian government bowing to Western pressure.[11] The Muslim Brotherhood, the Wafd Party, Al-Azhar University and various other actors led a passionate campaign against the reform of Egypt's procedural Personal Status Law (no. 1 of the year 2000) to grant women more rights. Hoda Abd el Moneim argued that the law 'annulled man's role in qawamah' as exemplified in article 20, dubbed in the Egyptian context the 'khul' law'. Article 20 stipulates that a woman has the unilateral right to a divorce, if she cannot stand living with her husband (she declares that she hates him), on condition she forfeits all her financial rights and returns her mo'akhar. Khul' is based on a hadith (considered by the jurists as authentic) in which the Prophet Muhammed was approached by a woman who appealed to him that she could not stand her husband and feared that this may drive her not to be able to observe God's laws. The Prophet asked her to return the garden that her husband had given to her and be divorced. Law 1 stipulates that if the court fails to convince the woman to return to her husband, she is to be granted a divorce. Abd el Moneim argues that the fact that the khul' is determined by the judge negates the agency of the husband, which is against the principle of qawamah. The Brothers advocate that a woman should only be allowed to pursue khul' with her husband's permission, which is required by all four schools of fiqh. Abd el Moneim argued that there is no need for khul' in the first place, given that a woman may appeal for a divorce on condition of harm.

Against the laws from the West

In 2000, the Brothers also objected vehemently to the annulment of a ministerial decree which required women to obtain the permission of their husbands to travel. There is a consensus among the jursists, argued Abd el Moneim, that travelling without permission is prohibited in accordance with the Shari'a and with the principle of qawamah. She refers to when the Prophet was asked regarding the rights of a husband over his wife, and he said 'Listen and obey' (al sam' wal ta'a).

Abd el Moneim was critical of the law for raising the age of a mother's custody of children to fifteen years of age for boys and girls (with the possibility of extending it for the latter until she marries). Abd el Moneim, Ismail and others argued that this was in violation of the Shari'a, which stipulated that boys remain with the mother until nine and girls until twelve. She argued that while such a change seems in favour of the mother, it is detrimental to the children, who need the authority of their father as they get older. She argued that in this day and age, when children are exposed to so many moral temptations, fathers will be capable of being more stern than mothers. Other objections to the law include allowing the divorcee to the right to the residential home while she is raising the children, the new condition that requires men to register their divorce (rather than rely on vocally telling their wives they are divorced).

The gender dimensions of the Child Law of 2008 also came under fierce attack by the ICC and the Muslim Brotherhood MPs in parliament. In 2008, the Muslim Brotherhood objected to twenty-four of the proposed revisions to the Child Law no. 12 issued in 1966 and the normative framework to which it refers. Farid Ismail, a Muslim Brotherhood MP and member of the health committee in parliament, argued that the proposed legislation is in conformity with the resolutions of the international women's conferences (Beijing and Cairo) and aims to undermine the family in the Arab and Islamic cultures, seeking to bring them down to the state of families in the West (Wagdy Islamonline 2008). The purpose of the law, argued Manal Abou el Hassan, candidate for the parliamentary elections of 2010 and a professor of media studies, is to make Egyptian law comply with international conventions and treaties (Child Convention and CEDAW), which are at odds with the normative values of Egyptian society and modern science (Hamdy 2008). Hazem Farouk, an Muslim Brotherhood MP, argued that USAID is behind the law, and that:

> we are now faced with two projects, one is the Islamic civilization project emanating from our values and authentic traditions and the other a western one that issues legislation in conflict with our culture and permits freedom in all things to children and homosexuals and makes women equal with men in all things.

(Hamdy 2008)

Ismail identified five articles in particular that are particularly harmful to Egyptian Muslim society. These include the article that raises the legal marriage for girls to eighteen, which he argued is in violation of the Shari'a as the only age criteria for marriage is reaching puberty. Since people reach puberty at different ages, it is unacceptable to set an age to be applied universally, he argued, warning that the impact of setting the age of marriage so high is to encourage sexual promiscuity and 'urfi[12] marriages.

Ismail and other Muslim Brotherhood MPs objected to mandatory medical tests as a requirement for marriage, and said that while there is nothing in Shari'a to prohibit having medical tests, nevertheless, since it should not be made a requirement. The Muslim Brotherhood also expressed its objection to the criminalisation of female circumcision which they said has no basis in the Shari'a. Ismail argued that it is permissible (according to the Shari'a) to circumcise one's daughter 'and the decision is up to the guardian and the doctor who decides on the extent to which the girl needs this operation'.[13] The Muslim Brotherhood MPs are in favour of 'organising' circumcision but they are not in favour of its criminalisation, arguing that 'the article imposes a prison penalty for whoever circumcises [a girl] and we are in favour of the matter being left for choice and does not reach the point of criminalization' (Hamdy 2008). The Brotherhood objected to the right of the child to report corporal punishment including that initiated by the parents. Ismail pointed out that raising children requires disciplining them, referring to a hadith by the Prophet in which he says 'Play with them in the first seven years, hit them in the next seven years and befriend them in the seven after that and then let them go to live life' (Hamdy 2008). The fifth article in the Law which was opposed is the right of the mother to give her name to her child, in the case where the child is illegitimate. Apart from being in contradiction with the Shari'a, this they said will encourage adultery.

The parliamentary session on 7 June 2008 saw a heated confrontation between the Muslim Brotherhood bloc and the government and NDP, in which what was at stake were not only the articles of the law but Egypt's very identity. While the government defended the law as being compatible with the Shari'a, the Brothers insisted it wasn't. The government insisted it can draw on international conventions to which it is signatory in guiding the formulation of the law, while the Brothers insisted these are the very instruments aimed at destroying Muslim families and society at large.[14]

The minister of culture and the veil saga

Few gender-related issues sparked such intense reactions among parliamentarians since the khul' as what became known as the minister of culture veiling saga. In November 2006, Farouk Hosni, the minister of culture, made an unofficial statement in an off-the-record conversation with a journalist in which he said: 'Women with their beautiful hair are like roses that should not be covered or veiled from people' (El Dakhany 2006). He added: 'Religion now is more about appearances only, despite the fact that a faith-based relationship between a servant and his Lord is not related to attire' (El Dakhany 2006). He reminisced about an Egypt where mothers went out to university and to work without wearing the veil and asked rhetorically why Egypt is going backwards. The minister commented that many crimes today are committed by those donning the veil and the niqab. He said that while the world was moving forwards, 'we will not progress as long as we think in a backward way and go to listen to sheikhs' fatwas worth three milliems [pennies]'. In his controversial interview he mentioned Arab countries such as Bahrain and Qatar where women are starting to remove the face veil (niqab) while in Egypt people are taking it up. The statement caused a furore and many politicians called for an immediate apology. Hosni never did. However, he sought to defend himself in parliament by insisting that the remarks represented no more than a personal opinion given in an informal conversation and in no way reflect the policy of the government or his ministry, where large numbers of women don the veil.

The Brotherhood, together with some members of the ruling National Democratic Party and independent MPs such as Mustapha Bakry, insisted that either the minister of culture resign or the head of Al-Azhar should resign for accepting the assaults waged against the sheikhs in such a manner. A deluge of articles followed, insisting that the veil is a fareeda (religious obligation).[15] The Brotherhood and other Islamist forces mobilised their female members to lead several massive protests in the streets to express their anger at Farouk Hosni's remarks and demand his removal. While the Brotherhood used a rights discourse to defend the rights of women to wear the veil in parliament,[16] the political battle was not about women's choice to wear the veil (which the minister did not challenge) but it was about the choice of influential actors to voice an opinion on the veil that runs counter to the normative values of society, values which regard the veil as an unquestionable requirement of Islam and as symbolic of the Islamic identity.

Political agency

The role of female members of the Muslim Brotherhood in the national parliamentary elections has been instrumental for securing Muslim Brotherhood victories in national elections. It is the women members of the Muslim Brotherhood who have access to people via mosques (in particular the women's section of the mosques), the welfare organisations run by the movement and access to homes. One study indicates that the high turnout of veiled voters at women's polling stations creates common knowledge about the popularity of Islamist candidates in a particular district, and the presence of female activists cut down on the likelihood and effectiveness of government repression. The participation of Islamist women in the face of repression and hardship also serves as a powerful and politically motivating symbol for both male and female voters who are inclined towards the Muslim Brotherhood (Blaydes and Tarouti 2009: 365). During the 2005 elections, female supporters and members of the Muslim Brotherhood defied the state security harassment and the thugs hired by the National Democratic Party in order to reach the polls and vote for the Muslim Brotherhood. Women donned the regular veil instead of the more conservative forms of veiling they often wore (including the niqab and the khimar). They would flash NDP pamphlets and campaign material as they were approaching the voting polls to indicate that they were supporters of the ruling party. At instances when the NDP men blocked the entrance to the polling station, they climbed through windows (Rab'e 2005).

In 2000, for the first time, the Brotherhood fielded one female candidate, Jehan al Hallafawy, who ran in the electoral district of El Raml in Alexandria (Al Hallafawy is the wife of prominent Muslim Brotherhood leader Ibrahim el Za'farany, who, in April 2011, resigned from the movement and formed his own party). She was subject to much security harassment and lost due to vote rigging. In 2005, the Brotherhood fielded one female candidate, Makarem el Deiry, a professor at Al-Azhar university, born in 1950 (whose husband was killed by the regime in 1965). El Deiry was fielded in the middle-class district of Madinet Nasr, and did well in the elections, scoring 6,000 voices, qualifying her to the second rounds of elections. Her main competitor, the ruling party's NDP candidate, businessman Moustapha El Sellab, won 9,000 votes (Sadaqa 2005). She lost and appealed against the results of the elections on the basis that there was vote rigging. The Brotherhood's fielding of a woman was to defy the public image that they were against women's nomination to political office. The fact that only one woman out of many candidates was fielded is not unique to the Muslim Brotherhood, other political parties did not fare much better, including the progressive leftist Tagammu Party. El Deiry said that many potential female candidates were hindered from participating in the elections because their husbands prohibited them on grounds of safety and security precautions. El Deiry, on the other hand, claims she was able to participate because her children 'permitted' her to do so.

While the Brethren were mobilising political support for Makarem el Deiry, convincing voters she would be the best candidate to represent them in parliament, Muslim Brotherhood supporters of Muslim Brotherhood candidate Mohammed Abd el Megeed Dessouky were distributing pamphlets in Toukh, Al Qalubiyya warning people that electing a woman to parliament would be in violation of Islamic law. They argued that the nomination of Gamalat Rafe', a woman, 'is null and void'. Their campaign drew heavily on the hadith 'a people cannot succeed if led by a woman'. In response Gamalat responded by also distributing pamphlets and other material highlighting how they are condemning women's representation while promoting a female candidate in the Madinet Nasr electorate district and making reference to a Koranic verse damning those who say what they do not know, and finally reciting Sheikh el Azhar's fatwa allowing women's representation in parliament. In the first round, Dessouky was ahead of her by 4,000 votes, however, in the second and final round she was ahead of him by 8,400 votes (27,400 votes in comparison to 19,000) ('Abd el Meguid 2005).

In view of the greater opportunities for political apprenticeship and leadership for Muslim Brotherhood women within the community compared to their counterparts in other political parties and forces, the pool of women who can potentially run for office, backed by a substantial constituency, is greater and, accordingly, the fact that so few are fielded by the Muslim Brotherhood is significant. It means that activist members have not been voicing a demand to assume leadership positions or that they have not collectively mobilised around this (the latter is the view expressed by El Deiry).

In 2009, the Egyptian parliament passed a new women's quota law setting sixty-four additional seats for women to the 454-seat parliament. While a quota was one of the main demands high on Egyptian feminists' agenda for women's equality, nevertheless many criticised the terms and design of the new legislation, which was clearly tailored to win more seats for the ruling regime – as opposed to enhancing Egyptian women's opportunities of acquiring more equitable representation in politics. Yet the Muslim Brotherhood MPs position was a rejection of the quota not because it fails to deliver on an enabling environment for women's political empowerment, but because they reject the principle of affirmative action in the first place. Their stance was that affirmative action undermines the constitutional principle of equality of opportunity for all citizens and that if the forms of political repression and corruption prevalent in the system were addressed (reforming electoral law and practice, eliminating violence, thuggery and seeking to control vote purchase), this would in and of itself create an enabling environment for women's political accession of power.

In an informal interview with a leading member of the Brotherhood prior to the elections of 2010, in which a women's quota was applied for the first time, he said that the difficulty was not in finding qualified women but that few women wanted to run. The problem, he argued, is that in view of the security harassments of Muslim Brotherhood candidates by the government, fielding a woman carries certain risks. A husband's or family's permission to allow women to field the elections is absolutely necessary if the Muslim Brotherhood were to extend support to a woman candidate, however, in view of the hardships entailed, such support is not always possible to secure. The fact that support for women candidates is conditional upon a husband's consent indicates the way in which the concept of qawamah at home has resonance on the ground.

In 2010, the Brotherhood fielded three candidates under the quota system, Manal Abou Hassan in Cairo and Manal Ismail and Bushra Al Samny in Alexandria. They did not win the elections but then none of the women candidates except those from the ruling National Democratic Party were able to win any seats!

The 2011 November parliamentary elections will be a real litmus test as to whether the Muslim Brotherhood will field more women: there is no longer an inhibitive political environment and there are is shortage of women candidates.

Post-Mubarak Egypt: reimagining women's agency?

While women in general participated fully in the revolution, male-biased accounts of the activism that instigated and sustained the revolt against the regime until the ouster of Mubarak have generally tended to ignore women's full agency. Where women have been most recognised in the public discourse has been in their capacity as 'mothers of martyrs', a role that sits comfortably with the patriarchal status quo. In Tahrir Square, women members of the Muslim Brotherhood joined the protests in the latter days, however, they always featured as participants, never leaders on the stage, which can be contrasted with leftist forces where women stood on the stage and addressed the public.

Moreover, although the revolution made known to us the names of Muslim Brotherhood youth who assumed leadership positions, there were no publicly recognised Muslim Brotherhood women youth leaders. This represents a significant gap in our knowledge of Muslim Brotherhood women's agency during the uprisings and in the millioniyyas that followed the demise of Mubarak. It may also reflect the bias in Brotherhood preference for delegating leadership positions to women who are older, whose children have grown, rather than young unmarried women or those with children.

However, there is evidence that many female members of the Muslim Brotherhood began to openly voice their desire for a greater recognition on the part of the leadership of their role. At a Muslim Brotherhood youth meeting in April

2011 attended by around 1,500 youth the issues around the movement's organisational structures were raised, including the necessity of establishing an organisational structure of the Sisters of the Brotherhood. Shortly afterwards, on 2 July, a conference was organised specifically on the theme 'Women from the revolution to renaissance'. This high level conference was attended by the Supreme Guide, Bad'i, Khayrat al Shatter, the deputy Guide, members of the Guidance Bureau, key actors and some 2,500 sisters. Bad'i praised the role played by women in the revolution as activists, mothers, sisters and wives of the protestors and started by paying tribute to the mothers of martyrs. The conference was a grand event without offering any major structural change either in relation to broadening their roles or their positioning in the Muslim Brotherhood internal organisational hierarchy. The discourse could have easily been that of the Brotherhood in Mubarak's Egypt. The recommendations spoke of enhancing women's political representation in syndicates, political parties and activism through NGOs, and raising women's awareness of the conspiracies aimed at undermining the family (presumably international actors plus local feminist organisations) ('Abd el Hafeez 2011).

This post-Mubarak period presents an opportunity to test the hypothesis that if the Muslim Brotherhood were not subjected to government repression, the justification for not rewarding capable women with more leadership opportunities within the organisation and in politics would not be so complacently accepted. In the absence of a political pretext to absolve the Brotherhood of their responsibility towards activist women, their real commitment to women assuming political leadership would be tested. So far, the response has been one of increased activities for the Muslim Sisters (such as meetings and camps) but no openings in formal leadership positions (either in the shura council or the Supreme Guide or even on a lower administrative level of the mainstream movement). It has also been characterised by a discourse very reminiscent of patriarchal post-independence forces, which urge that women's issues be delayed until the pressing priorities of building the foundations of a new socio-political order be laid For example, at the conference, Camillia Helmy advised the Muslim Sisters to apply fiqh al awlawiyyat (Qaradawy's jurisprudence of priorities) by prioritising home and children, and if there are no shortcomings in fulfilling this role, and there is a need in public life for a woman's capabilities and experience, then a woman should act accordingly, not so that she can benefit but so that she can be of benefit ('Abd el Hafeez 2011).

It is important to note that many of the rank and file do consider that the Muslim Sisters have an important role to play but they believe it is ultimately as homemakers and not as agents of political change. 'Abd el Latif's observation of the hegemonic prevalence of male resistance to women's full political and social agency, made in the Mubarak era, still stands today. 'Abd el Latif observes:

> The conservative view that women can best serve the cause through their traditional roles as mothers and wives but not as political actors or peers in the movement. Consequently efforts to expand the role of the Sister activists

in movement structures and political activities meet determined resistance, particularly from members living outside the capital. This conservative culture is being challenged to some extent by the younger generation of Brothers in the cities, but this group is a minority. Although they receive some encouragement from the reform-minded wing of the Brotherhood, they are frustrated. It appears that the majority of rank and file of both sexes hold a very conservative view of women's roles in the public sphere.

('Abd el Latif 2008: 14)

Such restrictions are not limited to the realm of political leadership but personal life choices as well. Sobhi Saleh, a lawyer and former MP said in a press conference in May 2011 that Muslim Brothers should only marry women from within the movement, and that they should not settle for less when they can have the best, referring to the group's female members. He explained that when a couple raised within the group get married, their children would adopt the group's ideology by inherence which would fortify the Brotherhood and their message in society. His comments provoked strong reactions from the liberal sections of society, and two lawyers filed a lawsuit against him on account of besmirching Islam's image in particular since Muslim men are allowed to marry Christian and Jewish women (Al-A'sar 2011).

However, while the Brotherhood said the views represent those of Saleh and not the movement, it seems that the pressure on marriage from within the movement is not a case of Sobhi Saleh propagating some outrageous idea. Fatma 'Abd el Hady in her autobiography proudly mentions the role of the Sisters in helping Muslim Brothers find the right partners, but she comments 'it was not a requirement that a Muslim Brother marry a Muslim sister as is the case today, there was not this rigidity' (2011: 40).

Noteworthy are issues of power, representation and voice which have been discussed in a highly conservative political environment towards women – even in the current revolutionary transitional period. It is a context in which the Islamisation of normative values had been promoted by the Islamists and the Egyptian government. While gains were being made on the legal front, in many respects, the normative values in society had become more conservative and the spaces for autonomous progressive women's agency had become more restrictive than they were.

Egypt faces one of the worst backlashes against women's rights in its contemporary history. A number of actors and factors have contributed to this, most notably the rise to power of the armed forces, the transitional government and the Islamist forces. All three hold highly patriarchal, gender-biased agendas. During the months following the ousting of President Mubarak, a number of laws and policies have been under attack. Like many other political forces, including liberal ones such as the youth coalitions, the Muslim Brotherhood called upon SCAF (Supreme Council for Armed Forces) and the government to annul the women's quota – and their request was granted. While the quota was controversial, it was expected that some other form of affirmative action would be instituted to recognise the gender gap in political representation, however, this was not the case.

The Muslim Sisters' advocacy work against the CEDAW and in favour of the repeal of Egypt's family laws was stepped up after the revolution, and they have sympathetic supporters among Egypt's leading Islamic Institution, Al-Azhar University. Opposition to women's empowerment agenda serves as a platform for unifying the Islamist forces. For example, the International Islamic Union of Muslim Scholars formed a committee comprised of all the Islamic waves in Egypt to promote cooperation among them. One matter upon which they reached agreement in the conference was to call upon Islamic countries to rethink their endorsement of the CEDAW and the Child's Convention and to revisit the family laws so as to address all matters that are in violation of the Shari'a. The conference called for the endorsement of the Islamic Charter of the Family and that of the Child that were issued by the International Islamic Committee on Woman and Child, so that it can become universalised ('Abd el Sallam 2011). A number of conferences, workshops and articles on Ikhwan online have been initiated in order to call for the repeal of what they dubbed 'Suzanne's Laws' (in particular the Personal Status Law and the Child Law), and for Egypt's abdication of its commitment to the CEDAW and other international treaties on women's rights (including the Beijing Platform). They called upon the armed forces to resist any UN pressure upon it to concede to women's empowerment agendas and criticised women's rights organisations as being no more than agents of the UN. Moreover, there was a call to remove all reference to international treaties as a reference for the development of family legislation and to rely instead on frameworks such as the Family Charter ('Abd el Hafeez and Ibrahim 2011).

So far, they have had some success. In July 2011, Al-Azhar recommended the repeal of the right of the mother to have guardianship over her children's education on account of its violation of the Shari'a.

In conclusion

It cannot be emphasised enough that the Muslim Sisters was established as a division and not an autonomous sisterhood. It was envisioned to be the helping hand of the Brotherhood and never a movement serving to advance the rights or interests of Muslim women per se. In that sense, it is as far as can be from an Islamic organisation intended to advance women's rights through an Islamic framework. Rather, it is an organisation intended to advance the Muslim Brotherhood's mission through women's agency. This is key to understanding several important dimensions of how women's agency plays out in the movement. First, it explains the lack of women occupying formal political leadership roles in the movement. Where women have any influence on the internal centres of decision-making powers, it has been through the exercise of informal power, rather than in any formal leadership capacity. Second, it explains the absence of women's roles in the development of the movement's religious and political thought. The

Sisters continue to function rigid patriarchal gender division of roles and identities and this has been reflected in the kind of pedagogy they have been exposed to. The content and scope of their instruction does not lay a foundation from which they can develop and grow to be faqihat or religious leaders. Third, because the Muslim Sisters are expected to be completely subservient and compliant to the Muslim Brotherhood leadership, one which has been very conservative throughout most of its eighty-year history, the women who emerge as leaders tend to espouse the same ideology. Moreover, in all of the cases that were encountered throughout this research, they happened to be the wives, daughters or sisters of renowned political actors in the movement. They also all happened to be in their senior years, relatively speaking (forties onwards).

It is noteworthy that, as compliant as the Muslim Sisters division has been to the Brotherhood, women's agency continues to manifest itself in highly complex and fluid ways. Women call upon other female members of the movement to dedicate themselves to their domestic mission, yet they themselves take on highly sensitive political roles in public life. As with many other conservative religious movements, there is a tension with respect to the role of Muslim Sisterhood members as proselytisers and home-makers. This tension is evident in the lives and writings of prominent members of the Muslim Sisterhood in terms of what they preach and what they do.

Engaging with the Muslim Sisters as a division of the Brotherhood and not as an autonomous movement of religious women is also important for understanding where the possibilities of coalitions and alliance work lie. Secular feminist actors who wish to partner with the Muslim Sisters to benefit from the latter's constituency may need to be reminded that the Muslim Sisters view their agency as promoting a higher good: the establishment of an Islamic state and not for the sake of achieving their full potential as individual women. In terms of ideological disposition and overall goals, it is likely that the points of convergence between the Muslim Sisters and the female members of the Salafi movement are likely to be far greater than those between them and the liberal feminist movements.

The position and standing of the Muslim Sisters within the movement will face a number of critical tests in the next phase. First is the question of whether the by-laws of the Muslim Sisters will change so that it is no longer a division but a fully fledged organisational structure. Second is whether the Muslim Brotherhood will choose to vote in the Sisters as members of the influential shura council and the power centre: the Guidance Bureau. Third is whether the voices of young Muslim Sisters will become more heard in the public arena. These issues are being discussed in an internal context full of challenges. The leadership is highly conservative and so are the rank and file. The voices of the 'progressives' are few and far between whether among women or men. It will be much easier to create these spaces in the Brotherhood's Freedom and Justice Party than within the internal organisational hierarchy of the movement.

The fact that the government's repression of the Muslim Brotherhood can no longer serve as a justification for protecting the Muslim Sisters from the wiles of the security apparatus means that there will be pressure on the Brotherhood to show their commitment to women on two important fronts: nominating them in the parliamentary elections and granting them greater visibility in the public sphere.

Where the Sisters' agency is likely to thrive is in da'wa and in national and international advocacy work against women's empowerment. It is expected that in the next phase the Muslim Brotherhood (including the Sisters) will step up their campaign to revoke all laws that were passed which granted women a modicum of rights. This is very much in tune with the historical role that the Muslim Brotherhood have played: they have consistently attacked and opposed any law put forward that sought to redress gender inequality whether it be in the political sphere (against all forms of affirmative action) or social (against all legislation that grants women more rights in marriage, divorce or custody) or economic (enhancing women's mobility by removing the restrictions on her travel with her husband's, father's or brother's permission). Historically and to the present day, the Brotherhood have consistently advocated against policies, practices and laws that would enlarge women's choices, spheres of influence or spaces.

Moreover, the Brotherhood have not only opposed the introduction of legislation that would redress some elements of inequality, they have also supported the introduction of laws, policies and decrees that would restrict women's choices such as the support shown in the 1970s for the enforcement of mandatory Islamic attire for women attending Al-Azhar University. Some of the ideological premises for endorsing such positions and policies as featuring in Muslim Brotherhood's political thought are addressed in the next chapter.

8 The gender agenda
Reformed or reframed?

The previous chapter discussed women's agency manifest within the Brotherhood and in wider society. It also discussed the way the Brotherhood shaped and responded to changing power relations in society, politics and government from the 1930s up to the period following the demise of Mubarak. This chapter traces the development of the Muslim Brotherhood's political thought on gender issues, with a focus on matters that have been raised in the movement's scholarship and official stances. These include gender identities and roles, marital relations, education and work, political leadership and sexual politics.

In discussing the Muslim Brotherhood's political thought, the work of three key actors bear much influence: the Supreme Guide Hassan El Banna, Youssef El Qaradawy and Mustapha el Seba'i whose book *Woman between Jurisprudence and Law* became a main textbook taught in the Brotherhood's curricula and a key reference in many of the brothers' writings on the subject. El Bahi el Kholy who taught the Muslim Sisters in the 1940s wrote *Islam and Women's Contemporary Issues*, which became a critical milestone in affirming the Brotherhood's thinking on gender roles and missions, but also allowing some space for rethinking the parameters of women's activism outside the home. The work of Sheikh Mohammed el Ghazaly has also been highly influential on Muslim Brotherhood political thought on gender matters.

Abd el Halim Abou Shouka, who spent more than twenty years studying the subject and produced the phenomenally sized encyclopedia on 'the liberation of women in the age of the message [resala]' is one of the key thinkers, although his work has had more resonance in the study of scholarship than in the political thought influencing policy. Many other Muslim Brotherhood members such as Farid Abd el Khalek (who also gave the Muslim Sisters lectures in the 1940s) Salem el-Bahnasawy, Sheikh Mohammed el Khattib (the Muslim Brotherhood's Mufti) and Tawfik el Wa'i have all had their imprints on relating fiqh on women's issues to the political vision of state and governance of the movement.

The chapter concludes by reflecting on the extent to which the official stances have deviated from the political thought of its key scholars, and the extent to which the gender agenda has been reformed.

Gender status and roles: different nature, different mission

Hassan El Banna highlighted his views on the position and role of Muslim women in a rare article published in 1940 titled 'resalet al mar'a al muslima' addressing the members of the Muslim Brotherhood. The basis for writing the *resala*, explained El Banna, is the need to remind believers of the decrees of Islam on women's role in society in the light of what he saw as the Muslim world's bid to emulate the West, a quest which has led them to seek ways of conforming the decrees of Islam to European orders and ways. 'In reality, this country [Egypt] and other Islamic countries have come under the shadow of a revolutionary and vicious wave', he wrote, explaining that this wave is 'the love of emulating Europe and immersing itself in it right to the chin' (1980: 4). He reflected that those that wish to be like the Europeans have not stopped there, 'but they try to deceive themselves by twisting the laws of Islam according to their Western liking and European orders/systems and to take advantage of the leniency of this religion [Islam] and the flexibility of its laws' (1980: 5). According to El Banna, such manipulation of Islamic texts

> totally removes these laws from its Islamic form and transforms [these laws] into other orders/systems that have nothing to do with it [Islam] under any circumstance. They totally ignore the spirit of Islamic jurisprudence [and they also ignore] many of the texts that do not agree with their liking.
>
> (1980: 5)

Hassan El Banna saw this is as doubly dangerous since it is not enough for them to deviate but that

> they try to find legal justification for this and they try to cover it up with pretense of it being *halal* and permissible. ... What is important now is that we examine the decrees of Islam with a view devoid of our personal inclinations, and prepare ourselves to accept Allah's orders especially in this matter which is crucial for our contemporary renaissance.
>
> (1980: 6)

El Banna broached issues that were the subject of intense debate at the time of the formation and spread of the Brotherhood: women's entry into tertiary education to study sciences and humanities, gender segregation being challenged, and increased visibility of women in public, urban space. Hassan El Banna made three principle arguments in his article, the first relating to women's status in Islam, the second addresses the religious premise behind the division of gender roles according to sex, and the third, the attraction between the opposite sexes and its role in preserving the complementarity in roles between men and women according to their sex. The first point relating to Islam's valuation of women is briefly broached in one paragraph. Hassan El Banna affirmed that Islam has elevated the status of woman, and recognises her as a partner to man in rights and duties. In the second point, he qualified the earlier statement by contending that the difference between man and woman in rights is attributable to their different biological natures and in accordance with the different roles assigned to each (1980: 7). This differentiation of roles according to sex, he affirms, is also for the maintenance of the rights granted to each. He suggested that where men were given more rights, women were compensated for this in other areas. He emphasised that this division of roles is derived from their biological natures.

Today, the ideas on gender roles espoused by the Muslim Brotherhood in relation to gender issues took a different framing to that of El Banna's rhetoric. However, the essence of the message vis-à-vis gender roles bears a striking resemblance to Hassan El Banna's exaltation of women's role as mothers and wives, especially in terms of a reference to the 'noble task' and 'noble mission' and in its presentation of the domestic realm as a sanctuary where she exercises her lordship and power. For example, the Muslim Brotherhood's election platform of 2006 states that:

> We must not forget that the woman has a noble and significant task entrusted to her by Allah Almighty, child-bearing and motherhood. A man cannot undertake this most noble of tasks, which is being denigrated today by some; furthermore the human race itself would disappear in the absence of this process. Moreover, it is the mother that suckles the baby with her milk, giving out of care, nurturing the child, the effects of which remain with him throughout his life. The woman is also the mistress of the house (*rabat al bayt*) and it is her task to care for the family and prepare the home as a place of comfort; her role is a huge responsibility and noble mission that must not be in any way neglected or underestimated.

The draft political party platform argues that while the Muslim Brotherhood recognise women's full equality with men in their humanity, nonetheless, there needs to be an emphasis on

> the importance of preserving the distinction between them in social and human roles, without this affecting the status of each of them. The role of women in the family is founded on the premise that she holds the primary/ main responsibility for raising the new generation … consequently we believe in the importance of finding balance in the roles of women and reviving her role in the family and public life without imposing on her duties which conflict with her nature or with her role in the family. We believe that the roles that women [should] espouse are an outcome of a social consensus built on the Islamic civilizational terms of reference (marja'iyya).

(2007: 103)

Women's education

The first Egyptian women enrolled in Egypt's premier university, Fouad 1 University, in 1929 and by the 1930s they were to be found in virtually all disciplines in the university on an undergraduate and postgraduate level, in a co-education system (Badran 1995: 148–150).

El Banna made the argument, referring to hadiths and the work of Muslim jurists, that fathers and guardians are encouraged, and indeed required, to raise girls according to principles of virtue. However, El Banna is cautious to set the rules for women's education: 'The proper raising of women requires that he [guardian or father] teaches them what is indispensable for them according to the requirements of their mission' (1980: 9). El Banna makes a list of skills indispensable for women's mission: 'reading, writing, numeracy, religion and history of the righteous predecessors, men and women. In addition to housekeeping, health issues, and principles of pedagogy and all that a mother requires for home management and child care' (1980: 9–10).

He adamantly warned that it was a waste of time to educate women outside these areas, and it is far more profitable for women to spend their time on what is useful (1980: 10). Here, too, he described different types of education that are unnecessary for a woman's role, one which he is keen to define more clearly:

> A woman is not 'in need of any special technical education for she will discover very soon that a woman is first and last for the home ... teach a woman what she needs with respect to her duty and her role which God created her for: running a home and raising children ... a woman does not need to study in depth different languages, or rights and laws and it is suffice that she knows what common people do.'
>
> (1980: 10, 11)

He concluded with the following: 'we say teach a woman what she is in need of according to her mission and her job which God created her for: house keeping and child care'. El Banna's emphasis is not just on women's role as mothers, but on the need to recognise that this role lies *within* the home. In other words when he asserts that woman is first and last for home, it is not just an affirmation of her maternal responsibilities and mission, it is also intended to highlight that this entails her association with the household.

On the issue of women's education, the contemporary official Muslim Brotherhood's position is slightly more relaxed than that espoused by Hassan El Banna. El Banna had suggested women should only be exposed to educational subjects that are conducive to their roles as mothers and wives. Mohammed Habib insisted that women have the right to pursue whatever education they wish, even in subjects that have nothing to do with their domestic roles. On the other hand, the idea that women should receive special education to prepare them for their role as mothers and wives has not been abandoned.

El Bahi el Kholy and El Seba'i, both strong advocates of education being a *farida*, believe that girls and women should be given special education to equip them for their roles as mothers and wives. While both acknowledge the importance of religious education, they do not see women excelling in the highest echelons of education as being an end in itself. Rather appropriate education should be allowed with a view to supporting women's domestic missions (El Kholy 1984; El Seba'i 2003).

In the *Mubadara* of 1994, one of the reform measures that the Muslim Brotherhood advocate is incorporating into the current educational curriculum material that is appropriate for 'women's nature, role and needs'. It is not surprising, therefore, that the idea of educating women to be leaders is rejected as unnecessary. On education, there is no reference in the draft party platform to gender-specific education. In the section on education, there is reference to enhancing the role of the girl in society 'through additional distinctive educational programmes' (Party Platform 2007: 37). Based on the political thought of the Muslim Brotherhood thinkers discussed above, it is not difficult to guess what kind of educational programmes would be appropriate!

Gender mixing

In the early 1930s, women began to engage publicly in sports events and activities and even gained access to the beaches where they could swim and be seen openly (Badran 1995: 159). The expansion of women's education, mixing of the sexes and women's increasing visibility in the public space caused intense reactions from conservative quarters and the rising tide of Islamists, particularly in the 1930s, yet feminists continued to advocate for women's emancipation, and they insisted that it is perfectly in accordance with religious values and precepts (Badran 1995: 159–163).

Women's entry into the public arena for other more worldly purposes is rejected by El Banna as anathema to Islam and its decrees:

> This fascistic[1] mingling of sexes among us in schools, institutes and public gatherings and their going out to places of entertainment, restaurants, parks … all of this is foreign goods which have absolutely no relation to Islam and has had the worst effects in our social life.
>
> (1980: 18)

El Banna explained why a Muslim society is one characterised by gender segregation, and why women's presence in the public sphere, except on certain exceptional occasions, is incompatible with the teachings of Islam. According to El Banna, Islam sees a real danger in the mixing between man and woman, 'for it divides between them except in the context of marriage' (1980: 11). 'Therefore Islamic society is a segregated not mixed society', he reiterates, contending that in Muslim societies that live in accordance with the precepts of Islam, 'Men have their gatherings and women theirs' (1980: 12). El Banna's objective is to refute the arguments made by those in favour of mixed societies, which he identifies as twofold: the first, the pleasure of being in the company of the opposite sex and the second, that it reduces the sexual desire between them since being in the company of the other becomes natural (1980: 11) However, any benefits incurring from women and men mixing, insists El Banna, are completely outweighed by the negative ramifications which he identifies as 'the loss of honour, a cunning inner self, corruption of souls, and breakdown of homes and the suffering of homes, and spread of crime'. Mixing also leads to 'a relaxation of morals, and the waning of manliness' (1980: 11–12).

El Banna argued that Islam allowed women to go out but under some very specific circumstances such as *shuhud al-'id* (shuhud al-'id refers to 'the permissibility of women's going out on 'id days towards the place of worship and their presence in the khutba (sitting) at a distance from men'. For further details, see the hadith as recounted in *Sahih Muslim* (Muslim n.d.: 418). Also women were allowed to go out to battle but 'it [islam] stopped at that' Under these exceptional conditions, El Banna defines the rules which women must comply with when outside the house. These include the necessity that women be covered, and not interact (or be present) with an *ajnabi* alone, etc. (an ajnabi man is 'distinguished from mahram, a man who cannot serve as the legal guardian of a woman; a marriageable person, according to Islamic law; any man to which the woman could potentially marry' (Abou el Fadl 2003: 299)). Even if a woman wants to leave the house to perform a religious duty, such as prayer, El Banna contends, with several *hadiths* to back his statement, that it is preferable for her to perform her prayers in the discretion of her own home.

In the 1990s, the Brotherhood advocated that gender segregation must be maintained at the voting polls and, if women were to be elected as MPs, in parliament as well:

> It is a duty to set aside election centres for women, which are already in effect in most Islamic countries. Women should be allocated special places in the representative councils so that there will be no fear of crowding or intermingling.
>
> (Muslim Brotherhood 2006)

In the light of the harassment that women are exposed to at overcrowded election polls in Egypt (although in recent elections such harassment was often perpetrated by government agents rather than the general population), it is understandable that calls for reserved areas for women in polls be made. However, given that women are highly unlikely to be exposed to any harassment inside parliament itself, the allocation of special places suggests that such a demand is not based on practical concerns, but on ideological grounds. The most liberal opinion expressed within the Muslim Brotherhood on the subject was given by Habib who suggested that while gender segregation in public life is no longer practical, nonetheless, it is still prohibited for a man and woman to be together alone (*kholwa*).

Work outside the home

Hassan El Banna was highly critical of women's work despite the fact that many of the Muslim Sisters were employed as headmistresses, nurses and government employees. El Banna refutes the argument that there is no Islamic text/verse to prohibit women from engaging in public works, arguing that just because there is no verse against hitting parents, it does not mean that it is permissible. El Banna recognised that under some 'social circumstances' a woman needs to go out to work, but if this occurs, he warned that, first, women must adhere to the conditions mentioned above (appropriate attire revealing only palms and face, etc.) and that it is a duty for her that her work be within the dire necessities, and 'not as a general rule/organization that it be for a woman to have a right to work in principle' (1980: 21).

The undesirability of women's work, in view of its encroachment on her supreme mission of household maker and nurturer, continues to be to this day a characteristic of many of the Brothers' political thought. El Khattib's fatwa affirms that the principle that 'women's work in itself is the exception and not the rule and what the Islamic society requires of woman in her home is many times more than what is needed of her outside home'. Interestingly, the Mufti's position was not substantiated by reference to any religious text, but by several social arguments. The first argument made is the hardship that women encounter in their journeys on public transport to and from work. Egyptian women commuting to work via public transport are susceptible to sexual harassment yet instead of demanding that appropriate action be taken to make the public space less hostile to women, the Muslim Brotherhood's Mufti suggests that this problem be addressed by women retracting to the private sphere. The second argument advanced by the Mufti is:

> if women's participation in the workforce is to share in relieving the cost of living for her family, this could be dealt with by increasing the wages of males so women's efforts can be saved for providing the comfort and excellent supervision over the internal affairs of her family and the moral, health, social and cultural upbringing of her children.
>
> (El Khattib 1977: 49)

The assumption implicit in this fatwa is that all households are male-headed households and that all men will channel any income earned to their households. Moreover, the responsibility of raising children seems to implicitly lie solely on the shoulders of women.

What is relevant here is the fatwa's response to the part of the question regarding being outside the home (fatwa in issue 9, February 1977). Sheikh Muhammad 'Abd Allah el Khattib in his fatwa stressed that 'women are not prohibited from going out to work if there is a need for it'. The concept that women's work should be in the strictest, most exceptional circumstances where dire need exists is stressed three times in the fatwa. The emphasis, like in the work of Hassan El Banna, is on women's role in the domestic sphere, one which is exonerated and exalted as the greatest contribution a woman can make for the sake of building a Muslim society. It is clear from the fatwa that a woman's role was determined primarily according to the Muslim Brotherhood's perception of what was needed for the establishment of a righteous Muslim society, not by her potential, talents or aptitude. Her role is predetermined for her by prescriptions of what is needed for building a righteous Muslim society. The establishment of a righteous Muslim society does not recognise a multiplicity of roles that women can espouse – only one is recognised and required: raising children according to a set of values and mores.

Other fatwas lay restrictions on the type of work women may be engaged in, and the terms of this engagement, in addition to appropriate modes of behaviour and attire for working outside the home. In case women are obliged by dire circumstances to be present in the public sphere, gender segregation is absolutely necessary, with clear resonances of Hassan El Banna's position. In response to a female Muslim research scholar that lamented the state of her generation's youth and their suffering from lack of values, etc., the fatwa issued in December 1978 (*Al Da'wa*) attributes the moral decay which is characteristic of their generation of youth to gender mixing. The mixing of the sexes was seen as an ill associated with many of the social problems of the time (see Chapter 7).

El Seba'i noted that there is no definitive text in Islam which prohibits women from working, however, the following Islamic principles must be complied with: that her job does not come in the way of her responsibilities at home; that it does not involve mixing with men and exposing what should not be exposed of her flesh; and that she be not found alone with one or more male employees. He added to this that in view of the scarcity of employment positions for men, women's employment in the state sector should be restricted:

> so that she is only hired in positions compatible with her mission and her nature like being a physician to other women, being a paediatrician, education in children's schools, in secondary schools for girls and similar work with a social leaning towards families.
>
> (2003: 135)

He argued that women should not be allowed to work unless they are poor and are not supported by their husband, father or relative until appropriate support is provided for them. Upon leaving for work, women should be appropriately dressed and laws should be implemented to punish the women who do not conform (2003: 136).[2]

Mohammed El Beltagui (2005: 245–246) adds to the list above the permission of the husband to work, not working in jobs entailing prohibitions in Islam such as maids in hotels (possibility of kholwa with men) and working in bars (serving alcohol) or hard arduous jobs incompatible with her nature. The permissibility of work if certain conditions were met has become the stance of the Brotherhood. While the official statement of January 2006 does not go specifically into the limitations and conditions of work outside the home, as is the case with Hassan El Banna's earlier message, nevertheless it reveals not only the undesirability of work for women, but also the need for regulating woman's work. A woman can work only if given permission by her husband. According to the statement:

These characteristics, duties and rights which have been allocated to women by Allah are in balance with the duties she has towards her husband and her children. These duties must be given precedence over other responsibilities and they are necessary for the stability of the family which is the basic cell of the society and the cause for its cohesion, strength, and efficiency. However, the husband has a right to permit his wife to work. This right is to be regulated by an agreement between the husband and the wife. Such rights should not be regulated by law and the authorities should not interfere with them except in some rare cases.

(Muslim Brotherhood 2006)

In other words, on a policy level, the Muslim Brotherhood is opposed to any constitutional guarantee of women's right to work as citizens. While the statement talks about the 'regulation' of a man's right to permit his wife to work through agreement between them, it is ultimately the man who has the right to allow or prohibit his wife from working. The draft party platform of 2007's discussion of the issue of women's roles and the question of work reflects more Mohammed Habib's framing of the argument in terms of complementarity of roles.

The 2007 platform argued that although women's role in the workforce was to be recognised, such a role had to 'balanced with the noble mission that a woman bears in her home and among her children for the sake of the uprightness of the first foundations of society' (2007: 103). The remaining paragraph, however, does not talk about complementarities between women's home and work roles, rather, it provides a typical Muslim Brotherhood justification for a woman's association with the domestic, premised on her biological nature and the division of roles deriving from it. The platform argues that while the Muslim Brotherhood recognises women's full equality with men in their humanity, nonetheless, there needs to be an emphasis on

the importance of preserving the distinction between them in social and human roles, without this affecting the status of each of them. The role of women in the family is founded on the premise that she holds the primary/ main responsibility for raising the new generation ... consequently we believe in the importance of finding balance in the roles of women and reviving her role in the family and public life without imposing on her duties which conflict with her nature or with her role in the family. We believe that the roles that women [should] espouse are an outcome of a social consensus built on the Islamic civilizational terms of reference (marja'iyya).

(2007: 103)

Of significance here is the use of the language of protection in terms of refraining from imposing duties outside her nature. Moreover, the language used in both the official stances and the political thought of the Muslim Brotherhood scholars discussed here indicates that women's work is not regarded as a matter of personal choice and entitlement, rather emanating out of personal economic need or society's need for female labour to cater for a female audience. Influential political thinker El Bahi El Kholy disputes the very notion of a woman's right to work. Women are entitled to – and have a duty towards – motherhood and raising children, but there is nothing in Islamic jurisprudence, he argued, to suggest that work is a right (1984: 252–253).[3]

Akef emphasised that although the social circumstances today have changed since the time of El Banna by for example forcing women out to work to earn a living, still, it remains that women's primary role is in the household. Hoda Abdel Moneim pointed out that 'the essence in Islam is that women's place is at home. We should never take too lightly the mission of woman in her home. Women are responsible for raising the new generation, girls and boys'.

Muhammad Habib rejected El Banna's emphasis on women's role in life being restricted to motherhood:

> El Banna saw that the home is better for the woman but we now see things differently. Women can go out and can have a role in the building, direction and development of society and so forth taking into consideration that this is subject to personality and personal capabilities.

Yet Habib was also careful to suggest that women's engagement in activities outside the home should not come at the cost of its neglect: 'This is not a question of privileging one over another but a question of establishing a balance between home and outside home.' If Habib's ideas were to be studied in their totality, it becomes clear that he is not suggesting that women can choose to play whatever role they wish, either in the domestic sphere *or* in the public. Rather, women's participation in the public sphere or work outside the home is coterminous to her ability to balance her domestic duties with other activities she may engage in outside the house. In other words, in no way is the concept of a woman's responsibility as a mother being compromised, challenged or contested. As the then Supreme Guide of the Muslim Brotherhood, Akef's emphasis on the legitimacy of El Banna's emphasis on women's domestic role probably is a closer representation of the position of the majority of the leaders and rank and file of the movement. Habib's emphasis on women being allowed to engage in a multiplicity of roles best illustrates the views of the reformist faction within the Brotherhood. However, it is noteworthy that the idea of recognising women's multiple roles is qualified upon women being able to fulfil their domestic role first. Moreover, while it shows a significant deviation from Akef's viewpoint, it is hardly expressed in terms of women's right to work, or women's right to choose between different roles.

Qawamah as a woman's right

Qawamah, as viewed by the Muslim Brotherhood,

> is merely a matter of leadership and directing in exchange for duties that should be performed. For it is the husband who pays the dowry in marriage,

it is he who provides the house, its furniture, and all its needs and it is he who provides for the wife and children. He cannot force his wife to pay for any of these expenses even if she is wealthy. In most cases, the husband is older and it is the husband who is usually the breadwinner of the family and mixes more, with a wider range of people. Every type of group including the family must have a leader to guide it within the limits of what Allah has ordained for there can be no obedience for a human being in a matter involving disobedience to the Creator. It is the husband who is qualified for that leadership.

(Muslim Brotherhood 2006)

Leading women members of the Muslim Brotherhood such as Helmy have framed men's qawamah over women in terms of a defence of women's human rights: 'We raise the banner of men's qawamah as a right for woman and not for man', she affirmed, explaining that it is men who are required and obligated to earn a living and provide for the household and not women.[4] The fact that a woman is not required to earn her bread is for Helmy one of the privileges accorded to women as a result of men's qawamah. In practical terms, while Helmy talks about a man's obligation to provide for the household as a woman's right, there are a plethora of personal and economic factors that would prevent a man from being able to provide for his family (such as unemployment) and for which it would be difficult for women to hold them accountable. In such a context, a man's qawamah over women in terms of power relationship does not change accordingly, unless a woman wishes to apply for a divorce.

On the other hand, while the principle of qawamah is applicable to both the domestic and the public spheres according to the fatwa of 1981, the current official Muslim Brotherhood position is that qawamah is only applicable to marital relations. 'The boundaries of men's *qawāmah* over their wives is restricted to marital partnership only and it is a *qawāmah* of sincerity and mercifulness and consultation in return for responsibilities born by the husband' (Muslim Brotherhood 1994).

This is also the position taken by El Qaradawy, El Beltagui, El-Bahnasawy and El Wa'i.[5] By narrowing the sphere of the exercise of men's qawamah over women to marital relations in the contemporary Muslim Brotherhood's discourse, it does mean in effect that it is not a case of universal qawamah of all men over all women. It is this logic of the universality of qawamah that Sheikh El Khattib, for example, used to prohibit women's political leadership.

However, in view of the fact that, in reality, the lines of demarcation between the public and the private are far more fluid than the neat classification of qawamah in the house, not outside, the implications of this domestic power hierarchy has a clear spillover effect on the public realm. If men exercise their qawamah at home to restrict women's sphere of influence and leadership to the household (vis-à-vis domestic responsibility), then the scope for agency outside the home is limited. This is a critical issue which some members of the Islamic movement face when they marry. In some cases, husbands have insisted that their spouses, highly active members of the movement prior to marriage, shift their energy into domestic responsibilities. Hence, in such circumstances, women's exercise of full agency may be severely hindered by the underlying ideologically framed gender division of roles and its manipulation by some members to advance their own personal agendas.[6]

What we see is the use of qawamah to restrict, inhibit and obliterate measures to grant women more rights, whether they be in the area of travel, divorce or reproductive health (see Chapter 7).

Power, politics and leadership

The position of the Muslim Brotherhood on women's political engagement varied from rejection of their leadership positions on religious and social grounds (i.e. Hassan El Banna and El Khattib), the permissibility of women in politics but with conditions (El Qaradawy) and, third, that the matter has nothing to do with Islam and is to be socially mediated (Farid Abd el Khalek and Sheikh Mohammed el Ghazaly).

We will start with the third position because it is very much on the margins. That this has been adopted by renowned political figures such as Farid Abd el Khalek contests that there is a definitive position from the Koran or the Sunna to prevent women from occupying positions of leadership. In addition to adopting the same position as that of Sheikh Ghazaly on women and leadership, he also emphasises that the principle of qawamah rests only in the household. In his detailed fiqh study, he arrives at the conclusion that the prohibition of women from occupying positions of leadership in the Islamic societies cannot be substantiated on religious grounds, it does not represent one of the thawabits. His stance however falls short of promoting women in leadership positions, and as heads of states. Other matters need to be taken into consideration, he argues, such as the readiness of society and the overall interest of the nation (Abd el Khalek 1998).[7] Sheikh Mohammed el Ghazaly, whose ideas heavily influenced the Muslim Brotherhood (but not on this point!) argued that the Prophet's hadith rejecting women's leadership is case specific and does not represent a general rule, and that history has seen women of competent leadership such as the Queen of Sheba.

A more common position, held in particular by the Muslim Brotherhood up to the 1970s, is that espoused by Hassan El Banna, Sheikh el Khattib and, to a lesser extent, El Seba'i. In 1944, Zoheir Sabry, an MP, put forward a proposal to parliament to allow women to vote. His proposal was rejected but it provoked Hassan El Banna to write a commentry on the matter.[8] El Banna was highly critical of Sabry's bid, and the feminist movement that applauded him. He argued that in the Egyptian context in which the majority of men do not care for elections and know nothing about how to exercise this right to vote, should not priority go towards providing these men with civil education (Amin 2006: 24–249). He probed rhetorically those who wish to give the vote to women: 'Do they not see with us that a woman's primary place is at home and that her most noble mission is to form a family and raise the young people and the building of the Ummah' (2006: 250). In view of the ignorance prevalent among women of raising children, spouse's rights, or house management, he urged that this be made a priority rather than wasting their time and that of people with an issue that is of no benefit (2006). In a public lecture, El Banna was even more forthcoming, saying to those

> promoters of westernization and followers of their whims in calling for the right [of women] to vote and to work in the law profession we say to them if men who have a more whole mind (akmal) than women have not mastered the exercise of this right then how will women and they are lacking in mind and religion?
>
> (El Banna 1999: 336)

In the 1970s, the then Mufti of the movement, Sheikh 'Abd Allah el Khattib, produced a fatwa in response to a question sent to *Al Da'wa* on the authenticity of the hadith stipulating that 'a people will not succeed if they are led by a woman'[9] and its relationship to women's occupation of positions of public authority. The fatwa issued objections to women holding leadership positions over men, especially with regards to the posts of president, ministers or members of the shura council (Khattib 1981). The fatwa validated the aforementioned hadith, classifying it as a *sahih* (valid, authentic, true). The fatwa pointed out that the hadith was mentioned in the *Sahih* of al-Bukhari and Ahmad (ibn Hanbal) and al-Nisa'I and al-Tirmidhi and also mentioned by Abu Bakra who recounted that when the Prophet was informed that the people of Persia made Bint Kisra, daughter of the king, ruler over them, he said 'A people ruled by a woman will not succeed'. Of significance is the fatwa's reference to the work of the renowned Muslim scholar the late Mawdudi who is considered the father of radical Islamism and whose political thoughts[10] influenced the Muslim Brotherhood (Barout 2003: 625–653). The Mufti quotes the late Mawdudi as saying:

> If this text – that is the *hadith* is compared by the words of Almighty 'Men are *qawwamun* [rulers over/preside over] women', then put together they would definitively establish that the leadership positions in the state – presidency or ministry or member of the parliament or the management of different government offices – are not delegated to women.

El Khattib's fatwa in *Al Da'wa* magazine then contests the idea that qāwamah (leadership) applies to family life and not to the politics of the state, reasoning:

> we ask this person who is objecting to the clear cut [verse from the] Koran and the Sunnah: If God did not make her [a woman] leader in her home over one family, will He allow her to be a leader over a state comprising millions of homes? No doubt leadership over the state is a more serious matter.

Hence, El Khattib's objection to women's political leadership rests on two fiqh principles, the first emanating from the above hadith from which the scholars decided that being a man is a necessary criteria for leadership, and the second emanating from the principle of qawamah over men, as many of the public positions (for example MP) would require.

Mustapha el Seba'i's interpretation of the aforementioned hadith was that it served to prohibit women from occupying the position of the wellaya 'uzmah which he interprets to be head of state. He argues that the hadith could not mean wellaya more generally because women enjoy legal capacity (ahleya) and exercise their wellaya over minors and those lacking in legal capacity as well as serving as a guardian over people's property and money. With reference to the head of state, he then highlights three dimensions which conflicts with women's psychological and social disposition and mission. The first is waging wars, leading in battles and ending them, the second is leading the Muslims in prayer as imam and the third is what the leadership of the state requires 'in making public interest override emotion, and the complete devotion to addressing the issues of the state which goes against the nature of the woman and her mission' (El Seba'i 2003: 30).[11]

El Seba'i argued that while there were no injunctions in Islam against a woman's right to become an MP in parliament, however, the overall principles of Islam and the general public interest require of a woman the following: that she devotes herself to her home and does not become preoccupied with anything else; that the prohibition of mixing with *ajaneb* and in particular *kholwa* with an *ajnabi be observed*; that no part of her body except her face and hands be exposed; that a woman never travel without a *mahram*. El Seba'i pointed out that these conditions make it practically impossible for a woman MP to pursue her job, in addition to the fact that, in his opinion, the general benefits were outweighed by far by the harms incurred from women's participation in parliament.

> Therefore I say it in all honestly that Islam is averse to women becoming engaged in politics ... not because of the absence of a woman's ahleya (legal capacity) but because of the social harm emanating from it and because it directly violates the general ethical principles of Islam.
>
> (2003: 110)

The third position, the most common, is that held by El Qaradawy, El Wa'i, El-Bahnasawy, Ghozlan and others. El-Bahnasawy takes El Seba'i's point about the four core Islamic principles but argued that they do not only apply to parliamentary representation but to all forms of public work. Hence, why proscribe parliamentary action in particular. He argues that these restrictions can be avoided by women voters as well as candidates for parliament and accordingly the Muslim Brotherhood have accepted the woman voter and candidate for parliament as long as she complies with the precepts of the Shari'a in all that she says or does (El-Bahnasawy 2004: 283).

This position was announced in the 1994 *moubadra* which announced that women are allowed to hold a variety of positions including that of member of parliament and shura and minister provided a number of conditions are met. In other words, women are allowed to not only vote but run for particular offices. The famous document written by Mahmoud Ghozlan, *Yes Islam is the Solution* (2005) which bore the Muslim Brotherhood stamp of approval as representing the movement's position, also confirmed this idea that women may not occupy the position of head of state or corresponding positions. This was justified on the premise that 'The boundaries of men's *qawamah* over their wives is restricted to marital partnership only and it is a *qawamah* of sincerity and mercifulness and consultation in return for responsibilities born by the husband' (Mubadara 1994).

The objection of women occupying the position of the Grand Imamate has rested principally on the hadith mentioned above by El Khattib. Abd el Kader Ouda considers 'maleness' as the second requirement for assuming the position of the Grand Imam, the first being that one is a Muslim (1951: 102). El Beltagui (2005), El Sawi (1992) and El-Bahnasawy (1995) have also considered the position of Grand Imam to be prohibited to women.

The Grand Imamate debate

The contemporary Muslim Brotherhood standpoint is that there are certain positions that a woman is not allowed to hold. For example, according to the *mubadara*, women are prohibited from assuming the position of the Supreme Imamate 'and positions corresponding to it',[12] i.e. the position that is equivalent to the highest leadership position in the country, such as president or prime minister, etc.[13]

Makarem Elldery defended the Muslim Brotherhood's prohibition of women holding the position of president on the basis that it relieves her of immense burdens. She suggested that wars are declared and waged by heads of governments (presidents) who sometimes have to engage in very bloody events. 'Hence, Islam does not want to expose her to any dangers or put her in a compromising position', she affirmed. Members of the reform wing in the Muslim Brotherhood such as Abou el Fotouh suggest that changes in the future may bring about a situation in which it is permissible for women to hold the position of president (a position that he has openly advocated).

The position of the Muslim Brotherhood today, of the prohibition of women from leading a Muslim country, is framed with strong paternalistic overtones of relieving women from undertaking a role for which nature has not equipped them:

> For our part, we believe that the responsibilities required of the head of state, and these are responsibilities of *wellaya* (governance) and leadership of the army which are considered responsibilities that should not be imposed on women to shoulder because they conflict with her nature and her other social and human roles.
>
> (2007: 103)

Despite the fact that this has been a position they have consistently held in all their political platforms from 1994 onwards, at the time of its issuance when there was much talk of the Muslim Brotherhood reforming, some pointed to this prohibition as indicative of their lack of commitment to women's full citizenship. An internal debate within the Muslim Brotherhood ensued, and a handful of politically renowned figures such as Gamal Heshmat, Abdel Moneim Aboul Fotouh and Essam El Erian came out to say that they do believe that a woman may lead. Gamal Heshmat, for example, opposed the position of the Muslim Brotherhood on women and non-Muslims' prohibition from the position of presidency as 'incompatible with reality and the circumstances in which we live and is incompatible with a civil state that the MB talk about in the introduction to their programme' (www.islamonline.net/Arabic/index.shtml). He added that:

> the election of a woman like Dr Noha el Zeiny – in my opinion – is better and more just than the election of Ahmed Ezz,[14] member of the Policy Council in the NDP. Also, there are some Coptic personalities which enjoy credibility, and are known for being just, and therefore if votes go to them this is better than to go to Muslims, many of whom are unjust.
>
> (www.islamonline.net/Arabic/index.shtml)

It is important to analyse Heshmat's case carefully. The election of Noha el Zeiny or some Coptic personalities with good reputations is deemed possible in a context in which their competitor represents the most unjust and oppressive leadership figure in governance possible. He enjoys the privilege of being a man, but nothing else. The question then becomes, what if the competitor for the position of state president/imam is a just Muslim man, who would then qualify more for election, a woman, a non-Muslim man or one who enjoys piety, the right religion and the right gender? In other words, does Heshmat's stance reflect fiqh al mouazanat, where the benefits of having a just non-Muslim or a pious woman in power outweigh the harms incurred from having a corrupt leader who neither abides by the precepts of the Shari'a nor acts justly? Whatever the interpretation, the consensus among jurists around the conditions of the Imamate remains a bone of contention in resolving the tension between equal citizenship, the civility of the state and Islamic Shari'a.

When this debate erupted, the Muslim Brotherhood turned to El Qaradawy for a definitive fatwa. El Qaradawy's earlier position on this matter had been clear: women are prohibited from occupying such a position based on the hadith mentioned above (Sa'dawy, A. 2006: 207). However, at that political juncture, El Qaradawy's fatwa was not so definitive, and a debate ensued over whether the presidency in the modern state is equivalent to wellaya 'uzmah. If it wasn't, then there was no prohibition to women assuming it. Essam el Erian said that at that time, El Qaradawy's stance was far from conclusive which therefore served to reinforce the stance that had already been expressed (personal interview). In 2009 El Qaradawy's stance was articulated more definitively and clearly:

there is ijma'a (consensus) among the jurists that a woman is unfit for the General Immate or Al Wellaya al 'uzmah, which is the general caliphate over all Muslims. However, does the regional presidency in current territorial states represent the Caliphate or is it more akin to the old regional wellayas?

('Abd el Gawad 2009)

When the interviewer asked him whether that follows that a woman may occupy the position of president, his answer was a categorical yes. While this reflects a major leap in the political thinking of El Qaradawy and is at odds with his earlier fatwas on the matter, it does not seem to, so far,[15] have led to a change in the Brotherhood's own stance on the matter.

The Brotherhood's prohibition of women from leading the country is a position analogous with that expressed earlier by Sheikh Ahmed el Tayeb, the former Grand Mufti of Al-Azhar and the current Sheikh of Al-Azhar, the country's leading Islamic establishment and one of the most renowned sources of authority for Sunni Muslims. When prominent Egyptian feminist Nawal el Saa'dawi announced that she would run for president in the presidential elections of 2004 (which she later retracted), the Grand Mufti of Egypt responded by issuing a fatwa that prohibited women from assuming the position of president. Sheikh Ali Gom'a, the Grand Mufti that followed later clarified that a woman could lead a modern Muslim state, although not after the earlier fatwa had been widely disseminated and gained much ground.[16]

The objections expressed by the secularists to such a compromise on women's full citizenship in the Muslim Brotherhood party platform were weak in particular in comparison to how vocal they were in their rejection of the Brotherhood's position on prohibiting non-Muslims from assuming the position of president. Moreover, despite a number of feminist activists' critiques, a weakened and fragmented feminist movement in Egypt failed to mobilise a unified collective platform to contest the Muslim Brotherhood's stance on women's assumption of political leadership of a country (this is despite the fact that the Brotherhood's platform was widely discussed for a sustained and prolonged period of several weeks, giving them plenty of time for organising politically).

The Muslim Brotherhood's announcement of a political stance against women's right to hold the position of president did not only generate minimal opposition from political and civil society, but was in harmony with the religious-patriarchal normative ideals entrenched in contemporary Egyptian society.

Sexual politics

In 2006, when Mahdi Akef was asked what is the current position of the Brotherhood on the permissibility of female circumcision[17] (interview with author, 2006), he responded that the issue was inconsequential in the light of the grander, more pressing political matters afflicting Egypt. He retorted that raising this matter illustrated shallowness on my part (interview, 2006). However, the issue did become one of high politics two years later when the Brotherhood took a position against the criminalisation of FGM (female genital mutilation, commonly referred to in Egypt as female circumcision) on the basis that there is no need for such action. While criminalising any social practice always bears a certain amount of risk of a social backlash,[18] the Brotherhood's resistance to the proposed legal reform was not premised on the best course of action to reduce the prevalence of the practice. It was strategically aimed to allow those who wish to continue the practice on religious grounds not to be penalised for this. A 'medical argument' was used in the debates in 2008 to support such a position, stating that in some cases some women do need to be circumcised.[19] In that sense, such a stance is closer to the fatwa that had been issued by Sheikh Khattib in 1981. In response to a question on the position of Islam on the practice of female circumcision, the fatwa published in 1981 (Khattib 1981) explained that female circumcision dates from the dawn of history and 'when Islam arrived, it approved this *operation* for males and females' (my italics). While El Khattib makes reference to a hadith to substantiate the circumcision of males, for females, he also assumed a medical position:

> There have been diverse views on circumcision. Some [views] see female circumcision as a religious duty for males and females, some see it as a sunna, and some see it as a requirement for males and not females, and that for females it is a *moukarama* [preferable, pleasing in the sight of God]. Some doctors believe that not circumcising females leads to sexual arousal and this would lead to the commitment of the unlawful. So circumcision is a duty for the protection of the honour of the believing woman and for the preservation of her chastity and purity.

The reference to FGM as 'an operation' throughout the fatwa is crucially important because it gives the impression that the practice has medical justification or is of a medical nature. It removes it from the realm of a social ritual or rite and introduces it to the reader as a procedure of a medical nature, especially since at the beginning of the fatwa, the parts of the body that are cut for males and females are described in a decisive manner. The reference to some doctors' opinion on the matter is to furnish the religious argument with greater authority and legitimacy. The manipulation of the medical argument is instructive because it entails a selective exclusion of the medical view, and the dismissal of the positions of Muslim doctors who emphasised the negative psychological and physical implications of female circumcision on the well-being of women and on marital sexual relations. What can be inferred from the above is that FGM is preferred, or at the very least condonable.

Several renowned fiqh scholars widely respected in Muslim Brotherhood circles, such as Mohammed Selim el Awa and Mohammed 'Emara, have categorically rejected the practice of female circumcision as anathema to Islam. The fact that the Muslim Brotherhood have chosen to ignore these stances is significant. It suggests that the spaces and possibilities for reform on gender matters is very limited, even when there are strong judicial evidence to allow them to do so. This speaks of a movement that chooses to comply with the most conservative positions compatible with its own patriarchal values.

This is not specific to FGM, it is characteristic of the Muslim Brotherhood's dealings with gender issues more widely. There seems to be very limited ijtehad exercised on gender issues that allow for stances that grant women more choices or remove the basis for discriminatory practices. These range from issues such as travelling with a mahram (which many jurists have argued is no longer needed if the conditions of travel are secured), or women leading general prayers (which some scholars have argued there is no injunction against) or the question of a woman's right to work, rather than the permissibility of her working under certain conditions.

Reformed or reframed?

When the draft party platform was issued in 2007 prohibiting women from occupying the position of president, some scholars (such as Tammam 2010) suggested that this represents a regression in the Muslim Brotherhood's thinking and a reflection of the extent to which the more conservative wing of the movement had taken over. This chapter suggests that the position taken in 2007 on leadership and other gender-related questions was consistent with previous stances adopted in official platforms as well as in contemporary Muslim Brotherhood political thought. Hence, there is neither a deviation from the core thinking, nor is there sudden hegemonic takeover from the conservatives. The views reflect the Muslim Brotherhood more generally. The impression that the revisionists were sidelined may have been because they were the ones that have been politically visible (certain members of the political office) and therefore some may have overestimated their influence on the wider constituency.

The overall ideological foundation of the Muslim Brotherhood's contemporary stance on gender issues has not changed: women and men have strictly defined gender identities based on their biological difference. All matters relating to men's and women's responsibilities and missions derive from this vision. While the contemporary Muslim Brotherhood discourse no longer advocates the restricted presence of women in the public sphere, where mobility is allowed, it is often conditional upon rigidly meeting a set of qualifiers. Perhaps the most important shift in the position of the Muslim Brotherhood has been in its delineation of the limits of qawamah, restricting it to the private domain. The pertinence of this position shift lies in its ramifications on women's occupation of leadership positions which necessarily entail women's direction/leadership over women as well as men. Yet in practice, the restriction of qawamah over women in the household does have a spillover effect on her powers to exercise her agency in accordance with her choices. Even when women's leadership in public space is allowed (a far cry from Hassan El Banna's stance), nonetheless, women's occupation of leadership positions excludes the presidency as well as the imamate in prayer, and is conditional upon the fulfilment of certain conditions (in terms of mode of conduct and appearance) as well as conditions guaranteed in society (no threats to women's modesty, etc.).

What this suggests is that a fundamental reform in their gendered approach to the position of women has not taken place. The Muslim Brotherhood's approach contests the notion that they are committed to the principles of universal citizenship since there are crucial challenges to the concept of women's personal and political rights. In this respect, widening the scope of women's inclusiveness in the public realm still falls significantly short of even securing the modicum of rights that women in Egypt currently enjoy in the constitution which is gender blind vis-à-vis the gender of the head of state.

If the agenda has not been reformed, it has been reframed in multiple ways. First, there is a far more sophisticated framing of arguments in a way that draws on political discourses in vogue. Hence, rather than framing positions in terms of 'it is prohibited for women to do x or y', it is now framed in terms of a human rights discourse – women's right to enjoy the benefits of men's qawamah, women's right to protection from assuming roles incompatible with their biological nature, which is also simultaneously framed in a paternalistic discourse of protecting women.

The reasons why the political thought of the Muslim Brotherhood has not changed are highly complex and due to a number of structural and agential factors. On a structural front, the Brotherhood had for many years lived under an authoritarian regime in which gender matters were relegated to the bottom of the priority list for the movement to address. Moreover, the Brotherhood is thriving in a highly patriarchal context in which women's rights advocacy is not part of the normative culture. The institutional culture within the Brotherhood promotes highly traditional approaches to the study of fiqh, and rejects reformist perspectives. Further, other influential religious actors in society tend to have a highly conservative agenda, no less reactionary than that of the Muslim Brotherhood. These include Al-Azhar University as well as the other Islamist movements who have a strong constituency on the ground. On an agential front, the highly conservative leadership in the Guidance Bureau but also among the Muslim Sisters undermines the prospect of quiet reform. The absence of a feminist constituency within the Brotherhood that can lead on ijtehad on re-interpreting fiqh has further undermined possibilities for change.

Conclusion

On 11 November 1954, a prominent Muslim Brotherhood leader, Hindawy Duweir, appeared in front of one of Nasser's military courts dubbed 'mahkamet el shaab', which were part of the regime's crackdown on members of the movement. During the long court trial, at one point, Duweir described how Supreme Guide Hassan el Hodeiby was chosen by recounting that when Hassan El Banna passed away, there were 100 persons or more who were very capable and committed who were qualified to assume the role of Supreme Guide. However, they were not positioned at the centres of power at the time of the death of the Supreme Guide because 'el Banna preferred having window showcases' around him 'such that the shop would be at the back but the window showcase would be in Fouad St.'[1] (1954: 33–34). In his account, Duweir pointed out that Hassan el Hodeiby was not a member of the Muslim Brotherhood but was known for his Islamist leanings and therefore was nominated for the position and elected by the Brothers (unauthored, Mahkamat el Shaab: a transcript of the proceedings, Part 1, 1954, pp. 33–34). What can be inferred from Duweir's words is that El Hodeiby was one of the figures displayed in the window showcase, but that, in effect, the real activity was happening backstage, where the movers and shakers were running the place. Duweir's account bears much insight into how the Brothers engage politically. The front cover does not necessarily reflect what is on the inside. However, it serves a purpose: the division of labour within the movement.

Division of labour and political thought

As with any heterogeneous movement, there is a high level of functional diversification within the Brotherhood. This enhances its ability to manoeuvre and navigate the power struggles on several fronts simultaneously. Such functionalism has been facilitated and enhanced by the plurality of ideological standpoints and their convergence within the Brotherhood (see Introduction).

This division of labour with the Muslim Brotherhood has manifested itself throughout the history of the movement. More recently, during the 25 January 2011 uprisings, the Muslim Brotherhood supported the role of youth members in participating in many of the emerging coalitions in order to keep a watch on the emerging agendas and the intensity of the revolutionary fervour while concurrently negotiating with the armed forces and the government the terms of the entente. During the 29 July millioniyya for the Shari'a, the Muslim Brotherhood rank and file synchronised much of the campaigning strategy together and Safwat Hegazy denied any agreeement on any deal with the other political forces, while Essam el Erian reaffirmed the Brothers' continued commitment to work with the other political forces. Within the movement, there are members of the political office who can use the 'right' discourse in engaging with a foreign audience, while renowned preachers can use a very different discourse appropriate for a prayer meeting in a packed mosque on a Friday.

In view of the division of labour, it would be very reductionist to focus strictly on what the members of the political office do and say. They have a role, and speak to a particular domestic and international audience concerned for democracy and freedom. The famous preachers (do'ah) also have a role in mobilising the constituency. And the rank and file have a role in outreach. This is not to suggest that each actor has a singular role: in many cases agency is expressed through multiple functions and on multiple fronts. However, ultimately, the division of labour is strategically instrumentalised to enable the Brotherhood to accede to power. Yet since there are many contextual factors that influence the struggle for power beyond only the Brotherhood's own agency, the path is never a linear one.

This approach of examining the Brotherhood's agency through the division of labour and the strategic position of different actors to varying degrees of visibility helps the movement survive. The movers and shakers working in the backstage 'shop' can function without the hassle of being under the scrutiny of the public eye. However, it makes studying the Brotherhood very complex because those who are most ready to engage with the press, the researchers, the activists and sometimes even the policy-makers, are not necessarily those whose perspectives, positions, orientations reflect – or influence – the rest of the movement.

This book has argued that in order to understand the political agency of the Brotherhood, it is not sufficient to examine those at the tip of the pyramid of political visibility. There are several approaches needed, all complementing each other, in helping us move beyond the tip of the pyramid. Ethnographic studies at the rank and file level are needed – and need to be 'read' against the backdrop of other sources on the movement's agency. One such source is the political thought of the Brotherhood figures. To engage with this influential group, a relational approach is needed: we need to examine their political thought in relation to the curricula being taught, in relation to the policy documents being issued and in relation not only to the discourses but to the day to day practices being played out.

An engagement with the political thought of the Muslim Brotherhood in constellation with policy and practice enhances our understanding of the contextual signifiers behind a particular policy. It shows for example that the notion of a civil state with an Islamic reference has no grounding in Muslim Brotherhood political thought, and its usage has been furthered through the political office of the Brothers for deployment in relation to a particular domestic and international audience. A study of the political thought of the Muslim Brotherhood, for example, paved the way for a more nuanced understanding of the Muslim Brotherhood's political stance of tolerating a multiparty system. It showed that the logic of fiqh al mouazanat meant that it is context-bound and temporal. While this book does not do justice to the diversity and breadth of Muslim Brotherhood political thought, it has sought to capture some important patterns in certain areas such as individual civil and political rights, religious and political pluralism, and gender equality – yet coverage is still very modest in terms of themes (judiciary and international relations for example are missing) as well as the scope of political thought (which can be expanded to include a wider array of political thinkers who have shaped the movement).

Conditional rights

The Muslim Brotherhood have increasingly adopted the language of human rights in articulating their belief in reconciling citizenship rights with the Islamic marja'iyya. Yet the use of the language of rights does not necessarily mean that the intention is to expand choices and entitlements. A classic example is the Muslim Sisters' claim to a 'right to men's qawamah' which would in essence restrict women's choices, in particular for those who do not wish to be ruled according to legislation that inhibits their entitlements under the premise of protection under men's qawamah. As was discussed in Chapter 3, using the language of rights to show that shura is democracy is highly problematic not only vis-à-vis the current system of governance but also for the Brothers' own constituency.

Hence the dilemma of the Muslim Brotherhood using human rights language is twofold. On the one hand, its ability to make a convincing argument that the Muslim Brotherhood perspective (i.e. qawamah is more conducive to women's well-being than empowerment) may not be persuasive to an audience that is probing in the substantive dimensions of human rights. On the other hand, the use of human rights language may not be convincing for an informed Islamist audience who are knowledgeable on Islamic fiqh. For example, from the time of El Banna up to present-day Bad'ie the Muslim Brotherhood leadership has affirmed its commitment to the principle of 'lahum ma lana wa 'aleihum ma 'aleina' (the same rights as we have and the same duties as we have) in relation to the Copts of Egypt. Such framing is intended to convey a commitment to equal citizenship founded on Islamic fiqh. Yet as suggested in Chapter 6, since the original hadith means the opposite of the much lauded slogan, its ability to gain buy-in from the Islamists who have a mastery over Islamic fiqh is very thin. In other words, framing messages in a way that is intended to convey an impression of Islamic authenticity as well as commitment to rights is highly problematic, on several fronts.

Whether we are engaging with issues of individual civil and political rights, religious and political pluralism or women's equality, all rights are, according to the Muslim Brotherhood's framework, exercised within an Islamic marja'iyya or in other words in compliance with the Islamic Shari'a. The Islamic marja'iyya has been justified on the premise that the majority of the citizens of Egypt are Muslim, that it is historically and culturally closer as a reference than its exported counterpart and that it does not undermine rights, to the contrary. However, what has been argued here is that the use of the Shari'a as the norm-ative framework means that rights are often accompanied by 'qualifiers/conditions/criteria' which dissolve them of their essence. In Chapter 3, it was argued that the idea of a civil state with an Islamic reference is an oxymoron because it is the full agency of God, enacted in codified legislation, that is to be considered the authoritative source, not the will of the people. In discussing the concept of shura, it was argued that there are significant restrictions or conditions on when it is to be applied, on what issues and by whom. Similarly in Chapter 4, it was argued that the commitment to a multiparty system under an Islamic state is tied to the parties' commitment to espouse no ideological premise or orienta-tion for their programme that violates Shari'a law. In Chapter 5, it was argued that by focusing on the rights of Copts as equal brothers in the nation, this was given as an indicator of a commitment to religious equality, when in fact, the right to choose one religion – or have no religion at all – was severely hampered, to the point of being almost non-existent. The mediation of citizen identity, rights and religion by the Islamic marja'iyya meant that there was a hierarchy of rights which determined which citizens were entitled to which rights. With respect to women's rights, policy positions on their right to learn, to work, to lead remain conditional upon observing a number of precepts which invariably limit the choices possible. A classic example is the Muslim Brotherhood's reformed position that qawamah is strictly related to the domestic affairs between husband and wife and not applicable to the public sphere more gener-ally. However, given a woman cannot work or travel or assume a political leadership position except with the permission of her husband, clearly no amount of rights discourse can change these constraints to choices.

The gravity of the Islamic marja'iyya in relation to issues affecting funda-mental freedoms is that if in power the Muslim Brotherhood will make it the only reference. In other words, it cannot co-exist with other references such as the international conventions of human rights, since the Islamic marja'iyya is considered to be superior to all of them and all-encompassing. Hence the current situation that we have now where liberal judges may seek to circumvent some dimensions of Shari'a law by pointing to the fact that Egypt is signatory to inter-national treaties (see Chapter 3) is unlikely to be the case if an Islamic state is instituted. From what is being advocated by the Muslim Brotherhood, it is likely to be a state in which not only is the Shari'a the principle source of legislation, but the only source of legislation.

The Brotherhood: a moderate/reformist movement?

Claims to the Muslim Brotherhood being a reformist/moderate movement were very high around the mid-2000s, when the movement was keen on representing itself as a democratising force in Egyptian political life. Akef's *moubadra* of 2005 and the statements of members of the political office then tended to convey the impression of a movement that is keen on edging closer to recognition of civil rights. Yet this was only one face of the Brothers. While the Brotherhood is by no means a homogeneous movement, and there are reformist/moderates elements in it, the hegemony of Salafism in it suggests that it is here to stay. The Salafisation of the Muslim Brotherhood, as Tammam refers to it, is insidious at the rank and file level with significant representation at the Guidance Bureau, the movement's power base. The curricula taught as part of the Muslim Brotherhood's religious learning process promotes Salafi ideology. The personal trajectories of many of the leaders in terms of their contact with Wahabi-Salafi Islam has deepened this.

In addition to ideological convergences, there are also political reasons as to why the Muslim Brotherhood would organisationally have synergies with the Salafi movement: the latter have a strong constituency on the street in Egypt and are able to mobilise thousands behind them. What has been suggested in the Introduction and Chapter 4 is that, on an ideological, organisational and personal level, there are strong associations between the Muslim Brotherhood and Salafism in Egypt. In the light of this Salafi diffusion, it becomes difficult to talk about the Muslim Brotherhood as a reformist movement.

In terms of political stances in parliament, the Muslim Brotherhood have consistently rejected laws that are based on more reformist readings of jurisprudence. One case that combines reformist perspectives on both gender and the non-Muslim other was Zeinab Radwan's, a jurist's, proposal to parliament in 2008 that a Christian/Jew wife be allowed to inherit from her Muslim husband when he dies. Although backed by some key scholars in Al-Azhar, the Muslim Brotherhood objected vehemently to the proposal. It did not pass. Throughout their history, the Brothers have consistently sought to block any law that would give women more rights whether on a personal level (family reform legislation in 1981 and 2000) or social level (child law in 2008) or political level (quota in 2009 and 2011). Some Muslim Brotherhood MPs also sought to block the introduction of an article on citizenship in the constitutional amendments of 2006 (see Chapter 5). While this is not to suggest in any way that these proposed legislations represent a yardstick for whether a movement is reformist or not, it is highly significant, however, that since their establishment, there is a pattern of consistently rejecting any reforms that would grant more rights to women or religious minorities, even in cases where there were strong jurists' justification for it. The Muslim Brotherhood have consistently sided with the most traditional and most conservative stances, often in alliance with the most regressive scholars of Al-Azhar.

Hence, an examination of a constellation of sites of engagement (internal curriculum, personal trajectories of key leaders, ideological leanings of a significant proportion of the rank and file, political stances on issues open for jurists' interpretation on women and non-Muslims, as well as organisationally, in terms of synergies with the Salafi movement), suggests that the Muslim Brotherhood leans more towards the conservative, traditional orientation than that of a progressive, reformist moderate Islamist movement.

Democratic flourishing for the Brotherhood after the demise of Mubarak? Current and future perspectives

During Mubarak's authoritarian era, some scholars argued (see Introduction) that the Muslim Brotherhood's full democratic credentials would only be unleashed if the shackles of political repression were removed and political legitimacy bestowed upon them like any other political force. At that time, no one predicted the uprisings of the Arab world, however, during the year following the demise of Mubarak, the Muslim Brotherhood has enjoyed full political legitimacy, thus allowing us to engage to a certain extent with some of the proposals regarding the relationship between the Muslim Brotherhood's agency and contextual factors.

One of the main contentions is that once the Muslim Brotherhood is allowed to function like a political party, a differentiation may ensue, such as political engagement occurs through the party on civil terms and the movement itself restricts its activism to da'wa. One year after the 2011 uprisings, this has not materialised. The Freedom and Justice Party has a different leadership from that of the Muslim Brotherhood (the leaders of the party had to resign for example from the Guidance Bureau). However, this does not mean that they are organisationally separate. The Brotherhood will continue to engage through da'wa with the understanding that this cannot be separated from politics because Islam combines both. The Freedom and Justice Party will also not abandon its religious foundations, and has declared clearly in its charter that it adopts a political platform with an Islamic marja'iyya. The mosque will continue to be the powerhouse of the movement. No amount of public conferences or work by local Muslim Brotherhood MPs can have the same impact on mobilising a constituency as the mosque. It is through the mosque in complementarity with other channels, that the Muslim Brotherhood can convey a message that they are the upholders of the true Islam. Nowhere was this more evident than in the constitutional referendum of March 2011, in which people were mobilised through the instrumentalisation of Islam to achieve the Brothers' political agenda (as described in Chapter 2).

The Freedom and Justice Party has served to present the political front of the Muslim Brotherhood, the window dressing showcase to borrow Duweir's expression. The platform does not present a radical departure from the earlier political platforms issued by the Brothers. Instead it strategically deals with the contentious issues (such as women and Copts in leadership positions and the place of the 'ulama in governance) by omitting reference to these specific questions altogether. Omission is one way to make them invisible, and therefore irrelevant. The specific qualifiers that are associated with rights can be glossed over by simply making the Islamic marja'iyya the overarching framework for their guarantee.

The second hypothesis regarding the Muslim Brotherhood's agency in a non-authoritarian setting which has also been challenged here is the notion that in a democratic environment, the reformist factions of the movement will rise to the surface and perhaps become its driving force. What Chapters 2 and 4 suggest is that the youth with reformist agendas, as well as key figures who personified the 'reformist' face of the movement, have had to exit the Muslim Brotherhood because they could not be accommodated internally. The internal dynamics are complex and certainly we only have snippets of the power struggles playing out. However, the change of political environment has not loosened the hold of the hard-core Qutbists or their offshoots (such as the Sororyeen). The composition of the Guidance Bureau, the central decision-making apparatus, has not changed in terms of the hegemonic representation of the hard-core actors (even though there were opportunities for voting in reform-oriented figures to fill two vacant seats in the Guidance Bureau, however, the shura council chose to elect figures known for their conservative stances).

The possibilities of the reform wing taking over are undermined by several factors. First, there are no domestic or international pressures on the Muslim Brotherhood to reform. Second, the leadership, as suggested above, continues to be dominated by the hard-core group. Third, the rank and file are not all in favour of the reformists leading the Muslim Brotherhood (otherwise they would have voted them into office). Fourth, the Brotherhood has to compete in a political context in which the ultra-conservative Islamist movements have built their constituency by showing they are more pious and more serious about the business of religion. Given that the Brotherhood has, with the government, contributed in the last forty years to the Islamisation of society, there is now a demand for more religion among a wide sector of the urban and rural populations – not less of it.

Finally, historically in periods when the Muslim Brotherhood flourishes (1940s, 1952–1954, the 1970s), it has consistently been the case that it is the conservatives within the movement that become most pervasive, not the reformists on the fringes.

What is proposed here is that the more politically free the environment, and the more the Brotherhood is allowed to flourish unhindered by any pressures, it will be the conservatives – not the reformists – who grow in power, whether internally within the movement or externally within the wider society. Reformers have to adjust or exit.

There are several possible scenarios in relation to Egypt's political future.

One is that the Muslim Brotherhood and the Islamists form a majority coalition government with tacit support from the armed forces. In which case, unless there are strong international and local sources of pressure upon them to reform, a political system that constrains choices and freedoms is likely to be promoted. Another possible scenario is that the Brotherhood may forge an alliance with a political force that is not Islamist leaning (but is not anti-Islamist either, such as Al Wafd Party) in some kind of power-sharing agreement. Another possible scenario is a military coup which would bring the armed forces to power on the pretext of protecting the civility of the state or any other justification, in which case we may have a repeat of the 1954 scenario in which a systematic crackdown on the Brotherhood follows. Whatever the political outcome, the Egyptian uprisings have shown that the Brotherhood is not the only political actor able to mobilise the Egyptian street. The ability of the youth movements in coordination with political parties and forces to mobilise hundreds of thousands into joining them in Tahrir Square (like they did on Friday 9 September 2011), in spite of the Brotherhood and the Islamists' refusal to participate, indicates that no one political force can exclusively claim the street as theirs.

There is a need to press the Brotherhood for removing the conditionality of rights. For example, since fatwas are recognised to be temporal, i.e. they are changeable according to changing circumstances, the Brotherhood could be pressed to openly pronounce its refutation of the fatwas that were issued by Sheikh el Khattib in the 1970s which comprise severe violations of the human rights of non-Muslims and women. To claim that Sheikh Khattib represented these views in his personal capacity is unconvincing when he held the title of the Mufti of the movement and his powers of influence were substantial.

Second, to continuously press for a clarification of the conditions set out in fine writing associated with rights. For example, what does it mean for Egypt's commitment to the Child Convention Act and the Convention on the Elimination of all Forms of Discrimination Against Women (CEDAW) if the Islamic Shari'a becomes the only marja'iyya of the nation?

Moreover, the idea that the Muslim Brotherhood is Islam, and Islam is the Muslim Brotherhood, conveyed by the movement needs to be constantly challenged. The Brotherhood's instrumentalisation of religion to justify its political agenda and quest for power has enabled it to create a normative environment in which critiques of its ideological foundations are interpreted as a critique on Islam itself. The obsession with Islamophobia has reached a point where by virtue of its association with Islam, critiques of the Brotherhood in particular in relation to international audiences are anathema. It is important to note that the former Egyptian regime and many other political forces have sought to also use religion to build legitimacy on the street but with far less effectiveness.

Finally, when the Brothers are in coalition with the Salafis (and this is subject to the political interests of both movements), it would be helpful if we can examine not just the agency of each political actor separately, but how is this collective agency exercised and what kind of joint platform is advocated – not just through the political statements but through the collective activism of their rank and file. To suggest that the Brotherhood is a political force whose vision of governance in Egypt is fundamentally distinct from that of the Salafis is to miss some of the more nuanced commonalities across movements.

Glossary

Al bay'a   Homage, pledge of allegiance. A pledge given by the citizens to their imam (Muslim ruler) to be obedient to him according to the Islamic religion.

Al-Siyassa al Shar'iyya   The study of politics in accordance with the principles of Shari'a and as set out in Islamic jurisprudence.

'badat   Devotions, devotional acts, acts of worship.

caliphate   Successor, vicegerent. The word is used in the Quran for Adam, as the vicegerent of the Almighty on earth. In Islam it is the title given to the successor of Prophet Muhammed, who is vested with absolute authority in all matters of state, both civil and religious, as long as he rule in conformity with the law of the Quran and hadith. It is absolutely necessary that the caliphate be a man, an adult, a sane person, a free man, a learned divine, a powerful ruler, a just person, and one of the Quraish.

Dar al Harb   'Domain of War'. Referring to the territory under the hegemony of unbelievers, which is on terms of active or potential belligerency with the Domain of Islam, and presumably hostile to the Muslims living in its domain.

Dar el Islam   'Domain of Islam'. It is a country in which the edicts of Islam are fully promulgated.

da'wa   Call to Islam.

Dhimma (People of)   Protected people who adhered to their old faith. The people with whom a compact or covenant has been made, and particularly the Kitabis, or the People of the Book, i.e. Jews and Christians, who pay jizyah. An individual of this class – namely, a free non-Muslim subject of a Muslim state, who pays jizyah, and in return the Muslims are responsible for his security, personal freedom and religious toleration – is called Zimmi.

farida   Duty, obligation, task. An enjoined duty, religious duty, ordinance.

Hisba   Enjoining what is right, and forbidding what is wrong.

huddud   Prescribed punishments.

ijma'a   Consensus.

ijtehad   An independent judgement in legal question, based on the interpretation and application of the four foundations (usul) as opposed to (taqleed) individual judgement. This method of attaining to a certain degree of authority in searching into the principals of jurisprudence is sanctioned by the Traditions.

jihad   Lit., exertion, striving. Struggle for the sake of God, whether for self-discipline or self-purification.

Jizya   Head-tax imposed by Islam on the people of the scriptures and other people who have a revealed book (non-Muslims) when they are under Muslim rule.

kufr   Literally: that which covers the truth. It is basically disbelief in any of the articles of Islamic Faith and they are: to believe in Allah (God), his angels, his Messengers, His revealed Books, the day of Resurrection, and Al-Qadar (i.e. Divine Preordainments whatever Allah has ordained must come to pass). Kufr consists of rejection of the Divine Guidance communicated through the Prophets and Messengers of Allah. More specially, ever since the advent of the last of the Prophets and Messengers, Muhammed rejection of his teaching constitutes kufr.

Marja'iyya   Reference or framework.

millioniyya   A term that was coined during the uprisings of the Egyptian people against Mubarak to indicate the mobilisation of one million plus citizens. The call for a millioniyya to voice various demands and agendas was made by both the civil political forces as well as the Islamists in the months following Mubarak's demise during the transition phase.

safka   Conclusion of a contract, deal, bargain, transaction.

shirk   'Idolatry; paganism; polytheism'. Ascribing plurality to the Deity. Associating anything or anyone with the Creator either in His being, or attributes or in the exclusive rights (such as worship) that he has against His creatures.

Shura   The consultation. In Quran: 'and consult them in affaires (of moment)'.

'Ulama   One who knows; a scholar. In this plural form the word is used as the title of those bodies of learned teachers in Islam and law, who headed by their shaikhu 'l-islam. This term usually includes all religious teachers, such as imams, Muftis and Qadi.

Ummah   A people, a nation, a race. The word occurs about forty times in the Quran.

Notes

Introduction

1 Or at least during the six months of transition that this research covered.
2 This word has a particular meaning and nuance in Sufi groups.
3 'Nation' but used not to refer to the nation-state but the community of Muslims beyond the boundaries of a particular state.
4 The Salafis believe in the fundamental centrality of the Quran and Sunna and the traditional sources of fiqh.
5 Wahabi ideology emanates from the political thought of Mohammed Abd Ibn el Wahab (1703–1791) in Saudi Arabia to revive the tradition of returning to the fundaments. There is no fundamental difference between Salafi and Wahabi ideology except that the latter tends to represent a less accommodating position towards any idea or act considered to be anathema to the fundamentals. It is rather ironic that the first Muslim Brotherhood established was in Saudi Arabia in 1912 by Imam Ab el Aziz Ibn So'ud to propagate Wahabi ideology. When Hassan El Banna established his own organisation, he chose the same name.
6 This was in a context in which there was a struggle between Egypt and Saudi Arabia over who would become the next centre of power for the establishment of a caliphate, following the demise of the Ottoman empire (see Chapter 3).
7 Although this does not preclude the fact that El Banna was also a recipient of American and British finances at different stages of the movement's history (see El Nimnim 2011 and Curtis 2011).
8 El Nimnim (2011).
9 El Banna (1996: 19, 23).
10 El Ess'ad (1986: 106).
11 Hassan El Banna is not only revered as the founder of the Brotherhood, but his vision for the movement and for Islamic rule continues to play a central role on several levels. His writings constitute the core of the curriculum taught to new members of the movement and to those aspiring to join. In a letter published on Ikhwan online, a woman asks: how can she follow the way of the Muslim Brotherhood? The response is that she must observe the five ordinances of Islam, excel in her studies and enhance her skills, and the first among the readings mentioned with which she must familiarise herself is 'the messages of Hassan el Banna'. *Ikhwan online*, http://ikhwanonline.com (accessed 1 September 2008).
12 With the exception of the question of use of violence which is not addressed in this book due to limitations of space and because it has been amply addressed through other literature.

1 Egypt and the Brotherhood in a pressure cooker

1 Although up until the mid-1990s he was living in London.
2 Which it would not have normally done in relation to the Muslim Brotherhood despite the fact that it is common practice in Egyptian politics.
3 When the Muslim Brotherhood defected from participation, one candidate refused to pull out and made it to parliament, however, the movement has, according to rumours, dropped his membership.
4 Further, the fate of four remaining seats, representing less than 1 per cent of parliament, was never confirmed since the Higher Election committee said they will be settled through another round due to irregularities. *Al-Ahram* online, 6 December, 'Official results: 16 opposition, 424 NDP, 65 "independents"', http://english.ahram.org.eg/NewsContent/1/5/1321/Egypt/Egypt-Elections-/Official-results-opposition,–NDP,–independents.aspx (accessed 10 May 2011).
5 The other event being the ousting of President Zein al Abiddin Ben Ali in Tunisia.

2 From the Friday of Fury to the Shari'a Friday

1 This was following a closed meeting held at the premises of El Ghad political party and attended by representatives from Al Wafd, Kefaya, the Nasserite Party and the Muslim Brotherhood.
2 The only local press sources that continued to point to the Brotherhood's Islamic rendering of the revolution were the national newspapers who had already lost all credibility in the eyes of the citizenry who were against Mubarak.
3 Opposition leader of Al Ghad Party, Ayman Nour, went even further, saying that in this private meeting the Brotherhood had also agreed to support Omar Suleiman's future nomination for president (*Al Bashayer* 2011).
4 This section relies heavily on Youssry el Ezzabawy's excellent study on the youth and the revolution (2012).
5 According to an AFP photographer's account.
6 El Wazeiry (2011).
7 Polytheism or the association of partners with God (Abou el Fadl n.d.: 307). Considered to be one of the gravest forms of idolatory.
8 See for example, *Stances against the Muslim Brotherhood* by Abou Abdallah Al Wahab Ben Ali Al Hagoury, in which the author compared beliefs and practices which he argues are prevalent among the Brothers such as their call for democracy, their participation in elections, demonstrations and practices, not growing their beard, and dressing in Western clothes, which are all condemned actions associated with the infidels, the People of the Book.

3 A civil state with an Islamic reference: an oxymoron?

1 See for example El Sanhoury (1988) and Mohammed Hussein Heikal, The Islamic government, El Ma'aref for Publ. Cairo, Egypt, 1984 and Ali Hosny El Khortoby Islam and the Caliphate, Dar Beirut for Publ. And Abu el Ela el Mawdudy, The Islamic government, The Islamic Dar el Mokhtar for Publ. Cairo, 1977. Even in Shia thought, reference was to an Islamic government, see for example, Khomeyni, Ayatollah Rohallah, 2005, Islamic Government: Governance and Jurisprudent, University Press of Pacific. And Bani Sadr, Abu Al-Hasan, 1981, Fundamental Principles and Precepts of Islamic Government, Mazda Publications.
2 Rafik Habib, a political counsellor to the Muslim Brotherhood and the deputy head of the Freedom and Justice Party and one of the key actors to have influenced the Brotherhood's thinking on this concept contributed to the formulation of the 2007 Muslim Brotherhood platform.

3 El Qaradawy argues that both terms can be used interchangeably.
4 A constitutional theocracy, is defined by its four main elements: (1) adherence to some or all core elements of modern constitutionalism, including the formal distinction between political authority and religious authority, and the existence of some form of active judicial review; (2) the presence of a single religion or religious denomination that is formally endorsed by the state as the 'state religion'; (3) the constitutional enshrining of the religion, its texts, directives and interpretations as a, or the main, source of legislation and judicial interpretation of laws – essentially, laws may not infringe upon injunctions of the state endorsed religion; and (4) a nexus of religious bodies and tribunals that not only carry symbolic weight, but that are also granted official jurisdictional status and operate in lieu of, or in an uneasy tandem with, a civil court system. Hirschl (2008).
5 A term used for a command of Allah which relates to the life and conduct of an adult Muslim (Al-Khudrawi n.d.: 128).
6 Text from the Koran, the hadith or sunna or fiqh or ijma'.
7 The legitimate in politics, governance and the reform of the constitutional institutions, al Maktab al masry publ. 2005.
8 Muslim Brotherhood (n.d.).
9 Ghozlan (2011).
10 Teleimah (2011).
11 Ouda (1951).
12 When a commotion was stirred up regarding the Brotherhood's draft platform in 2007, many members went back to Sheikh El Qaradawy for his opinion on the contentious points of the document. Shortly thereafter, he published *Religion and Politics*, in which he rethought the relationship between shura and democracy.
13 I have not mentioned Iran here since El Qaradawy already argued that it is a Shi'a country that is founded upon different governance principles than those prescribed by the Sunnis.
14 The same viewpoint was also expressed by another leading Salafi preacher, Al Aziz belallah, when asked for a fatwa on Sunday 20 March 2011 over the permissibility of talking about a civil state with an Islamic reference (Fatawa Varied fiqh questions, Sunday, 20 March, 2011, lecture in Aziz bellaah, Helmia, Zeitoun). Sheikh Mohammed Ismail Muqaddem, the Salafi leader in Alexandria speaking on Al Nass television channel, and El Heweiny took the same position (the latter was removed from YouTube) – the general gist of it is that a civil state is not a theocratic state as it was known in Europe and is not one where a military leader is imposed upon the people against their will, because of the Islamic concept of al bay'a. http://faisal1624. com/2011/07/11/%D9%86%D8%B9%D9%85-%D9%84%D9%84%D8%AF%D9%8 8%D9%84%D8%A9-%D8%A7%D9%84%D9%85%D8%AF%D9%86%D9%8A%D 8%A9-%D8%A7%D9%84%D8%B4%D9%8A%D8%AE-%D8%A7%D9%84%D8% AD%D9%88%D9%8A%D9%86%D9%8A-%D9%81%D9%8A%D8%AF%D9%8A/, the same recording is also to be found on www.youtube.com/watch?v=l38ZeBGoOqQ (accessed 31 July 2011).

4 Political pluralism with an Islamic reference

1 The famous leader and member of the shura council for the Muslim Brotherhood speaks to Islamonline, Salah El Din Hassan, 13 March 2011, Islamonline.net.
2 The Brotherhood warn its members who have joined a party other than Freedom and Justice: resign or be expelled, Shorouk, 24 June 2011, Mohamed Khayal. www. shorouknews.com/contentdata.aspx?id=487130 (accessed 19 August 2011).
3 Qawa'ed koliyya.
4 One of the key Muslim Brotherhood figures who is one of the leaders of Hamas.

5 The expression used in Arabic wa'ada derives from the practice of burying a living being alive.

5 The Copts and the Brothers from El Banna to Bad'i

1 Abou al Abbas Mohammed *Roz al Youssef* magazine, ibid.
2 See for example Kamal (2011: 13) and Shoukry (2011).
3 Ashour (2011).
4 *Al-Masry Al-Youm* (2011).
5 *Al-Dustour*, 12 May 2011.
6 Interview with Milad Hanna, *Al Araby*, 20 November 2005.
7 *Al distour*, 20 December 2006.
8 See for example Guirgis (1981).
9 El Kady (1981).
10 These were told by the author through oral histories of Copts, who wish to remain anonymous.

6 Islamic citizenship and its qualifiers

1 Some translate it as they are to have the same rights and the same duties.
2 There no Koranic injunctions to this effect, however, the hadith is considered the second most important source of jurisprudence.
3 The translation of 'lahum ma lana wa 'aleihum ma 'aleina'. However, I have chosen to use the word duties instead of responsibilities which I believe reflects a more accurate translation.
4 A renowned book of jurisprudence.
5 Meaning it is fabricated.
6 See Hamido Allah (2001). There is reference to this principle in the Patrilogia Orientalis version of the treaty with the Christians of Nagran, however, there is a consensus among Muslim scholars that this is a fabricated version.
7 See article 1 of the Egyptian constitution amended in 2007, www.constitutionnet.org/files/Egypt%20Constitution.pdf (accessed 3 August 2011).

7 The Sisters of the Brotherhood and the woman question

1 The branch is the second smallest administrative unit, it is followed by a district, then an administrative office which reports to the general headquarters. The smallest unit is the family.
2 Fatma 'Abd el Hady, a 25-year-old teacher of Upper Egyptian origins living in Cairo first came into contact with the Muslim Sisters in 1942 and found herself drawn to their piety and emphasis on religious mores and values. 'Abd el Hady then became one of the twelve committee members that revived the 1940s Muslim Sisters division. Her autobiography, quoted in this chapter, provides an important account of the Muslim Sisters from one of its surviving founders.
3 El Bahi el Kholy wrote a highly influential book, *Between Home and Society*, which became a key text for the Muslim Sisters and for the Muslim Brotherhood more generally on gender matters.
4 Here nakedness does not refer to the absence of any clothes, but being clothed in what the Muslim Sisters considered revealing attire. The fashion at the time was clothes at or slightly above the knee.
5 Wearing revealing attire.
6 Eventually, after the death of Sadat, the law was deemed unconstitutional on technical grounds.
7 See for example Lasheen (1979: 12–13) and *Al Da'wa* (October 1979: 17–19).

8 On a detailed discussion of the Koranic principle of qawamah, see Chapter 8.

9 The Council comprises eighty-five Islamic organisations from around the world.

10 For more information on the ICC, visit their website at http://iicwc.org/lagna/iicwc/iicwc.php?id=476.

11 Her position is taken from her article on 'Changes in the Personal Status Laws in Egypt' (2011) which she told me in a conversation represents the Muslim Brotherhood's stance on this issue.

12 'urfi marriages are non-certified marriages, that may be in compliance with the Islamic requirements for marriage (public announcement, witnesses) or not (if done in secret).

13 Ibid.

14 For an excellent coverage of the Muslim Brotherhood's voices in the parliamentary debates on the Child Law, see Adel (2008).

15 Abdel Moneim Aboul Fotouh, *Al-Masry Al-Youm*, 18 November 2006, 'The brotherhood call upon the president to remove Farouk Hosny', unauthored.

16 Hamzawy in Brown and Hamzawy (2010: 40) spoke about the Muslim Brotherhood as 'defending the right of women to veil'.

8 The gender agenda: reformed or reframed?

1 The word he used is 'fashi' and it was removed in the edited version of this article which appeared in the collection of his articles that was published by the second largest publishing house owned by the Muslim Brotherhood, Dar el Da'wa (1990: 304). The removal of the word does not indicate that his reverential position in the movement is challenged (the Muslim Brotherhood held a grand event to mark 100 years of his birth in 2006), only that there is a more conscious attempt to 'repackage' his ideas to make them more palatable to a wider audience today.

2 Interestingly, El Seba'i argued that women must be equipped for war, since we are exposed to bloody regional and international wars and they must master the skills of first air, use of weapons and defence (135). Given that the first edition of this book was written in 1998 at which time Egypt was not exposed to any hostile assaults, this is one of the perplexing recommendations made in his study.

3 Kholy (1984).

4 Interview with Camillia Helmy, June 2005.

5 The *mubadara* addressed issues relating to the position and role of women in its tenth point.

6 This is also an issue that was critiqued by renowned Sheikh Youssef El Qaradawy, a figure held in high esteem by the Brotherhood and one of the informal leaders of the movement. See www.witnesspioneer.org/vil/Books/Q_Priorities/ch2p1.htm#A%20 Potential%20Objection%20and%20Its%20Rebuttal (accessed 16 October 2010).

7 F Abd el Khalek, From the Islamic political jurisprudence Constitutional Principles Dar el Shorouk 1998, Cairo Egypt.

8 Women achieved universal suffrage in 1956 following a long struggle led by the Egyptian feminist movement among whom Dr Doria Shafik went on a strike in the jouralists' syndicate to press the government to grant women the right to vote and nominate herself for political office.

9 *Al Da'wa* issue no 58, February 1981.

10 Especially on the principle of hakemya with respect to governance.

11 El Seba'i (2003).

12 Translated from the arabic '*ma fi hokmaha*'.

13 Although only the government leadership position is prohibited to women, there are other positions too from which women are prohibited such as leading men in prayer as imam. All members of the Muslim Brotherhood confirmed that a woman cannot lead men into prayer. Habib made the concession that she can preach to men, as

Aisha, the wife of the Prophet did, but that she cannot act as imam because there is an order in prayer in which men are to be in front followed by young boys, then women.

14 Ahmed Ezz being a business tycoon friend of Gamal Mubarak, see Chapter 1.

15 Up to September 2011 when this manuscript was submitted.

16 Tadros (2010), http://freedomhouse.org/template.cfm?page=384&key=253&parent=2 4&report=86.

17 The practice of removing the clitoris and part of the labia minora, believed to be widely observed in Egypt for thousands of years, although it was on the decline in some parts of the country in the past ten years.

18 Although in this particular context at that particular moment, a massive awareness campaign had been sustained over many years, disseminating the message that female circumcision is not required by religion or for the protection of a girl's chastity.

19 A position which has no grounding in mainstream international medical scholarship.

Conclusion

1 Fouad St. is a very well known street in the heart of the city centre of Cairo.

Bibliography*

*All references are in Arabic except where indicated otherwise. Names of books have been translated from Arabic to English, names of publishing houses have been translated into English where appropriate.

'Abd El Fattah, N. (1997) *The Thief and the Bullets: Political Islam, Copts and the Crises of the Modern State in Egypt*, 1st edn. Beirut: Dar el Nahr.

'Abd el Gawad, M. (2009) 'El Qaradawy in an interview: the woman may [lead] Iftaa, judiciary and head of state', 14 December, El Qaradawy website. http://qaradawi.net/2010–0 2–23–09–38–15/7/4746–2009–12–14–04–37–01.html (accessed 20 August 2011).

'Abd el Hady, F. (2011) *My Journey with the Muslim Sisters from Imam Hassan el Banna to the Prisons of 'Abd el Nasser*, edited by Hossam Tammam, Cairo: Dar el Shorouk.

'Abd el Hafeez, H. (2011) 'Gomaa to the Muslim Sisters: the Ummah is watching out for your role', *Ikhwan online*, 2 July. www.ikhwanonline.com/new/Article.aspx?SecID=211&ArtID=87007.

'Abd el Hafeez, H. and Ibrahim, S. (2011) 'Suzanne's laws for the family … annulment is the answer!', *Ikhwan online*, 20 April. www.ikhwanonline.com/new/article.aspx?ArtID=82905.

'Abd el Halim, M. (n.d.) *The Muslim Brotherhood: Events that Made History. A View from Inside (Part 1)*, Alexandria: Dar el Da'wa.

'Abd el Halim, M. (1994) *The Muslim Brotherhood: Events that Made History. A View from Inside (Part 2)*, Alexandria: Dar el Da'wa.

'Abd el-Haq, O. (2005) *Neo-Islamists to Where?* Cairo: Centre for Arab Civilization.

'Abd el Khalek, F. (1998) *On the Islamic Political Fiqh: The Principles of Constitutional Shura – Justice – Equality*, Cairo: Shorouk Publisher.

'Abd el Khalek, F. (2011) 'Introduction', in F. 'Abd el Hady, *My Journey with the Muslim Sisters from Imam Hassan el Banna to the Prisons of 'Abd el Nasser*, edited by Hossam Tammam, Cairo: Dar el Shorouk.

'Abd el Khateeb, M. (1989) *Fatwas on Religion and Life on Issues Facing the Contemporary Muslim*, Cairo: Islamic House for Distributing and Publishing.

'Abd el Khateeb, M. (1990) *Education Principles (Part One)*, Cairo: El Manar Modern Publisher.

'Abd el Khateeb, M. (1990) *Education Principles (Part Two)*, Cairo: El Manar Modern Publisher.

'Abd el Latif, O. (2008) *In the Shadow of the Brothers: The Women of the Egyptian Muslim Brotherhood*, Carnegie Papers 13, Washington, DC: Carnegie Endowment for International Peace.

'Abd el Meguid, W. (2005) 'Gamalat defeated the Brothers', *Roz al Youssef*, 2 December.

'Abd el Meguid, W. (2011) *The 25th of January Revolution: A Preliminary Reading*, Cairo: Al Ahram for Publishing, Printing and Dissemination.

'Abd el Moneim, H. (2011) 'Changes in the Personal Status Laws in Egypt', The International Islamic Committee on Woman and Child. http://iicwc.org/lagna/iicwc.php?id=304.

'Abd el Qodous, M. (1981) 'Honest assessment of the reasons behind sectarianism', *Al Da'wa*, Issue 64, August.

'Abd el Razek, A. (1978) *Islam and the Fundamentals of Rule*, Beirut: Dar Maktabat al Hayat.

'Abd el-Salam, F. (n.d.) *The Fiqh of the Movement in the Balance*, Cairo: New Dawn Bookshop.

'Abd el Sallam, M. (2011) 'A committee to unify the Islamic groups in Egypt', *Ikhwan online*, 30 July. www.ikhwanonline.com/new/Article.aspx?ArtID=88596&SecID=230.

'Abd el Sami', O. (1992) *The Islamists, Conversations Regarding the Future*, Cairo: Dar el Tourath Al Islami.

'Abd elsattar, A. (2009) *My Experience with the Muslim Brotherhood: From the Dawa'a to the Secret Organization*, Cairo: Zahra for Arab Media.

'Abd ullah, S.A.Y. (1995) *Mahmoud Fahmy Nokrashy and His Role in Egyptian Politics and Liquidation of the Muslim Brotherhood (1888–1948)*, Cairo: Madbouli Books.

'Abd ul-Majid, A. (1991) *Muslim Brotherhood and 'Abd el-Nasser: The Full Story of the Organization of 1965*, Cairo: Zahra for Arab Media.

Abou el Fadl, K. (2003) *Speaking in God's Name. Islamic Law, Authority and Women*, USA: One world.

Abou el Fotouh, A. (2006) 'Abd el Moneim *Response to the Paper on Islamists*. www.carnegieendowment.org/files/FutouhEnglishFullText__5_.pdf (accessed 21 June 2006).

Abou el Fotouh, A. (2011) *Al Youm al Sab'i*, 2011. www.youm7.com/News.asp?NewsID=36659.

Abou El Nasr, M. (1988) *The Truth about the Dispute between the Muslim Brothers and 'Abd el Nasser*, Cairo: Islamic House for Distributing and Publishing.

Abou Faris (1988) *The Stance on Shura in Islam and its Result*, Amman: Dar el Forqan.

Abou Faris, M. (2001) *The Change Approach [Curriculum] of the Two Martyrs Hassan el Banna and Sayed Qutb*, 1st edn, Cairo: Islamic House for Distributing and Publishing.

Abou Khalil, H. (2011) 'A suspect pact between the Brotherhood and Omar Soliman', *Al Bashayer*, 31 March. www.elbashayer.com/news-133673.html (accessed 5 May 2011).

Abu Dawood, A. (1997) *The Islamic Movement: A View from Inside (Explicit Interviews with the Symbols of Awakening)*, Cairo: Eetesam Publishing House.

Adeeb, M. and Deish, H. (2011) 'The Gama' Islamiyya: delegating the Brothers with securing Tahrir in the millioniyya of "identity and stability"', *Al-Masry Al-Youm*, 27 July, p. 6.

Adel, H. (2008) 'Parliament approves Child Law and the Brothers reject it and warn [against it]', *Ikhwan online*, 1 June. www.ikhwanonline.com/Article.asp?ArtID=37711&SecID==230.

Adel, M. (2011) 'Pope warns Copts against participation in the demonstrations', *Ros Al Youssef*, 25 January.

Agence France-Presse (AFP) (2011) 'Egypt protest hero Wael Ghonim barred from stage', 18 February. www.hindustantimes.com/Egypt-protest-hero-Wael-Ghonim-barred-from-stage/Article1-663996.aspx.

Ahmed, F. (2008) *What if the Brothers Rule?* Cairo: Roz al youssef Publisher.

Ahmed, H.H. (2005) *The Muslim Brotherhood and the Parliamentary Elections of 2005: A Documentary Study*, no publisher.

Ahmed, M. (2011) 'A speck of light, Makram Mohamed Ahmed', *Al Ahram*, 25 January.

Akef, M. (2004) *The Brotherhood's Moubadra on the Principles of Reform in Egypt*, Cairo: no publisher.

Akladious, W. (2003) *The Full Works of Farag Foda*, part 1, Cairo: name of publisher unknown.

Al Ahram (2011) 'Dr "'Abd el Moneim Abou el Fotouh: there is no religious state ... but it is a civil state"', 23 February.

Al Akhbar (2011) 'The opposition parties refuse the invitation to participate in the day of demonstration tomorrow, except al Wafd', 25 January.

Al Alzkm, A.A. (1988) *From Muslim Brotherhood to Communism, and a Dialogue with Islamic Groups*, Cairo: The Arabi for Publishing and Distribution.

Al Bashayer (2011) 'Nour: the Brotherhood endorsed Omar Soliman as president', 4 April, www.zenadanet.com/t3234-topic (accessed 5 May 2011).

Al Da'wa (October 1979) 'Once again, the Personal Status Law in confronting the fiqh articles', Issue 41, pp. 17–19.

Al Dostor (2011) 'The Brotherhood stage plays national anthem and the Salafists reply', 29 July.

al Khateeb, A. and Adeeb, M. (2011) 'The Brotherhood participate in the dialogue and proposes 8 demands including 'Abdication [of President Mubarak], annulment of Emergency [Law] and the dissolution of parliament', *Al-Masry Al-Youm*, 7 February.

Al Shorouk (2011) 'The demonstrations of the protests "a gift" to the policemen on their feast day', 24 January.

Al Albany, M. (1988) *The Series of Weak and Fabricated Hadiths and their Negative Impact on the Ummah*, Vol. 3, 2nd edn, Riyadh: Al Ma'aref for Publishing and Distribution.

Al Albany, M. (1995) *The Authentic Hadiths Series*, Vol. 1. El Riyadh: Al Ma'aref for Publication and Dissemination.

Al Albany, M. (2005) *The Series of Weak and Fabricated Hadiths and its Negative Impact on the Ummah*, Vol. 5, 2001–2005, 2nd edn, Riyadh: Al Ma'aref for Publishing and Distribution.

Al 'Awadi, H. (2004) *In Pursuit of Legitimacy, the Muslim Brothers and Mubarak, 1982–2000*, London: Tauris.

Al-Antony, A. (2002) *The Patriotism of the Coptic Church and its Contemporary History*, Part 3, Cairo: publisher unknown.

Al-Aqeel, A. (2000) *The Main Figures of the Islamic Movement*, Cairo: Islamic Publication and Distribution.

Al-A'sar, M. (2011) 'Brotherhood denies questioning Sobhi Saleh', *The Daily News*, 5 June.

Albas, A. (1987) *The Muslim Brotherhood in the Egyptian Countryside*, Cairo: Islamic Publication and Distribution.

Al-Gabar, S. (2007) *They and the Muslim Brotherhood*, Cairo: Hala for Publishing and Distribution.

Al-Gabry, A. (1977) *Why Shahid Hasan al-Banna was Assassinated*, Cairo: Eetesam Publishing House.

Al-Gabry, A. (1983) *The Crime of Marrying with a Non Muslim Woman: Jurisprudence and Policy*, 3rd edn, Cairo: Wahba Publishing.

Al-Gabry, A. (1984) *The Order of Government in Islam*, Cairo: Wahba Publishing.

Al-Gendi, A. (1978) *Hassan al-Banna: The Preacher, the Imam, the Renewal and the Martyr*, Beirut: al-Qalam Publishing House.

Al-Ghazali, Z. (1999) *Days from My Life*, Cairo: Islamic Publication and Distribution.

Al-Hajory, A.A. (2006) *Stops with the Muslim Brotherhood Organization*, Cairo: Dar Al-Imam Ahmad.

Al-Hakeem, S. (1996) *The Secrets of the Special Relationship between Nasser and the Muslim Brotherhood*, Cairo: Center of Arab Civilization for Media and Publishing.

Ali, A. (2004) *Scenarios Before a Fall*, Cairo: Mahrousa Center for Publication, Press and Information.

Ali, A. (2005) *Al Ikhwan al Moslimoon Fatawi fi Al Akbat wal Dimoukrateyya wal mar'a wal fan*, Cairo: Al Mahroussa Publisher.

Ali, A. (2005) *The Muslim Brotherhood: The Crisis of the Reformist Trend*, Cairo: Al mahrosa Press.

Ali, A. (2007) *The Muslim Brotherhood from Hassan al-Banna to the Mahdi Akef*, Cairo: Mahrousa Center for Publication, Press and Information.

Ali, A. (2011) *The Muslim Brotherhood: Reading in the Classified Files*, Cairo: The Egyptian General Book Organization.

Ali, H.I. (1996) *Islamic Movements and the Cause of Democracy*, Beirut: The Centre for Arab Unity Studies.

Ali Zalat (2010) 'Emad El Din Adeeb: the elections spawned opposition outside the institutions', *Al-Masry Al-Youm*, 26 December.

Al-Khudrawi, D. (n.d.) *Dictionary of Islamic Terms*, 3rd edn, Damascus: Al Yamama Publisher.

Allam, F. (n.d.) *Muslim Brothers and I*, Cairo: Dar Akhabar el-Youm.

Allam, F. and Gabr, K. (1996) *The Most Dangerous Brigade for State Security Tells His Story: Sadat – Detective – and Muslem Brotherhood*, Cairo: Dar el-Khayal.

Al-Masri, S. (1992) *Muslim Brotherhood and the Egyptian Working Class*, Cairo.

Al-Masry Al-Youm (2009) 'Akef speaks on internal conflict, elections and the future' (English), 24 October.

Al-Masry Al-Youm (2011) 'Brotherhood leaders announce they will implement Shar'ia, set off storm' (English), 17 April, www.almasryalyoum.com/en/node/403687 (accessed 4 July 2011).

Al-Miligy, A.A. (1994) *The History of the Islamic Movement in the Arena of Education (1933–1993)*, Cairo: Wahba Publisher.

Al-Said, R. (1990) *Hassan Al-Banna: When, How and Why?*, Cairo: al-Ahali Books.

Al-Said, R. (2002) *The Political Movements in Egypt: A Critical View (Marxist/Muslim Brotherhood/Nasyrion/Leftist Tagamo'a)*, Cairo: The Egyptian General Book Organization.

Al-Said, R. (n.d.) *The Islamised Terrorism: Why, When and How? Part Two: The Armed Shekh*, Cairo: Dar Akhbar Alyum.

Al-Said, R. (2004) *The Islamised Terrorism: Why, When and How? Part One: The Muslim Brotherhood*, Cairo: Al-Amal for Printing and Publishing.

Al-Said, R. (2004) *The Islamised Terrorism: Why, When and How? Part Three: The Islamised Coming from the Brotherhood*, Cairo: Dar Akhbar Alyum.

Al-Shawi, T. (1987) *The Rule of Islamic law (Shari'a) in Egypt*, Cairo: Zahra for Arab Media.

Al-Shawi, T. (1998) *Memories of a Half-century of the Islamic Work (1945–1995)*, Cairo: Shorouk Publisher.

Amin, G. (2003a) *The Brotherhood and Egyptian and International Society within the Period 1928–1938*, Cairo: Islamic House for Distribution and Publishing.

Amin, G. (2003b) *The Beginnings of Formation and Internal Organization*, Cairo: Islamic House for Distribution and Publishing.

Amin, G. (ed.) (2004) *From the Heritage of Imam al-Banna, Book I: Faith and Hadeth*, Alexandria: Dawa House for Printing, Publishing and Distribution.

Amin, G. (ed.) (2004) *From the Heritage of Imam al-Banna, Book V: Sermons and Speeches*, Alexandria: Dawa House for Printing, Publishing and Distribution.

Amin, G. (ed.) (2005a) *From the Heritage of Imam al-Banna, Book II: Interpretation of the Quraan*, Alexandria: Dawa House for Printing, Publishing and Distribution.

Amin, G. (ed.) (2005b) *From the Heritage of Imam al-Banna, Book III: Thoughts Inspired by the Qur'an*, Alexandria: Dawa House for Printing, Publishing and Distribution.

Amin, G. (ed.) (2005c) *From the Heritage of Imam al-Banna, Book IV: Fiqh and Fatwa*, Alexandria: Dawa House for Printing, Publishing and Distribution.

Amin, G. (2005d) *The Formation Stage 1943–1945 Fifth Book from the History of the Muslim Brotherhood Series*, Cairo: Islamic House for Distribution and Publishing.

Amin, G. (2006a) *The Role of the Muslim Brotherhood in Egyptian Society 1938–1945*, Cairo: Islamic House for Distribution and Publishing.

Amin, G. (ed.) (2006b) *From the Heritage of Imam al-Banna, Book VI: Islamic Events*, Alexandria: Dawa House for Printing, Publishing and Distribution.

Amin, G. (ed.) (2006c) *From the Heritage of Imam al-Banna, Book VII: To the Nation's Rising*, Cairo: Islamic Publication and Distribution.

Amin, G. (ed.) (2006d) *From the Heritage of Imam al-Banna, Book XII: On Dawa and Islamic Education*, Cairo: Islamic Publication and Distribution.

Amin, G. (ed.) (2006e) *From the Heritage of Imam al-Banna, Book XIII: On the Dawa, the Governments and other Bodies*, Cairo: Islamic Publication and Distribution.

Amin, G. (ed.) (2006f) *From the Heritage of Imam al-Banna, Book VIII: Social Reform*, Alexandria: Dawa House for Printing, Publishing and Distribution.

Amin, G. (ed.) (2006g) *From the Heritage of Imam al-Banna, Book X: Issues of the Islamic World*, Cairo: Islamic Publication and Distribution.

Amin, G. (ed.) (2006h) *From the Heritage of Imam al-Banna, Book XIV: Conversations, Correspondence and Literature*, Cairo: Islamic Publication and Distribution.

Amin, G. (ed.) (2006i) *From the Heritage of Imam al-Banna, Book IX: Political Reform*, Cairo: Islamic Publication and Distribution.

Amin, G. (ed.) (2006j) *From the Heritage of Imam al-Banna, Book XV: Collection of Letters of Imam al-Banna*, Cairo: Islamic Publication and Distribution.

Amin, G. (ed.) (2006k) *From the Heritage of Imam al-Banna, Book XI: Essays on the Palestinian Issue*, Cairo: Islamic Publication and Distribution.

Amin, G. (2007) 'Summary of our vision in reform and change', in Salah 'Abd el Maksoud (ed.), *Research Papers of the Millennium Conference of Hassan el Banna: The Reformist Project of Hassan el Banna*, Cairo: Arab Media Centre.

Amin, M. (2010) 'The state security investigations MPs', *Al-Masry Al-Youm*, 14 December.

Arkoun, M. (n.d.) *Islamic Thought*, translated from French to Arabic by Hashem Saleh, Algiers: National Institute for Books Publisher.

Ashour, A. (ed.) (1999) *The Tuesday Lectures*, Hassan el Banna, compiled and edited by Ahmed Eissa, Cairo: El Koran Publisher.

Ashour, H. (2011) 'Freezing Mikhail's releases the Qena protest', *Al Shorouk*, 27 April.

'Ashmawy, S. (1981) 'When will these voices disappear?', *Al Da'wa*, Issue 59, March.

Ashour, H. (2011) 'Freezing Mikhail's releases the Qena protest', *Al Shorouk*, 27 April.

Azzouz, S. (1997) *The Muslim Brotherhood: The Face and the Mask*, Cairo.

Bad'i, M. (2011) 'The Muslim Brotherhood … we will not negotiate with the existing regime', *Al-Masry Al-Youm*, 3 February.

Badran, M. (1995) *Feminists, Islam, and Nation. Gender and the Making of Modern Egypt*, Princeton: Princeton University Press.

Barout, M. (2003) 'Hakemeya in contemporary Islamic thought', in Salma Al Giussy (ed.), *Hozouk al Insan fi al fikr al arabi*, Beirut: Centre for Arab Unity Studies.

Bayat, A. (2011) 'Egypt, and the post-Islamist Middle East', *Open Democracy*, 8 February. www.opendemocracy.net/asef-bayat/egypt-and-post-islamist-middle-east (accessed 28 August 2011) [in English].

Bayoumi, Z.S. (1979) *The Muslim Brotherhood and Islamic Groups in Egyptian Political Life (1928–1948)*, Cairo: Wahba Publishing.

Bayoumi, Z.S. (1987) *The Muslim Brotherhood between Nasser and Sadat: From Mansheya to the Podium (1952–1981)*, Cairo: Wahba Publishing.

Bianchi, R. (1989) *Unruly Corporatism*, New York: Oxford University Press [in English].

Blaydes, L. and Tarouti, S. (2009) 'Women's electoral participation in Egypt. The implications of gender for voter recruitment and mobilization', *Middle East Journal* 63(3).

Brown, B. and Hamzawy, A. (2010) *Between Religion and Politics*, Carnegie Endowment for International Peace, Washington, DC [in English].

Brown, N., Hamzawy, A. and Ottoway, M. (2006) *Islamist Movements and the Democratic Process in the Arab World, Exploring the Gray Zones*, Carnegie Endowment for International Peace, Washington, DC.

Cairo, February 18, 2011, www.hindustantimes.com/Egypt-protest-hero-Wael-Ghonim-barred-from-stage/Article1-663996.aspx [in English].

Carter, B. (1986) *The Copts in Egyptian Politics*, London: Croom Helm [in English].

Cooke, Miriam (2001) *Women Claim Islam*, London: Routledge [in English].

Curtis, M. (2011) *Britain's Collusion with Radical Islam*, London: Serpent's Tail.

Daifallah, S.I. (ed.) (2004) *Islam and Democracy*, Cairo: The Cairo Center for Human Rights Studies.

Daly, S. (2011) 'The Brotherhood's Big Brother', World Policy Blog, 15 March. www.worldpolicy.org/blog/2011/03/15/brotherhoods-big-brother [in English].

Deish, H. (2011) 'Attack on the Kefaya stage with empty bottles', *Al-Masry Al-Youm*, 30 July.

El Anani, K. (2007) *The Muslim Brotherhood in Egypt: The Senility of Time's Struggle?* Cairo: El Shorouk International Publisher.

El Anani, K. (2009) 'Centrist political parties can be a bulwark against extremism', *Islamica Magazine*, 24 November. www.islamicamagazine.com (accessed 20 October) [in English].

El Ansari, A. (ed.) (1999) *The Muslim Brotherhood, 60 Burning Issues, Confronting Ma'moun el Hodeiby*, Cairo: Islamic Publishing and Distribution.

El Bahi, M. (1980) *Religion and State*, 2nd edn, Cairo: Wahba Publisher.

El Banna, G. (2009) *From the Unknown Documents of the Muslim Brotherhood*, Part 4, Dar al Fikr Al Islamy.

El Banna, H. (n.d.) *Collection of the Letters of the Martyr Imam Hassan el Banna*.

El Banna, H. (1980) 'Al Mar'a al muslima', in Muhammad Nasser el Din (ed.), *Al Mar'a al muslima*, Beirut: Al Albani and Dar el Jeel.

El Banna, H. (1986) *Memoirs of the Da'wa and the Preacher*, Cairo: Islamic House for Distribution and Publishing.

El Banna, H. (1990) 'El Mar'a al muslima', in *Magmou'at Rasael Al Immam Al Shaheed Hasan al-Banna*, new edited version, Cairo: Dar el Da'wa Publisher.

El Banna, H. (1999) 'It is a war against Islam and not against the daw'a people', in H. el Banna, *Jurisprudence of Reality (fiqh al wake')*, Part 1, Cairo: The Word Centre for Studies and Researches.

El Banna, H. and Ashour, A.I. (eds) (1979) *Looks at the Sirra*, Cairo: Eetesam Publishing House.

El Bishri, T. (1972) *Al Haraka el Siyassiya fi Misr 1945–1952*, 1st edn, Cairo: Egyptian General Organization for Books.

El Dakhany, F. (2006) 'Hosni: veiling is a return backwards ... and we are now listening to fatwas worth three millems', *Al-Masry Al-Youm*, 16 November.

El Dellal, A. (2007) *The Islamists and Democracy in Egypt*, Cairo: Madbouli Press.

El Erian, E. (2011) 'The days of the revolution', *Al Dostor*. www.dostor.org/opinion/11/february/19/36527.

El Es'ad, A. (1996) *Saudi Arabia and the Muslim Brothers*, Cairo: Centre for Legal Studies and Information for Human Rights.

El Ghazali, M. (1989) *Fanaticism and Tolerance between Christianity and Islam*, Cairo.

El Ghobashy, Shoeib (2000) *Sahafet el Ikhwan el muslimeen*, Cairo: Islamic Printing and Distribution House.

El Guindy D. and Masoud, R. (2010) '90 former MPs announce the establishment of a "people's parliament"', *Al Shorouk*, 12 December.

El Hindy, H., Al Goushi, Y., Badr, M. and Tarek, M. (2011) 'Brotherhood slogans on their stage Thank you thank you Al Mosheer, a thousand greetings from Tahrir', *Al Dostor*, 29 July.

El Kady, A. (1981) 'Family planning between Islam and Christianity', *Al Da'wa*, 62, 40.

El Khateeb, M. and Hamed, M. (1990) *Perspectives on the Mission of Education*, Cairo: Islamic House for Distribution and Publishing.

El Kholy, E. (1984) *Islam and Women's Contemporary Issues*, Cairo: Dar el Tourath.

El Masry, M. (2006) *Participation in Political Life in the Light of Contemporary Political Systems*, Mansoura: Al-Kalima for Publication and Distribution.

el Mouawfy, A. (2007) 'The Brotherhood play the role of the victim...', *Nahdet Misr*, 16 January.

El Nimnim, E. (2011) *The Hassan el Banna Whom Nobody Knows*, Cairo: Madbouli Publisher.

El Qaradawy, Y. (1973) *The Lawful and the Prohibited in Islam*, 8th edn, Cairo: Dar al 'tesam.

El Qaradawy, Y. (1997) *From the Fiqh of the State in Islam*, 4th edn, Cairo: Dar el Shorouk.

El Qaradawy, Y. (1999) *Islam's Doctrinal Position from the Apostasy of the Jews and Nazarenes*, Cairo: Wahba Publisher.

El Qaradawy, Y. (2001) *Fatwas of Muslim Women*, Beirut: Resalah Foundation.

El Qaradawy, Y. (2007) *Religion and Politics*, Cairo: Dar el Shorouk.

El Rahman, M. (2006) *The Reform and Change Approach of the Muslim Brotherhood*, 1st edn, Cairo: Islamic House for Distributing and Publishing.

El Rouwein, M. (2007) *Political Pluralism in the Shura State*, 2nd edn, Cairo: Wahba Publisher.

El Sanhoury, A. (1988) *The Jurisprudence of the Caliphate and its Development to Become the Cornerstone of the Nations of the East*, Cairo: Egyptian General Organization for Books.

El Sawi, S. (1413 H) *The Confrontation between Islam and Secularism*, 1st edn, Cairo: International Horizons for Media.

El Sawi, S. (n.d.) *The Thawabit and Mutaghayerat in the Pathway of Contemporary Islamic Work*, Sanaa: El Quds for Publication and Distribution.

El Sawi, S. (1992) *Political Pluralism in an Islamic State*, Cairo: Dar al Illam Al Dawly.

El Seba'i, M. (2003) *Woman between Jurisprudence and Law*, Cairo: Dal al Salam for Publishing and Distribution.

El Shamach, A. (2008) *The Brothers and Copts: Who Reassures Whom?* Cairo: Wahba for Printing and Publishing.

El Shobashy, S. (2000) *The Muslim Brotherhood's Press: A Study in its Establishment and Content*, Cairo: Islamic House for Distribution and Publishing.

El Shobky, A. (ed.) (2009) *The Crisis of the Muslim Brotherhood*, Cairo: Al Ahram Centre for Political and Strategic Studies.

El Sissy, A. (1978) *Hassan el Banna Situations in Da'wa and Education*, 1st edn, Alexandria: Dar el Da'wa.

El Sissy, A. (1983) *From the Massacre to Field of Da'wa*, Cairo: World Federation of Student Organizations.

El Sissy, A. (1987) *Gamal 'Abd el Nasser and the Mansheya Accident in Alexandria October 26, 1954*, Alexandria: House of Printing and Publishing.

El Sissy, A. (1987) *In a Convoy of the Muslim Brotherhood (Part Two)*, Alexandria: Dar al-Qabas for Publication and Distribution.

El Sissy, A. (1989) *In a Convoy of the Muslim Brotherhood (Part One)*, Alexandria: Dar al-Qabas for Publication and Distribution.

El Sissy, A. (1990) *In a Convoy of the Muslim Brotherhood (Part Four)*, Alexandria: Dar al-Qabas for Publication and Distribution.

El Souweify, H. (2010) 'The Brotherhood's Mufti: withdrawal is Hallal, rigging is haram', *Al Distour*, 11 December.

El Tahan, M. (2002) *Contemporary Islamic Political Thought: A Study in Muslim Brotherhood Thought*, Cairo: Islamic House for Distribution and Publishing.

El Telmesany, O. (1977) *The Religious Government*, Cairo: El 'Tesam Publisher.

El Telmesany, O. (1982) *Some of what the Muslim Brotherhood Taught Me*, 2nd edn, Cairo: Eetesam Publishing House.

El Telmesany, O. (1984) *Days with Sadat*, Cairo: Eetesam Publishing House.

El Telmesany, O. (1985) *Memories not Autobiography*, Cairo: Islamic House for Distribution and Publishing.

El Wa'i, T. (1990) *Islam in the World of Reason*, Mansoura: Wafaa for Printing, Publishing and Distribution.

El Wa'i, T. (1995) *Landmarks on the Road*, Beirut: Ibn Hazm Publishing House.

El Wa'i, T. (1996) *The Islamic State between Heritage and Contemporary*, Beirut: Ibn Hazm Publishing House.

El Wa'i, T. (2001) *Contemporary Political Thought in the Muslim Brotherhood: An Analytical Study, Field Documented*, Kuwait: Al-Manar Islamic Bookshop.

El Wa'i, T. (2006) *Major Islamic Reform Groups in the Contemporary World: Communities – Movements – Political Parties (Part I)*, 2nd edn, Mansoura: Shorouk Foundation for Publication and Distribution.

El Wa'i, T. (2006) *Major Islamic Reform Groups in the Contemporary World: Communities – Movements – Political Parties (Part II)*, 2nd edn, Mansoura: Shorouk Foundation for Publication and Distribution.

El Wa'i, T. (2006) *Plans of the Enemies of Islam*, Mansoura: Dar Al-Badr for Printing and Publishing and Distribution.

El Wa'i, T. (2006) *The Islamic Understanding between Extremism and Moderation*, Kuwait: Al-Manar Islamic Bookshop.

El Wa'i, T. (2007) *A Major Reform Movements: Suspicions and Reactions*, 2nd edn, Mansoura: Shorouk Foundation for Publication and Distribution.

El Wa'i, T. (2007) *The Comprehensive Vision of the Muslim Brotherhood's Reform Attitudes*, Kuwait: House of Scientific Research.

El Wa'i, T. (2007) *Political Terms*, Cairo: El Shorouk Publisher.

El Wazeiry, H. (2011) 'The Brothers and the Salafis mobilize 50,000 in a conference in Hara', *Al-Masry Al-Youm*, 9 May.

El Zanaty, Fatma and Way, Ann (2005) *Egypt Demographic and Health Survey*, Cairo: Ministry of Health and Population.

El Zeiny, N. (2011) 'The intelligence of el dahya Omar Soliman and the idiocy of the Brothers' leaders', *Al Jazeera Arabic*, 7 February.

El-Adawi, M. (1980) *Facts and Mysteries, Muslim Brotherhood: Events Made History*, Cairo: Dar al-Ansar.

El-Assal, F. (n.d.) *The Muslim Brotherhood Between Two Eras: The Story of Religious Corruption*, Cairo.

El-Bahi, M. (1970) *Islam, in the Contemporary Ideological Reality*, Beirut: Dar al-Fikr.

El-Bahi, M. (1973) *Islam in the Life of a Muslim*, 2nd edn, Cairo: Wahba Publishing.

El-Bahi, M. (1979) *Clouds Obscured Islam*, 2nd edn, Cairo: Wahba Publishing.

El-Bahi, M. (1979) *The Approach of the Qur'an in the Development of Society*, 2nd edn, Cairo: Wahba Publishing.

El-Bahi, M. (1982) *Islamic Thought and Contemporary Society: Problems of Governance and Guidance*, 3rd edn, Cairo: Wahba Publishing.

El-Bahi, M. (1991) *Islamic Modern Thought and its Relationship with Western Colonialism*, 12th edn, Cairo: Wahba Publishing.

El-Bahnasawy, S. (1991) *Caliphs and the Caliphate between Shura and Democracy*, Cairo: Zahra for Arab Media.

El-Bahnasawy, S. (1992) *Islam not Secularism: A Debate with Dr. Fouad Zakaria*, Kuwait: Dawa House for Publication and Distribution.

El-Bahnasawy, S. (1994) *Government and the Issue of Atonement of Muslims*, Mansoura: Wafaa for Printing, Publishing and Distribution.

El-Bahnasawy, S. (1995) *The Slandered Islamic Law*, Mansoura: Wafaa for Printing, Publishing and Distribution.

El-Bahnasawy, S. (2003) *Freedom of Opinion: The Reality and the Controls*, Mansoura: Wafaa for Printing, Publishing and Distribution.

El-Bahnasawy, S. (2004) *Basic Rules of Dealing with Non-Muslims*, Mansoura: Wafaa for Printing, Publishing and Distribution.

El-Banna, G. (2009) *From the Unknown Documents of the Muslim Brotherhood (Volume I)*, Cairo: House of Islamic Thought.

El-Banna, G. (2009) *From the Unknown Documents of the Muslim Brotherhood (Volume II)*, Cairo: House of Islamic Thought.

El-Banna, G. (2009) *From the Unknown Documents of the Muslim Brotherhood (Volume III)*, Cairo: House of Islamic Thought.

El-Banna, G. (2009) *From the Unknown Documents of the Muslim Brotherhood (Volume IV)*, Cairo: House of Islamic Thought.

El-Baz, M. (n.d.) *The Brotherhood's Guns: What did the Sons of Hassan al Banna do for Muslim?* Cairo: Konoz for Publication and Distribution.

El-Beshri, T. (2011) *Toward a Basic Stream of the Nation*, Cairo: Shorouk Publisher.

El-Deeb, A. (2008) *The Muslim Brotherhood Secret Actions and Violence: Scientific and Methodological Reading*, Mansoura: Wafaa for Printing, Publishing and Distribution.

El-Dokki, H.A. (2005) *The Features of the Islamic Project in the Second Quarter of the Fifteenth Century Hijri*, Beirut: Al Rayyan Foundation for Printing, Publishing and Distribution.

El-Ghazali, A. (1992) *The Change Law and the Islamic Solution*, Cairo: Islamic Publication and Distribution.

El-Ghazali, A. (2000) *On the Basics of the Islamic Project for the Renaissance of the Nation: Reading in the Thought of Imam Shahid Hasan al-Banna*, Cairo: Islamic Publication and Distribution.

El-Ghazali, A. (2007) *The Economic Thought of the Muslim Brotherhood*, Cairo: The Universities' Publishing House.

El-Maghrabi, K. (1997) *The Muslim Brotherhood from Hassan al-Banna to Sayed Qutb*, Cairo.

El-Messiri, A. (2004) *The Papers of the New Wasat Party*, Cairo.

El-Nadim, A.A. (2010) *Islam and the Secular State*, Cairo: Merit Publishers.

El-Sharif, K.I. (n.d.) *A Page of Islamic History: The Muslim Brotherhood in Palestine (1984–1949)*, Cairo.

El-Tawell, M. (1992) *The Muslim Brotherhood in the Parliament*, Cairo: The Modern Egyptian Office.

El-Wekeel, M.E. (1986) *The Major Islamic Movements in the Fourteenth Hegri Century*, Mansoura: Wafaa for Printing, Publishing and Distribution.

'Emara, M. (2006) *Dictionary of Schools [of Jurisprudence and Islamic Terminology]*, Cairo: Nahdet Misr for Distributing and Publishing.

'Emara, M. (2007) 'Revival in the civilizational project of the Imam Hassan el Banna', in The Arab Media Centre (ed.), *The Reformist Project of Hassan el Banna*, Cairo.

Encyclopaedia of Islam (2007) *Encyclopaedia of Islam*, edited by P. Bearman, Th. Bianquis, C.E. Bosworth, E. van Donzel and W.P. Heinrichs, Brill [in English].

Ezzabawy, Y. (2011) 'The role of the youth's new protest movements in the January 25th revolution', in M. Tadros (ed.), *The Pulse of Egypt's Revolt*, IDS Bulletin 43.1.

Farouk, A. (19994) *Religious Extremism and the Future Change in Egypt*, Cairo: Center of Arab Civilization for Media and Publishing.

Fisk, R. (2011) 'Egypt's revolutionary youth are being sidelined', *Independent*, 2 August 2011. www.independent.co.uk/opinion/commentators/fisk/robert-fisk-egypts-revolutionary-youth-are-being-sidelined-2330213.html (accessed 2 August) [in English].

Gaweesh, M. (2011) 'Closed meeting between the political forces at Al Ghad premises', *Al-Masry Al-Youm*, 26 January.

Geneidy, A. (2011) 'The performance of the police force', in A. Rabie (ed.), *25th of January: A Preliminary Reading and a Futuristic Vision*, Cairo: Centre for Political and Strategic Studies.

Ghallab, M. (2011) 'Angry protests return to the pavements of the People's Assembly and a rise in the protests and sit-ins in the governorates', *Al Wafd*, 24 January.

Ghanem, I.B. (1992) *Political Thought of Imam Hasan al-Banna*, Cairo: Islamic Publication and Distribution.

Ghozlan, M. (2005) *Yes Islam is the Solution*, 1st edn, El Mansoura: Dar el Wafaa for Publishing and Distribution.

Ghozlan, M. (2011) 'Why we did not nominate or support one of us in the forthcoming presidential elections?', *Ikhwan online*, 21 May. www.maktoobblog.com/redirectLink. php?link=http%3A%2F%2Fwww.ikhwanonline.com%2Fnew%2FArticle.aspx%3FArt ID%3D84747%26SecID%3D390.

Greisha, A. (1986) *Islamic Thinking Approach*, Cairo: Wahba Publishing.

Greisha, A. (1986) *The Contemporary Intellectual Trends*, Mansoura: Wafaa for Printing, Publishing and Distribution.

Greisha, A. (1987) *The Shareah of Allah is Governing Not Only the Hodoud*, Cairo: Wahba Publishing.

Guirgis, G. (1981) *Sadat and the Copts*, California: American Coptic Association, Southern California.

Habib, R. (1996) *Papers of AlWasat Political Party*, Cairo.

Habib, R. (2010) *The Cultural Centrism: The Challenges of the Idea and Movement*, Cairo: Madbouli Books.

Habib, R. (n.d.) 'The Islamic state a secular distortion of the Islamic movement', *Islam online*. www.islamonline.net/cs/Satellite/IslamOnline/IslamOnline/ar/IOLStudies_C/1 278407350079/1278406725771/IOLStudies_C (accessed 20 August 2011).

Hamido Allah, M. (2001) *Collection of Political Documents for the Prophet's Era and the Rightly Guided Caliphate*, 7th edn, Beirut: Dar el Nafa'es.

Hamouda, H.M.A. (1985) *Secrets of the Relationship between the Free Officers Movement and the Muslim Brotherhood*, Cairo: Zahra for Arab Media.

Hamzawy, A. (2005) *The Key to Arab Democracy: Moderate Islamists*, USA: Carnegie Endowment for International Peace. Policy Brief August. Issue 40 [in English].

Haqqani, H. and Fradkin, H. (2008) 'Going back to the origins', *Journal of Democracy*, 19(3) [in English].

Hasan, A. ()Sunan Abu Dawud, English translation with explanatory notes by Prof. Ahmad Hasan. Vol. 2, [in English].

Hassan, A.A. (2006) *Political Reform at the Altar of Al-Azhar and the Muslim Brotherhood*, Cairo: Cairo Center for Human Rights Studies.

Hassan, S. (2003) *Christians versus Muslims in Modern Egypt*, New York: Oxford University Press [in English].

Hassan, S.A. (2011) *An Organization in Crisis: Interviews with Leaders and Rebels*, Cairo: Madbouli Books.

Hathout, H. (2000) *The Unique Decade (1942–1952): Ten Years with Imam Hassan Al Banna*, Cairo: Shorouk Publications.

Hawai, S. (n.d.) *Soldiers of God: The Culture and Morals*, Cairo.

Hawai, S. (1979) *To Move a Step Forward on the Path of Blessed Jihad*, 2nd edn, Cairo: Wahba Publishing.

Hawai, S. (1980) *In the Prospects of Teaching: A Study in the Prospects of the Call of El-Banna and its Organizational Theories (Through the Letter of Teachings)*, Cairo: Wahba Publishing.

Hawai, S. (1984) *An Introduction to the Call of Muslim Brotherhood: A Library and a Gift*, 2nd edn, Cairo: Wahba Publishing.

Hawai, S. (2004) *Soldiers of God: The Organization*, Cairo: Wahba Publishing.

Hawai, S. (2005) *Soldiers of God: The Planning*, 2nd edn, Cairo: Wahba Publishing.

Heshmat, G. (2005) *Memoirs of an MP from Egypt*, 1st edn, El Mansoura: El Wafaa for Printing, Publishing and Distribution.

Hirschl, R. (2004) 'Constitutional courts vs. religious fundamentalism: three Middle Eastern tales', *Public Law and Legal Theory Research Paper* no. 04–08, vol 82. http://ssrn.com/abstract=557601 [in English].

Hirschl, R. (2008) 'The rise of constitutional theocracy', *Harvard International Law Journal Online*, 49, 16 October.

Howeidy, A. (2006) Interview with Mahdi Akef, *Al Ahram Weekly*, 21–27 September, p. 4 [in English].

Howeidy, F. (2011) *Al Shorouk*, 27 April, p. 16. http://aljazeeratalk.net/forum/show-thread.php?t=311655 (accessed 5 May 2011).

Hudaibi, H.I. (n.d.) *Preachers Not Judges: Researches in Islamic Belief and Approach to the Call of God*, Cairo: The Islamic Printing and Distribution House.

Ibn-Kathir, H. (n.d.) *The Interpretation of the Great Qur'an (Volume two)*, Cairo: el-Shaab Books.

Ibrahim, K. (1985) *Omar el-Telmesani Witness to the Times: The Muslim Brotherhood in the Circle of Missing Truth*, Cairo: Almokhtar al-Islami for Printing, Publishing and Distribution.

Ibrahim, S. (1988) 'Egypt's Islamic activism n the 1980s', *Third World Quarterly*, April [in English].

Ibrahim, S. (2006) 'The "new Middle East" Bush is resisting', *Washington Post*, 23 August. www.washingtonpost.com/wp-dyn/content/article/2006 (accessed 21 October 2006) [in English].

Ibrahim, Z. (1985) *The Muslim Brotherhood: Historical Papers.*

Idris, M. (2011) 'Precursors to the revolution', in A. Rabie (ed.), *25th of January: A Preliminary Reading and a Futuristic Vision*, Cairo: Centre for Political and Strategic Studies

Imam, H. (2005) *The Muslim Brotherhood and Authority: Bloody Conflicts and Secret Alliances*, Cairo: Center of Arab Civilization for Media and Publishing.

Imam, H. (2005) *The Muslim Brotherhood and the Americans*, Cairo: Madbouli el-Sagheer.

Imam, H. (2006) *Mubarak and the Muslim Brotherhood: Public Conflicts and Secret Deals*, Cairo: Hewar Publishing House.

Imam, H. (2007) *The Muslim Brotherhood and the Copts: From Playing with Religion to Playing with the Homeland*, Cairo: Hewar Publishing House.

Islamic Centre for Studies and Research (1994) *The Muslim Woman in Muslim Society, Shura, and Mutipartyism*, Cairo

Islamic, Islamic" ' July 29th, unauthored.

Ismail, S. (2011) 'The paradox of Islamist politics', *Middle East Report*, Winter, no. 221, 34–39 [in English].

Jaber, H.M.A. (1987) *The Way to the Muslim Community*, Mansoura: Wafaa for Printing, Publishing and Distribution.

Kamal, A.A. (1987) *The Dots Above the Letters: Muslim Brotherhood and the Secret System*, 5th edn, Cairo: Zahra for Arab Media.

Kamal, E.M. (2006) *The Road to the Summit: The Rise of the Muslim Brotherhood*, Cairo: Freedom for Publication and Distribution.

Kamal, K. (2011) 'The case of Qena: "We want him Muslim" ', *Al-Masry Al-Youm*, 21 April.

Kamel, R. (2011) 'We have warned those who called for the Day of Rage of the necessity of obtaining a permit', *Al Akhbar*, 25 January.

Kassem, M. (2006) *Coptcs and Political Participation (the Brothers and the Copts)*, 1st edn, Cairo: Dar el Fikr Al Islami.

Khalaf, A.R.A. (1984) *Educational Thought of the Muslim Brotherhood and its Applications*, Cairo: Wahba Publishing.

Khallaf Allah, M. (1987) 'The Islamic revival in Egypt', in *Al Harakat al Islamiyya al Mou'assra fi Al Watan Al Arabi*, Beirut: Centre for Arab Unity Studies.

Khan, M. (ed.) (2007) *Debating Modern Islam: The Geopolitics of Islam and the West*, Utah: Utah Press.

Khateeb, A. (2011) 'Warning', *Al-Masry Al-Youm*, 27 January.

Khattib, H. (1981) Fatwa section of *Al Da'wa*, Issue 61, May, p. 46.

Khayal, M. (2010) 'The Supreme Guide: no alternative to dissolving the parliament', *Al Shorouk*, 12 December.

Khayal, M. (2011) 'The Brotherhood youth: we refused to obey the leaders' order to retreat from the Square', *Al-Shorouk*, 2 June.

Khayal, M. and El Gohary, M. (1993) *The Muslim Sisters and the Building of a Koranic Family*, 2nd edn, Alexandria: Dar el Da'wa Publisher.

Kholy, B. (1978) *Wealth in the Shadow of Islam*, 3rd edn, Cairo: Eetesam Publishing House.

Kholy, B. (1984) *Islam and Contemporary Women's Issues*, 4th edn, Cairo: Al-Torath Publishing House.

Langohr, V. (2001) 'Of Islamists and ballot boxes: rethinking the relationship between Islamism and electoral politics', *International Journal of Middle East Studies*, 33(4) [in English].

Lasheen, M. (1979) 'What the Shariah says about the Personal Status Law', *Al Da'wa*, August.

Lombardi, C. and Brown, N. (2006) 'Do constitutions requiring adherence to Shari'a threaten human rights? How Egypt's constitutional court reconciles Islamic law with the liberal rule of law', *American University International Law Review*, 21, 379–435.

Louer, L. (2011) 'A decline of identity politics', *International Journal of Middle East Studies*, 43 [in English].

Mabrouk, M.I. (n.d.) *Liberal Islam: Between the Muslim Brotherhood, Centrists and Seculars*, Cairo: National House for the Publication and Distribution.

Madi, A. (2005) *The Vision of the Wasat Party in Politics and Society*, Cairo: International Shorouk Publisher.

Mahdawy, T. (1986) *The Muslim Brotherhood on the Altar of Maneuver (1928–1986)*, Beirut: Dar Azal for Printing and Publishing and Distribution.

Mahmoud, M. (2008) *The Jurisprudential Differences among the Different Contemporary Islamic Trends*, Cairo: El Wafaa for Printing, Publishing and Distributing.

Mardini, Z. (1986) *The Two Arch Enemies: The Wafd Party and the Muslim Brotherhood*, 2nd edn, Cairo: Dar Iqra'a.

Mashour, M. (2002) *Lessons in Da'wa (Part Two)*, Cairo: Islamic House for Distribution and Publishing.

Mashour, M. (2004) *Lessons in Da'wa (Part One)*, *Cairo*: Islamic House for Distribution and Publishing.

Mazin, O. (2011) 'Islamophobia rears its ugly head following Foreign Office visit to MB', *Ikhwanophobia*, 22 April. http://ikhwanophobia.com/2011/04/islamophobia-rears-its-ugly-head-following-foreign-office-visit-to-mb/ (accessed 8 August 2011).

Metwali, M. (1989) *The Muslim Brotherhood and Political Action: A Historical Study*.

Mitchell, R. (1969) *Society of Muslim Brothers*, Oxford: Oxford University Press [in English].

Mohammed, A.M.S. (2007) *The Attempts to Reform and Change in the Contemporary*

Arab World and the Position of the Islamic Dawa'a, Mansoura: Shorouk Foundation for Publication and Distribution.

Mohammed, M. (1987) *Who Killed Hassan el Banna?* Cairo: Dar al Shorouk.

Moursy, S.A. (1993) *You all are Shepherds*, Cairo: Wahba Publishing.

Moustapha, H. (1992) *Political Islam in Egypt: From a Reform Movement to Violent Groups*, Cairo: Centre for Political and Strategic Studies.

Munson, Z. (2001) 'Islamic mobilization: social movement theory and the Egyptian Muslim Brotherhood', *The Sociological Quarterly*, 42(2), 487–521 [in English].

Muslim, Imam (n.d.) *Sahih Muslim*. Translated by Abdul Hamid Siddiqi. Beirut: Dar el Arabia Publisher.

Muslim Brotherhood (n.d.) 'Our internal problems in the light of the Islamic order, the governance system' (unedited version), Cairo: Islamic House for Distribution and Publishing.

Muslim Brotherhood (1994) *Al Mubadara*, http://ikhwanweb.com/home (accessed 1 June 2006).

Muslim Brotherhood (2004) *Press Releases and Public Statements During the Year (2003–2004)*.

Muslim Brotherhood (2005) *Muslim Women in Muslim Society, the Shura and the Multiplicity of Political Parties*, Cairo: Islamic Publication and Distribution.

Muslim Brotherhood (2005) *Press Releases and Public Statements During the Year (2004–2005)*.

Muslim Brotherhood (2006) *Press Releases and Public Statements During the Year (2005–2006)*.

Muslim Brotherhood (2006) *Al Mubadara*. http://ikhwanweb.com/home (accessed 1 June 2006).

Muslim Brotherhood (2006) *The Role of Muslim Women in an Islamic Society and the Stand of the Muslim Brotherhood Regarding Women's Rights to Vote, be Elected, Occupy Public and Governmental Posts, and Work in General*. www.ikhwanweb.com/Home.asp?zPage=Systems&System=PressR&Press=Show&Lang=E&ID=3787 (accessed 20 August 2006).

Muslim Brotherhood (2011) Media message (the Brotherhood's stance), 19 January 2011.

Muslim Brotherhood (2011) Statement from the Muslim Brotherhood regarding the events of 25th January 2011 and its aftermath.

Muslim Brotherhood (2011) 'The Muslim Brotherhood and the on-going events: the Tunisian Intifida and the demands of the Egyptian People', Cairo, 19 January.

Muslim, Imam (n.d.) *Sahih Muslim*, Vol. 2, translated into English by 'Abd ul Hamid Siddiqi, Beirut: Dar el Arabia Publisher.

National Book Committee (1965) *The Muslim Brotherhood Gang Crimes*, Cairo: Al National House of Printing and Publishing.

Ouda, A. (1949) *The Islamic Criminal Legislation Compared with the Human Law (Part One)*, Cairo: Heritage Publishing House.

Ouda, A. (1949) *The Islamic Criminal Legislation Compared with the Human Law (Part Two)*, Cairo: Heritage Publishing House.

Ouda, A. (1951) *Islam and Our Political Situation*, Cairo: Dar el Kettab al Arabi Publisher.

People's Court (1954) *The Minutes of the Official Sessions of the People's Court, Part I*, Cairo.

Phelps, T. and Murphy, K. (2011) 'Omar Soliman warns of a coup as tension rises between demonstrators and army', *Los Angeles Times*, 10 February. http://articles.latimes.com/2011/feb/10/world/la-fg-egypt-unrest-20110210 [in English].

Pieretti, D. (2008) 'Islamism and democracy in Egypt: converging paths', *Washington Report on Middle East Affairs*, 27(2) [in English].

Rab'e, S. (2005) 'Women's issues and the Brethren MPs', *Afaq Arabiyya*, 29 December.

Rab'ie, A.H. (ed.) (2011) *The Revolution of January 25: Initial Reading and Vision for the Future*, Cairo: Center for Political and Strategic Studies.

Raef, A. (1989) *Black Gate: Pages from the History of the Muslim Brotherhood*, 5th edn, Cairo: Zahra for Arab Media.

Raef, A. (1989) *The Satan's Basements: The Secret History of the Prison*, Cairo: Zahra for Arab Media.

Ramadan, A. (n.d.) *The Muslim Brotherhood and the Secret Organization*, Cairo: Rose Al Youssef bookshop.

Ramadan, A. (1982) *The Muslim Brotherhood and the Secret Apparatus*, Cairo: Roz Al Youssef Pub.

Rashwan, D. (ed.) (2006) *Daleel al harazakat al Islamiya fi al Allam*, 2nd edn, Cairo: Centre for Political and Strategic Studies.

Rashwan, D. (2011) 'The greater fears from the constitutional referendum', *Al Shorouk*, 21 March, Issue 779, p. 10.

Reyad, M.A. (n.d.) *Kerdasa's Nights*, Cairo: Al-Mokhtar Books.

Rizk, G. (1978) *The Real Secrets of the Assassination of Hassan al-Banna*, Cairo: Dar Al-Ansar.

Rizk, G. (1986) *Massacres of the Muslim Brotherhood in the Prisons of Nasser, (Volume I, II)*, Mansoura: Wafaa for Printing, Publishing and Distribution.

Robinson, M. and White, G. (1998) *The Democratic Developmental State*, Oxford: Oxford University Press.

Romeih, T. (n.d.) *The Wasat Party and the Muslim Brotherhood: The Full Story and Documents*, Cairo: Jaffa Center for Studies and Research.

Saadawy, A. (2006) *Women's Issues in E Qaradawy's Jurisprudence*, Cairo: Qutr el Naby Publisher.

Sabry, A. (2007) 'In the hearing committee of the constitutional amendments the Brotherhood refuse the article on citizenship being the foundation of the state', *Al Wafd*, 1 March.

Sadaqa, H. (2005) 'A hot repeat in Madinet Nasr between Al Sellab and Makarem', *Al-Masry Al-Youm*, 15 November.

Sadek, M. (2002) *Is the Movement Over? The Muslim Brotherhood and the Crisis of Fragmentation*.

Said, A. (2008) *Religion and the State in Egypt: The Thinking, Politics and Muslim Brotherhood*, Cairo: Nahdet Misr.

Sedeak, A. (1977) *The Muslim Brotherhood between Terrorism and Farouk and 'Abd el Nasser*, Cairo: Eetesam Publishing House.

Seqr, A. (1987) *The Diseases of the Islamic Movement*, Cairo.

Shady, S. (2006) *Pages of History: The Age Harvest*, Cairo: Islamic Publication and Distribution.

Shalaby, R. (1978) *Sheikh Hassan al-Banna and the School of Muslim Brotherhood*, Cairo: Dar al-Ansar.

Shallatah, A. (2011) *The Contemporary State of Salafism in Egypt*, Cairo: Madbouli Publisher.

Shamakh, A. (2008) *The Muslim Brotherhood and the Copts: Who Must Assure Whom?* Cairo: Wahba Publisher.

Shamakh, A. (2008) *The Muslim Brotherhood and Violence: Reading in the Thought and the Reality of the Muslim Brotherhood*, Cairo: Al-Saad for Publication and Distribution.

Shamouk, A.M. (1981) *How does the Muslim Brotherhood Think?* Beirut: Dar el-Geel.

Shobky, A. (ed.) (2004) *Islamists and Democrats: Current Problems of Building an Islamic Democracy*, Cairo: Center for Political and Strategic Studies.

Shobky, A. (2006) 'The future of the Muslim Brotherhood', *Strategic Papers*, Al-Ahram Centre for Political and Strategic Studies, Issue 163, May (in Arabic).

Shoukry, N. (2011) 'Qena burns under the of through the hands of the Islamists and the Military council faces a dilemma', *Watany*, 22 April. www.wataninet.com/ArticleDetailsEX.aspx?A=492 (accessed 28 April 2011).

Shuaib, S. (2010) *The Toz Dialogue: The Sins of the Muslim Brotherhood*, Cairo: Sefsafah House for Publication, Distribution, and Studies.

Shuker, A. and Siam, E. (2010) *Political Parties and the Crisis of Pluralism in Egypt*, Cairo: Gezeret el-Ward for Publishing and Distribution.

Shukr, A. (2011) 'Protest movements', in A. Rabie (ed.), *25th of January: A Preliminary Reading and a Futuristic Vision*, Cairo: Centre for Political and Strategic Studies.

Shukrallah, S. (2011) 'Political groups denounce violation of unity agreement in Egypt', *Al-Ahram online*, 29 July. http://english.ahram.org/News/17654.aspx [in English].

Slackman, M. (2011) 'In Mid East activism, new tilt away from ideology', *New York Times*, 22 January. www.nytimes.com/2011/01/23/world/middleeast/23egypt.html?pagewanted=1&sq=Egypt&st=nyt&scp=2 (accessed 2 May 2011) [in English].

Stacher, J. (2011) 'Egypt without Mubarak', *Middle East Report Online*, 7 April. www.merip.org/mero/mero040711 (accessed 6 June 2011).

Statement from the Muslim Brotherhood on the 11th day of the blessed people's revolution, 5 February, Mohammed Bad'i. [in English].

Sultan, M. (2009) *The Muslim Brotherhood and the National Community (2003–2007)*, 1st edn, Cairo: House of Knowledge and Faith for Publishing and Distribution.

Tadros, M. (2000) *Hadithi, Breaking the Silence: An Egyptian Experience*, USA: Rainbo Publications, Issue no. 2 [in English].

Tadros, M. (2010) Egypt country report, in *Women's Rights in the Middle East Freedom House Report 2010*, www.freedomhouse.org/template.cfm?page=444 (accessed August 2010).

Tadros, M. (2011a) 'Religion, rights and gender at the crossroads', *IDS Bulletin*, 42(1), np.

Tadros, M. (2001b) 'The securitization of civil society', Journal of Security, Conflict, and Development, 11(1), np.

Tadros, M. (2012) 'The pulse of Egypt's revolt', *IDS Bulletin*, 43(1), np.

Talkhan, A.A.H. (1996) *The Issues of Contemporary Muslim Society: The Problem and Solution*, Cairo: Wahba Publishing.

Tammam, H. (2008) 'The Muslim Brotherhood and the road to a political party', *Al Badeel*, 22 August.

Tammam, H. (2010a) *The Salafization of the Muslim Brothers*, Alexandria: Alexandria Public Library Publisher.

Tammam, H. (ed.) (2010b) *'Abd el Moneim Abul Fotouh: Witness on the History of Islamic Movement in Egypt (1970–1984)*, Cairo: Shorouk Publisher.

Teleimah, E. (2011) 'Slowly slowly Dr Ghozlan!', *Ikhwan online*, 25 May.

Telema, E. (ed.) (2005) *Friday's Talks of the Imam Hasan al-Banna*, Cairo: Islamic Publication and Distribution.

Torki, I. (2006) *The Collection of Rasa'el Hassan el Banna*, Cairo: Islamic Distribution and Publishing Inc. [in Arabic].

Wagdy, D. (2008) 'The revisions of the Child Law ... landmines to explode society', *Ikhwan online*, 26 March. www.ikhwanonline.com/Article.asp?ArtID= 35815&SecID=230.

Watany (2011) 'Religious slogans dominate in Tahrir Square', 29 July.

Wickham, C. (2002) *Mobilizing Islam: Religion, Activism, and Political Change in Egypt*, New York: Columbia University Press [in English].

Yakin, F. (1997) *Basics for Organizational Projection of Islamic Work*, 12th edn, Beirut: Resala Publisher.

Youssef, A. (1994) *Muslim Brotherhood: Is it an Islamic Revival, Part One: Hassan al-Banna and Building Organization*, Cairo: Center of Arab Civilization for Media and Publishing.

Youssef, A. (1994) *Muslim Brotherhood: Is it an Islamic Revival, Part Two: Hassan al-Banna and Intellectual Construction*, Cairo: Center of Arab Civilization for Media and Publishing.

Youssef, A. (1994) *Muslim Brotherhood: Is it an Islamic Revival, Part Three: The Organization and the Use of Violence*, Cairo: Center of Arab Civilization for Media and Publishing.

Youssef, A. (1997) *Muslim Brotherhood: Is it an Islamic Revival, Part Four: The Organization and National Liberation Movement*, Cairo: Center of Arab Civilization for Media and Publishing.

Youssef, A. (1997) *Muslim Brotherhood: Is it an Islamic Revival, Part Five: The Organization and the Political Parties*, Cairo: Center of Arab Civilization for Media and Publishing.

Youssef, A. (1998) *Woman and Her Rights in the Perspective of the Muslim Brotherhood*, Cairo: Arabi Publishing and Distribution.

Youssef, A. (1999) *Muslim Brotherhood and the Roots of Religious Extremism and Terrorism in Egypt*, Cairo: The Egyptian General Book Organization.

Youssef, A. (2011) 'Salafis abstain', *Al Shorouk*, 25 January.

Zaghloul, A. (2011) *One Hundred Steps from the Revolution*, Cairo: Merit Publisher.

Zaki, M. (n.d.) *The Muslim Brotherhood and Egyptian Society*, Cairo: Islamic House for Distributing and Publishing.

Zalat, A. (2010) 'Emad El Din Adeeb: the elections spawned opposition outside the institutions', *Al-Masry Al-Youm*, 26 December.

Zeghal, M. (2011) 'Resistance movements, the state and national identities', *International Journal of Middle East Studies*, 43, 390 [in English].

Zeidan, A. (1976) *The Fundamentals of el Daw'a*, Baghdad.

Index